Pro SQL Server 2008 Analytics

Delivering Sales and Marketing Dashboards

■ ■ ■

Brian Paulen and Jeff Finken

Apress®

Pro SQL Server 2008 Analytics: Delivering Sales and Marketing Dashboards

Copyright © 2009 by Brian Paulen and Jeff Finken

ISBN-13 (pbk): 978-1-4302-1928-6

ISBN-13 (electronic): 978-1-4302-1929-3

Lead Editors: Mark Beckner, Jonathan Gennick
Technical Reviewer: Vidya Vrat Agarwal
Editorial Board: Clay Andres, Steve Anglin, Mark Beckner, Ewan Buckingham, Tony Campbell, Gary Cornell, Jonathan Gennick, Michelle Lowman, Matthew Moodie, Jeffrey Pepper, Frank Pohlmann, Ben Renow-Clarke, Dominic Shakeshaft, Matt Wade, Tom Welsh
Project Manager: Sofia Marchant
Copy Editor: Heather Lang
Associate Production Director: Kari Brooks-Copony
Production Editor: Katie Stence
Compositor: Susan Glinert
Proofreader: April Eddy
Indexer: BIM Indexing & Proofreading Services
Artist: April Milne
Cover Designer: Kurt Krames
Manufacturing Director: Tom Debolski

Distributed to the book trade worldwide by Springer-Verlag New York, Inc., 233 Spring Street, 6th Floor, New York, NY 10013. Phone 1-800-SPRINGER, fax 201-348-4505, e-mail orders-ny@springer-sbm.com, or visit http://www.springeronline.com.

For information on translations, please contact Apress directly at 2855 Telegraph Avenue, Suite 600, Berkeley, CA 94705. Phone 510-549-5930, fax 510-549-5939, e-mail info@apress.com, or visit http://www.apress.com.

Apress and friends of ED books may be purchased in bulk for academic, corporate, or promotional use. eBook versions and licenses are also available for most titles. For more information, reference our Special Bulk Sales–eBook Licensing web page at http://www.apress.com/info/bulksales.

The source code for this book is available to readers at http://www.apress.com. You will need to answer questions pertaining to this book in order to successfully download the code.

Contents at a Glance

Contents

Foreword

Most of you have long since started a promising analytics journey and have experienced the deceptively rocky road firsthand, with only fleeting glimpses of the promise of fully realized analytics. These challenges vary by organization, and issues can be data-driven, process-driven, technology-driven, or often people-driven.

The result is that one or more of these obstacles, left unchecked, can lead to poor decision making and operational misalignment with business strategy, which can be catastrophic for a business, especially in the current economic climate where there is very little room for error.

Using applications, like Microsoft Dynamics CRM, that are designed to work the way your people work, through familiar Microsoft Office and Outlook user interfaces, is one of the key ways in which you can ensure that end users rapidly adopt your solution to capture necessary customer data and context.

Oftentimes, organizations build analytics and dashboards solely for executives to monitor and track historical activities. Keeping with the theme that analytics is a journey, this is similar to driving a Maserati in first gear on a straight road—while fun to do, it doesn't take advantage of the car's full potential or the reality of curved and winding roads. As a result, these organizations can be left far behind. Analytics and dashboards are not only the province of the executive suite but have tremendous value to managers and individual sales and marketing professionals. Implemented correctly, these can help users make better decisions and find root causes, empower front-line marketing and sales users, improve operational efficiency, and drive action. The right analytics delivered to the right users at the right time ensures organizational alignment for executives, accountability for managers, and agility for end users. Business insight requires an approach that is as sophisticated as the results you are trying to achieve.

Analytics is a journey on which your organization cannot afford to be left behind. Effective and fully realized analytics will help you measure the past, understand the present, and even project the future. Unlike using a Magic 8 Ball, marketing and sales analysis and forecasting is a legitimate way for organizations to see a potential future based on today's reality and to help you make better decisions now to avoid upcoming disasters or improve capacity plans for impending success.

To help in this journey, Microsoft Business Intelligence provides flexible and powerful low-cost analytical tools that can help organizations of all sizes with a wide variety of analytical needs. Because this journey is different from organization to organization, relevant guidance on how to take the key concepts and tasks associated with successful analytics projects and implement them efficiently is required.

Pro SQL Server 2008 Analytics: Delivering Sales and Marketing Dashboards combines important functional concepts with technical information on the available Microsoft Business Intelligence tools to form an end-to-end guide for individuals and organizations looking to successfully implement a powerful analytics solution. While Microsoft has always been committed to providing powerful analytics tools, with the release of Microsoft SQL Server 2008, the tools, graphics, and capabilities available to users and developers grew significantly.

In the end, being able to appropriately set the stage for your analytics engagement by correctly defining requirements, selecting the appropriate Microsoft technologies, and working through a proven implementation methodology will position you on the road to success. Brian Paulen and Jeff Finken have written this book with you, the reader, in mind.

For analysts and executives, this book will provide the planning, requirement-gathering, and project management tools necessary to ensure your implementation goes smoothly.

Developers, this book will enable you to further understand the tools available from Microsoft and how they can most successfully be implemented in your organization by beginning with basic steps and progressing to more advanced concepts.

Finally, for those using Microsoft Dynamics CRM 4.0 and Microsoft Office SharePoint, additional exercises are provided to further enhance your usage of these applications.

This book is full of sensible concepts and direction for a successful analytics deployment based on the authors' real-world analytics and CRM projects and experiences. I'm confident that this book can help your organization run a little smoother, and I hope you find this guide as informative and useful as I have.

I wish you every success with your marketing and sales analytics journey.

Bryan Nielson
Director, Worldwide Product Marketing
Microsoft Dynamics CRM and CRM Analytics
Microsoft Corporation

About the Authors

BRIAN PAULEN cofounded Madrona Solutions Group in July 2005. He has overall responsibility for the firm's growing business and for managing client and partner relationships. Additionally, Brian works to ensure that Madrona can offer an exciting and challenging "work" environment for its employees.

Prior to founding Madrona Solutions, Brian was the director of the CRM practice at a large consulting firm in the northwest, where he had responsibility for sales and client delivery of CRM solutions. Earlier, Brian was a member of the CRM team at Equarius (now EMC), working primarily with clients in the pacific northwest. His career began at Accenture (formerly Andersen Consulting), working out of their New York office.

Throughout his career, Brian has developed extensive project and program management experience and is an expert in delivering strategic sales and marketing solutions for organizations large and small.

JEFF FINKEN cofounded Madrona Solutions Group in July 2005 and brings years of experience to Madrona's Business Intelligence practice. He brings a particular focus on working with sales, marketing, and IT leaders to define key performance indicators that drive improved organizational performance.

Jeff spends much of his time working hands-on with clients on both the development of metrics as well as the technical implementation leveraging the most appropriate tools from Microsoft's Business Intelligence platform.

Throughout his career, Jeff has worked to deliver technology-driven sales and marketing solutions for large organizations while working with Deloitte Consulting and Onyx Software.

About the Technical Reviewer

VIDYA VRAT AGARWAL is a Microsoft .NET purist and an MCT, MCPD, MCTS, MCSD.NET, MCAD.NET, and MCSD. He is also a lifetime member of the Computer Society of India (CSI). He started working on Microsoft .NET with its beta release. He has been involved in software development, evangelism, consultation, corporate training, and T3 programs on Microsoft .NET for various employers and corporate clients. He has been the technical reviewer of many books published by Apress and an author for the Apress titles *Beginning C# 2008 Databases: From Novice to Professional, Beginning VB 2008 Databases: From Novice to Professional*, and *Pro ASP.NET 3.5 in VB 2008: Includes Silverlight 2Pro*. His articles can be read at www.ProgrammersHeaven.com and his reviews of .NET preparation kits at www.UCertify.com.

He lives with his beloved wife, Rupali, and lovely daughter, Vamika ("Pearly"). He believes that nothing will turn into a reality without them and that his wife is his greatest strength. He is the follower of the concept "no pain, no gain." He is a bibliophile, and he blogs at http://dotnetpassion.blogspot.com. You can reach him at Vidya_mct@yahoo.com.

Acknowledgments

We would like to begin by thanking the team at Madrona Solutions Group for their assistance and patience as we worked through this process for the first time. Specifically, we would not have been able to complete the work without technical guidance and extensive editing support from Katie Plovie, Tri Pham, Phong Nguyen, and Megan Conyers. We truly appreciate the long hours you have committed to make the book what it is. We can't imagine how this could have come together without your dedication, insight, and knowledge of SQL Server. We'd also like to thank Julie Paulen for taking the time to review the book and helping us improve the overall structure and flow. Finally, we would like to thank the team at Apress for giving us this opportunity. Particularly, we are grateful for the work that Mark Beckner did getting us engaged in the process. You have all been great people to work with.

Brian Paulen and Jeff Finken

I would like to thank my wife, Phoebe, for giving me the time and freedom to work on this project. It took more time than I'd ever imagined. I want to also thank my daughter, Zoe, who continues to grow and motivate me every day. Finally, I would like to thank Jeff for owning the tough parts of this book. As always, it was a pleasure working with you on this project.

Brian Paulen

Deb, you are the best. You have been incredibly patient with the amount of time it took for this project to come to completion, and I can't tell you how much I have appreciated your support every day. Gracie, you are always an inspiration, and your skeptical glances always cause me to double-check my work. Finally, Brian, it is always enjoyable. I really did not know how this would come together in the beginning, but it has been a great project, and I can't tell you how thankful I am for the steady approach you have brought to coordinating all the moving pieces.

Jeff Finken

CHAPTER 1

An Overview of Analytics

Most organizations' existing business applications deliver the capacity to store a wealth of valuable data. The challenge is that this data loses its value when it is not readily available to information workers and business executives in the right format on demand. Far too often, sales managers don't have visibility into their pipeline, and they can't make clear decisions about discounting, hiring, and resource allocation. Equally challenging are the situations when finance professionals can't effectively break down revenue and costs by product line and geography. Yet, with client after client, we encounter situations where significant time and effort have been spent designing and deploying business applications without putting any investment into the reporting. The result is that executives have little visibility into how their business is performing, and information workers and IT professionals spend exorbitant amounts of time manually pulling reports that become outdated almost as soon as they are delivered.

Understanding Analytics

A practical definition of "analytics" would be to think of them as the ways an organization arrives at its decisions. Long-time organization employees may base decisions on historical experience or gut feelings, while those more focused on data analytics or financials will focus on the reports or information generated by frequently used applications.

Throughout this book, we will utilize the terms "business intelligence" (BI) and "analytics" interchangeably. At the most fundamental level, we will be discussing the ability to leverage the available Microsoft tools and data from within an organization to improve the decisions that are made by people or groups of employees. Information can be accessed via a wide range of tools in BI environments. On the simple end, for operational or ad hoc reporting, Microsoft Office products (like Excel) can be combined with reports available within line of business applications to gather enough data to make more informed decisions. Should more complex reporting (often referred to as performance management) be necessary, products like SQL Server Reporting Services, Microsoft SharePoint Server, and even Vista gadgets can be used to provide varying views of information. Finally, analytics, or BI if you prefer, includes the ability to present information to consumers where it makes the most sense for them, whether that is via a desktop PC or a mobile device.

Projects involving analytics frequently include data from a wide range of sources. In addition to the standard sources like customer relationship management (CRM) or enterprise resource planning (ERP) applications, initiatives support the inclusion of data from an organization's web site, disparate spreadsheets, and single-purpose applications like dispatching tools or e-mail marketing technologies.

While some of an organization's data exists in these formats, much of it exists in an unstructured format. Merrill Lynch estimates that more than 85 percent of all business information exists as unstructured data, commonly appearing in e-mails, notes, web pages, instant message discussions, letters, general documents, and marketing information. With the growth of the Internet, considering unstructured data is important. However, this book will focus primarily on structured data and on providing the most valuable information to end users.

The Value of Analytics

Imagine running a business without the benefits of monthly financial information:

Put yourself in sales representatives' shoes: what if they don't have access to customer satisfaction information before they head into a sales call?

Picture running the same marketing campaign over and over again, without being able to completely understand the results, conversion rate, and overall return on investment.

These scenarios are examples of struggles that many organizations have when they're not able to synthesize data and present it in a manageable fashion.

Analytics are valuable because they can help individuals within an organization make well-informed decisions. Whether evaluating employee performance, judging the historical and predicted success of the business, or identifying the next investment opportunity, without intelligent information people are simply guessing at the correct answer.

Why Analytics Implementations Fail

One significant source of concern is the ultimate failure of business intelligence initiatives once the data has been gathered and presented. While this and other concerns seem obvious, many implementations fail because of the following reasons:

- *Differing priorities*: End users, managers, and executives within an organization frequently have varying priorities when it comes to managing data. Finding a solution that addresses all user needs is critical. This can be accomplished by identifying a solution that delivers the right level of analytics for each role within an organization, specifically:

- End users want information in a timely fashion that helps them better perform their day-to-day activities. This data must be easy to find, specific to a role, and available whenever and wherever the employee needs it.

- Managers need information that helps them evaluate the performance of their specific business and/or employees. This information must be a summary but contain enough detail for managers to provide feedback or change course as needed.

- Executives want data at a very high level. Information is often presented in a data-dense format and at a high, rolled-up level.

- *Data explosion*: Organizations are capturing increasing amounts of data across a broad array of locations. Many companies now have customer and prospect data spread between business applications located on premises, in the cloud, and on local hard drives in Excel and Access files. One of the great challenges facing analytics initiatives is the need to standardize applications that serve as the system of record for key customer interactions. At the same time, those organizations must architect analytics solutions that are adept at pulling data from local servers and cloud-based web applications while applying effective approaches to scrub and standardize this data to ensure that it performs well in business metrics.

  Failure to appreciate the need to define the system of record for key business data and to architect for a heterogeneous data environment will lead to a failed analytics implementation: users won't waste their time with scorecards and dashboards that report on only a subset of key business data. As more and more data is introduced into an analytics solution, the complexity of developing the solution and making the results consistent rises. Identifying quick wins and a manageable set of data for each phase will greatly improve the likelihood of project success.

- *Trust*: Employee trust in the data available to them and willingness to work with the results are crucial to the ultimate success or failure of an analytics solution. While the direct problem of having to work through reporting issues during a meeting is significant, the permeation of the subsequent distrust throughout the organization should be given equal weight when addressing issues.

- *Application adoption*: Many times, BI initiatives fail because the underlying systems have either poor-quality or incomplete data, which leads to limited usefulness from the analytics tools. Failures of this kind demonstrate the need for BI projects to be concerned with having a focus on delivering tools that help drive adoption of key underlying business systems.

- *Software-driven projects*: Frequently, we're asked to visit a client who is struggling to adopt an analytics solution. Invariably, the client has implemented the latest and greatest business intelligence tool but hasn't focused on deciding which metrics really matter for the business and delivering these metrics in a role-based context. One thing this book will do is to heighten the recognition that successful analytics projects must be driven by the business and enabled by good technology choices. Both the software and the business are critical for success, and neither alone can lead to successful analytics projects.

Environment Preparations

To successfully navigate the exercises and code presented in future chapters, you need to familiarize yourself with SQL Server 2008. You may already have a SQL Server 2008 environment to use throughout this book; if you don't, Microsoft also publishes a trial version of SQL Server 2008 Enterprise Edition for use. Please navigate to www.microsoft.com/sqlserver/2008/en/us/trial-software.aspx to download the software and install it in your environment. Additionally, for many of the scenarios presented in this book, having a platform or an application on which to build reports and dashboards is important. Based on our experiences, we have chosen Dynamics CRM and SharePoint as the tools used in these application-specific exercises. If you're using these tools, you will be able to implement the exercises in your environment. If you're using a different CRM or SharePoint-like application, the same concept can be implemented using your application.

As anyone familiar with analytics knows, good data often makes or breaks reports, so as we move through the exercises in the rest of this chapter, we will focus on setting up the SQL Server environment and associated data to allow for the best exercises and examples in future chapters.

Finally, from time to time, Microsoft releases a 180-day trial Dynamics CRM Virtual PC environment for evaluation by prospects and partners. If you would like to use this application, please navigate to www.microsoft.com/downoads/en/default.aspx and search for Dynamic CRM v4.0 to see if the VPC is currently available.

Exercise 1-1. Restoring the Database

Exercise 1-1 walks you through the steps associated with restoring a database in your SQL Server environment. This data will be used in subsequent chapters to build reports and provide a structure for upcoming exercises.

1. Restore the CRMDB.bak file located on this book's page of the Apress web site. Navigate to Start ➤ All Programs ➤ SQL Server 2008 ➤ SQL Server Management Studio.

2. Create a new database by right-clicking the databases folder and clicking New Database. Type **Contoso_MSCRM** in the "Database name" field, as shown in Figure 1-1.

3. Restore the backup file by right-clicking the database and navigating to Tasks ➤ Restore ➤ Database (see Figure 1-2).

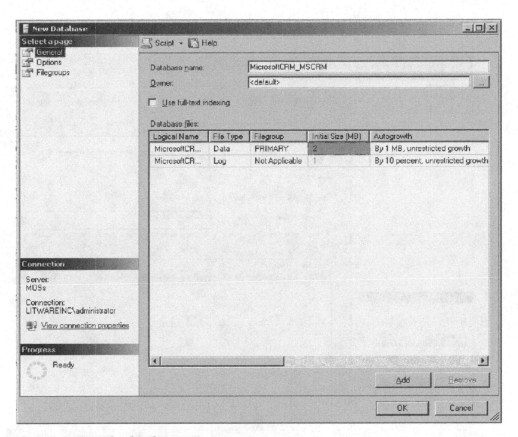

Figure 1-1. *Type the database name.*

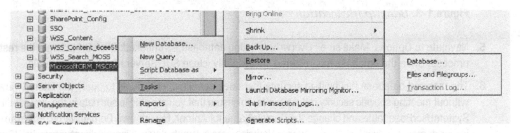

Figure 1-2. *Restore the database.*

4. Select "From device", and navigate to the location of the .bak file (see Figure 1-3).

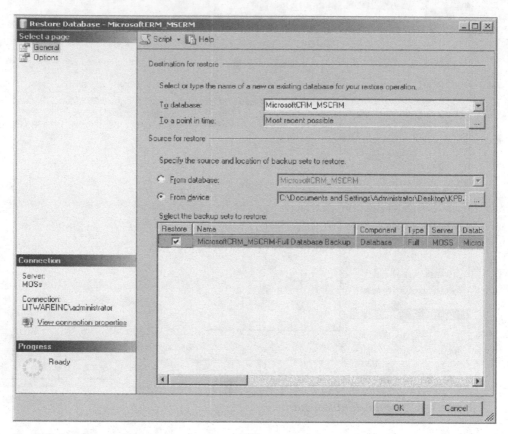

Figure 1-3. *Backup file location*

5. Navigate to Options. Make sure "Overwrite existing database" is checked. Click OK to begin the restore process. Once the database has restored successfully, close SQL Server Management Studio.

6. The restored database has built-in security that does not allow individuals to query the filtered views without meeting specific security requirements. To ensure that you are able to see data in the views, edit the SystemUserBase table and change the DomainName for AntonK to your own DomainName. For example, if your domain is Adventureworks and your domain name is jsmith, you will input **Adventureworks\JSmith** for the DomainName column of the SystemUserBase table on the row associated with AntonK.

Exercise 1-2 will enable you to familiarize yourself with another important reporting tool, Microsoft Office Excel. This exercise will focus on installing the Data Mining Add-In. We've found that, in deploying analytics solutions, most users are familiar with Excel's pivot tables, but more advanced functionality like data mining remains a mystery. Our goal with this example is to provide a baseline for some of the advanced Excel functionality that we will delve into more deeply in later chapters.

Exercise 1-2. Installing the Data Mining Add-In in Excel

This exercise will walk through installation and use of the Data Mining Add-In in Excel. To use the Data Mining Add-In outside of the demonstration environment, Microsoft Office 2007 and Microsoft .NET Framework 2.0 must be installed.

1. Open Internet Explorer in your environment. Type the URL **http://www.microsoft.com/DOWNLOADS/ details.aspx?familyid=896A493A-2502-4795- 94AE-E00632BA6DE7&displaylang=en**. Download the item displayed in Figure 1-4.

Download

Quick Details

File Name:	SQLServer2008_DMAddin.msi
Version:	10.00.1600.22
Date Published:	8/6/2008
Language:	English
Download Size:	17.6 MB
Estimated Download Time:	Dial-up (56K) ▼ 43 min
Change Language:	English ▼ [Change]

Figure 1-4. *The Data Mining Add-In download*

2. Run the Windows Installer Package you just downloaded. Accept the license agreement, and fill out any remaining questions appropriately. In the Feature Selection page, click the drop-down next to each item displayed in Figure 1-5, and select "This feature, and all subfeatures, will be installed on local hard drive."

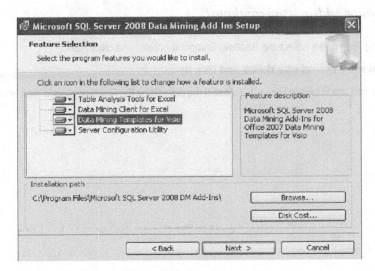

Figure 1-5. *Data Mining Add-In setup*

3. Configure SQL Server 2008 for the Office 2007 Data Mining Add-ins by navigating to Start ➤ All Programs ➤ Microsoft SQL 2008 Data Mining Add-ins ➤ Server Configuration Utility. Accept all the defaults and click Next on each screens until Finish. Install the Microsoft SQL Server Data Mining Add-In by navigating to Start ➤ All Programs ➤ Microsoft Office ➤ Microsoft Office Excel 2007. Open the file 'DMAddins_SampleData.xlsx'. Navigate to the Data Mining tab. Click the sample data button to run the Sample Data Wizard. Click Next to get past the introductory page. The screen in Figure 1-6 will be displayed.

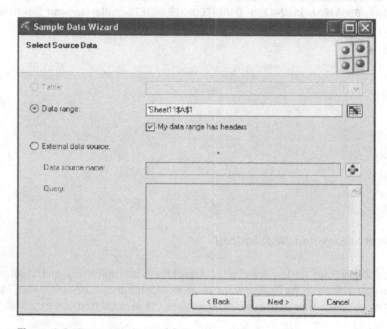

Figure 1-6. *Data Mining Add-In setup continued*

4. On the Select Sampling Type page, select the Random Sampling option, and click Next.

5. Select the Table option and a table of your choice, and click Next.

6. The next page is the Finish page shown in Figure 1-7. Accept the defaults on the Finish page, and click Finish.

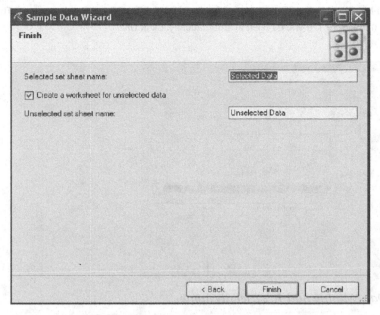

Figure 1-7. *The final setup step for the Data Mining Add-In*

7. Exit the Configuration Wizard.

8. Exit the Data Mining Add-In introduction page.

9. The sample data will be launched into the selected page. Take some time to look over the information provided.

10. Click the Data Mining tab, and navigate to the No Connection icon shown in Figure 1-8.

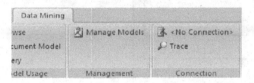

Figure 1-8. *The No Connection icon*

11. Click New, and type **localhost** in the "Server name" field and **DMAddinsDB** in "Catalog name." The friendly name shown in Figure 1-9 will be filled in automatically. Click OK.

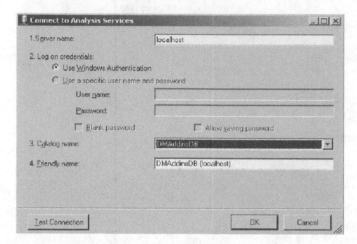

Figure 1-9. *The Data Mining Add-In's friendly name*

12. When the "Connect to Analysis Services" window is closed, the Analysis Services Connections window will open automatically. Utilize this window to make the sure that DMAddinsDB (localhost) is the current connection by clicking the Make Current button displayed in Figure 1-10. Click Close.

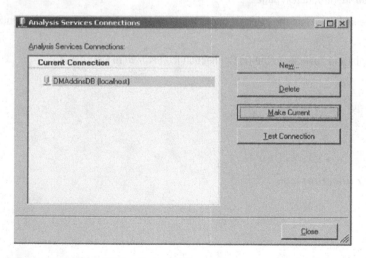

Figure 1-10. *The Make Current button*

13. Navigate to the Training Data sheet and the Analyze tab. This can be found by looking at the sheet names at the bottom of the workbook. The sheet will be called Training Data. Click a cell in the table, and click Detect Categories.

14. Review the columns shown in Figure 1-11, and decide which columns to select. In this case, everything but the ID column should be selected.

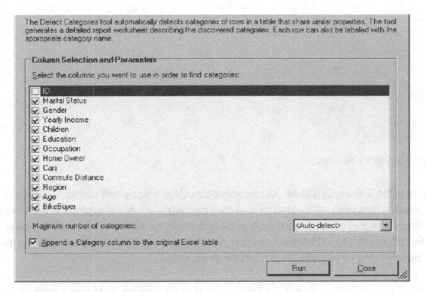

Figure 1-11. *Column selection*

15. Click Run, and the window displayed in Figure 1-12 will be shown.

Figure 1-12. *Detecting categories*

16. Once the Detect Categories dialog closes, a series of graphs and charts will be displayed. Use the filter on the category characteristics to see different categories outlined in Figure 1-13. Rename the categories to something more fitting by editing the entries in the Category Name column of the category graph shown in Figure 1-14.

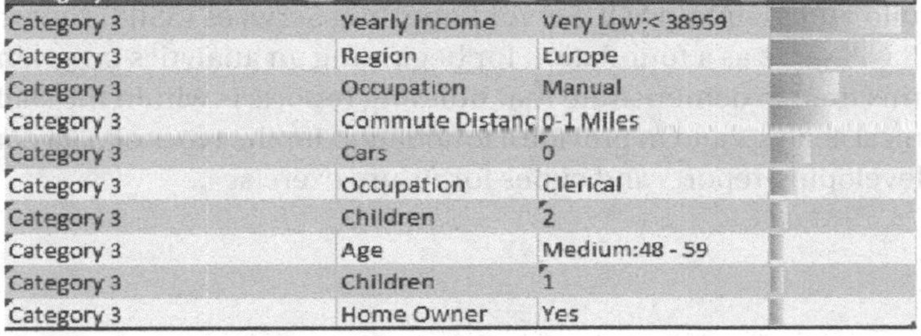

Category	Column	Value	Relative In
Category 3	Yearly Income	Very Low:< 38959	
Category 3	Region	Europe	
Category 3	Occupation	Manual	
Category 3	Commute Distanc	0-1 Miles	
Category 3	Cars	0	
Category 3	Occupation	Clerical	
Category 3	Children	2	
Category 3	Age	Medium:48 - 59	
Category 3	Children	1	
Category 3	Home Owner	Yes	

Figure 1-13. *Category characteristics*

Category Name	Row Count
Educated, Short Commute	1259
Low Income, Long Commute	1096
Low Income, Short Commute	840
High Income, Long Commute	762
Low Income, Young	788
Educated, High Income	670
Low Income, Children	650
Low Income, Many Cars	495
Medium Income, Children	440

Figure 1-14. *Category names*

17. Navigate back to the Training Data sheet. All customers are categorized by their names. Customers can be filtered based on categories and targeted for marketing campaigns. For example, people in the "Medium Income, Children" category could be sent e-mails at the winter holidays describing new children's bikes. People in the "Educated, Short Commute" category could be sent e-mails in the spring detailing the benefits of bicycle riding for individual health and the environment.

Occupation	Home Owner	Cars	Commute Distance	Region	Age	BikeBuyer	Category
Professional	Yes	4	1-2 Miles	Pacific	41	No	Medium Income, Children
Professional	Yes	0	0-1 Miles	North America	47	Yes	Medium Income, Children
Professional	Yes	0	0-1 Miles	North America	37	Yes	Medium Income, Children
Professional	Yes	0	2-5 Miles	Pacific	40	Yes	Medium Income, Children
Professional	Yes	0	0-1 Miles	North America	48	Yes	Medium Income, Children
Professional	Yes	0	0-1 Miles	Pacific	36	Yes	Medium Income, Children
Professional	No	1	0-1 Miles	Pacific	38	Yes	Medium Income, Children
Professional	No	4	10+ Miles	Pacific	32	Yes	Medium Income, Children
Professional	Yes	0	1-2 Miles	Pacific	39	Yes	Medium Income, Children
Professional	No	3	10+ Miles	Pacific	34	Yes	Medium Income, Children
Professional	Yes	2	10+ Miles	Pacific	30	Yes	Medium Income, Children
Professional	Yes	0	0-1 Miles	Pacific	36	Yes	Medium Income, Children
Professional	Yes	4	10+ Miles	Pacific	38	Yes	Medium Income, Children
Professional	Yes	4	10+ Miles	Pacific	35	Yes	Medium Income, Children

Figure 1-15. *Additional information*

18. Spend some time navigating through the other tabs and information shown in Figure 1-15. Explore the different ways the tools can be used.

The final exercise in this chapter, Exercise 1-3, helps you to familiarize yourself with the Microsoft tools used to build and maintain SQL Server Reporting Services (SSRS) reports. For many organizations, SSRS will serve as a foundation for beginning an analytics program. We like to introduce SSRS at this time to demonstrate that building reports is within the skill set of both developers and technical analysts and to provide a foundation for the types of data connections you will use when developing reports and cubes for future exercises.

Exercise 1-3. Building a Basic SQL Server Reporting Services Report

The exercise will walk through the initial creation of a reporting services report. The report, entitled Sales Report, will render information regarding opportunities won in the past year and any open opportunities. Selected parameter values will determine the data displayed.

1. SQL Server Business Intelligence Development Studio (BIDS) ships with SQL Server 2008. When you install SQL Server you must make an active decision to install BIDS. Navigate to Start ➤ All Programs ➤ SQL Server ➤ SQL Server Business Intelligence Development Studio.

2. Navigate to File ➤ New ➤ Project. Select the Report Server Project, as shown in Figure 1-16.

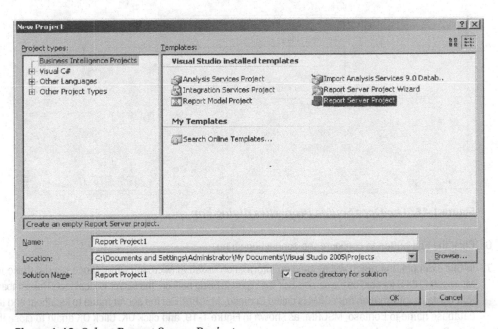

Figure 1-16. *Select Report Server Project.*

3. Give the report a name, and click OK.

4. When the Solution Explorer window shown in Figure 1-17 opens, right-click Reports, click Add, and then click Add New Item.

Figure 1-17. *Adding a new item*

5. Select Report, and type **Opportunities.rdl** for the report name. Click OK. The report will open to the dataset page. Click the New drop-down in the Report Data section to create a new data source. The Data Source Properties dialog box, shown in Figure 1-18, is used to create a connection to the database.

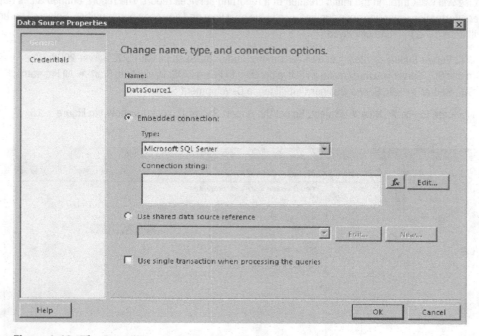

Figure 1-18. *The Data Source Properties dialog box*

6. Click the Edit button to configure the connection string.

7. In this example, the report will be built on information based in Microsoft CRM. Since the database for Microsoft CRM is located on the same sever the report is being built on, the server is localhost. The database that contains information from CRM is called Contoso_MSCRM. Set the server name to localhost and the database name to Contoso_MSCRM, as shown in Figure 1-19, and click OK. Click OK again to close the Data Source Properties window.

8. Right-click the newly created data source, and click Add DataSet. Change the name of the dataset to **OpenOpportunities**. In the query window, type the following text:

```
SELECT AccountIDName AS AccountName,
Name AS OpportunityName,
EstimatedValue AS EstimatedValue,
EstimatedCloseDate
AS EstimatedCloseDate
FROM FilteredOpportunity
WHERE StateCodeName = 'Open'
  AND OwnerID IN (@SalesRep)
```

When these tasks are complete, the dataset will resemble Figure 1-20.

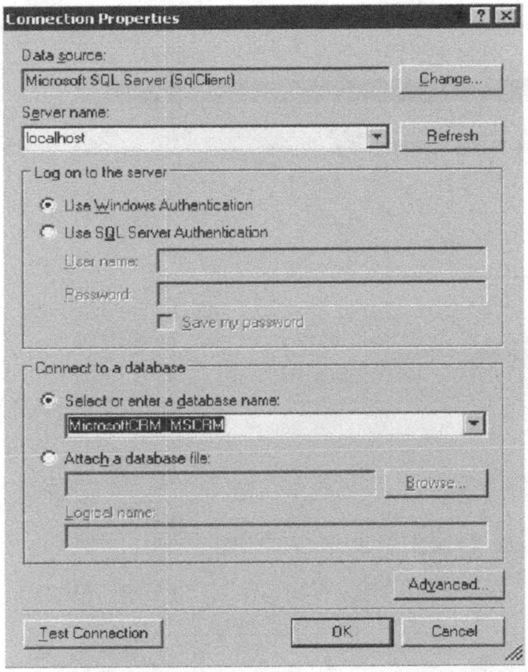

Figure 1-19. *The Connection Properties dialog*

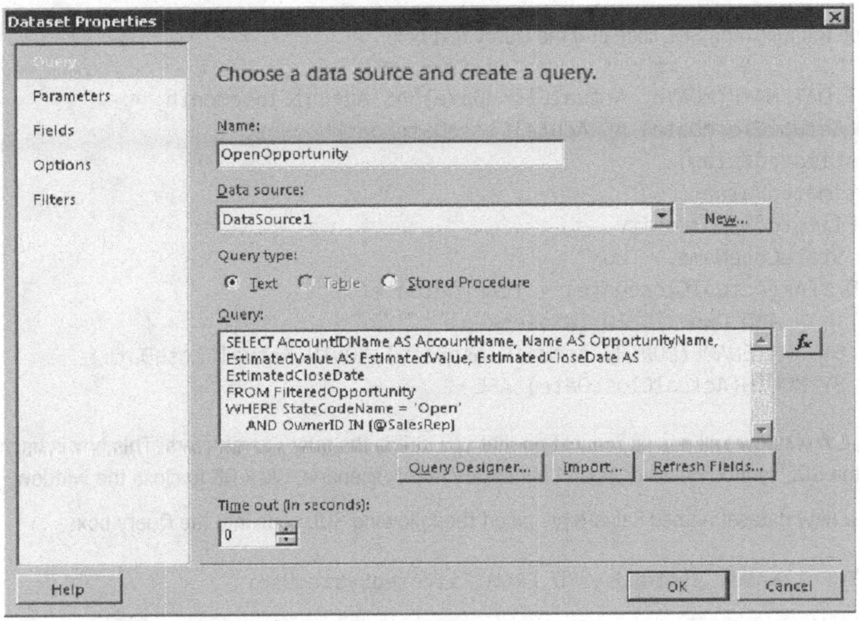

Figure 1-20. *The Dataset Properties dialog*

9. Click OK to close the window.

10. Create a new dataset by right-clicking the data source and clicking New Dataset. In the dialog displayed
    in Figure 1-21, type **WonOpportunities** in the Name field.

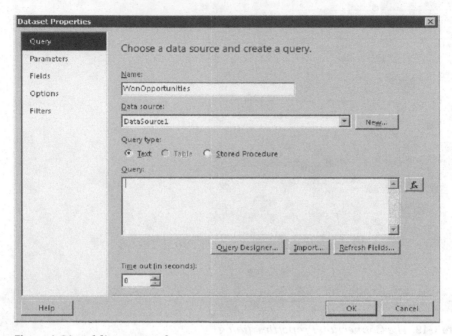

Figure 1-21. *Adding a new dataset*

And type the following SQL code into the Query text box:

```
SELECT DATENAME(MONTH, ActualCloseDate) AS ActualCloseMonth,
MONTH(ActualCloseDate) AS AcutalCloseDateMonthNumber,
SUM(EstimatedValue)
AS EstimatedValue
FROM FilteredOpportunity
WHERE StateCodeName = 'Won'
   AND YEAR(ActualCloseDate) = YEAR(GetDate())
          AND OwnerID IN (@SalesRep)
GROUP BY  DATENAME(MONTH, ActualCloseDate),MONTH(ActualCloseDate)
ORDER BY MONTH(ActualCloseDate) ASC
```

11. Click OK. A window will pop up requesting that you define the query parameters. This box is useful to
    check the SQL syntax. However, it isn't necessary in this scenario. Click OK to close the window.

12. Create a new dataset named SalesReps. Insert the following SQL code into the Query box:

```
SELECT FullName, SystemUserID FROM FilteredSystemUser
```

13. Click OK to close the window. Expand the Parameters folder in the Report Data window. Double-click the SalesRep parameter to configure the parameter properties.

14. Figure 1-22 shows the general screen for the parameter properties. Set the properties of the SalesRep parameter, which will list all of the sales representatives in the SalesRep dataset. Users will have the ability to select one, all, or a few representatives. The report's default behavior will be to run for all sales representatives. Set the values in the Report Parameter Properties dialog as follows:

The General tab:

- For Name, type **SalesRep**.

- For Prompt, type **Sales Rep**.

- For "Data type," type **Text**.

- Check "Allow multiple values," and leave "Allow null value" and "Allow blank value" blank.

- Set the parameter visibility to Visible.

The Available Values tab:

- Set available values to From Query.

- Set the Available Values to "Get values from a query," the Dataset field to SalesRep, the Value field to SystemUserID, and Label field to FullName.

The Default Values tab:

- Set the Default Values to "Get values from a query." Set the dataset to SalesReps and the Value field to SystemUserID.

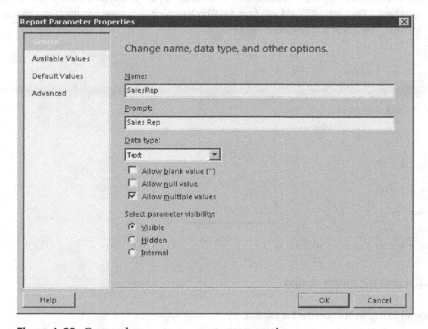

Figure 1-22. *General report parameter properties*

15. Click OK to leave this screen. Check to see if the toolbox is located on the left-hand side of the project. If it is not, navigate to View ➤ Toolbox to add the toolbox to the view.

16. One informative and visually appealing way to display revenue from won opportunities over time is to chart the information in a graph. Click the chart icon, and drag it onto the canvas. Once the chart is on the canvas, a window will automatically be displayed that requires the report creator to select a chart type. Select the smooth area chart. Click OK. The results are shown in Figure 1-23.

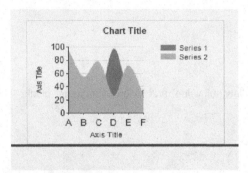

Figure 1-23. *A smooth area chart*

17. Change the chart title from Chart Title to Won Opportunities by clicking the chart title and typing in the new title. Set the title format to Calibri. Right-click the graph, select Chart Properties, and set the color palate to "pastel."

18. Drag the EstimatedValue field from the WonOpportunites dataset on to the section of the graph entitled "Drop data fields here." Drag ActualCloseMonth from the WonOpportunities dataset into the "Drop category fields here" section. The graph will resemble Figure 1-24.

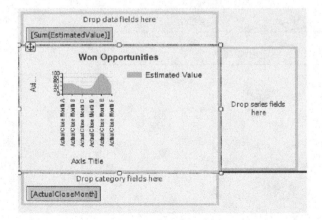

Figure 1-24. *A sample graph design*

19. Click the legend to highlight it. Delete the legend.

20. Delete both axis titles by highlighting each title and clicking the Delete key on the keyboard.

21. Right-click the y axis, and navigate to the properties. Navigate to the Number tab. Select Currency. Set the decimal places to 0, and check the "Use 1000 separator (,)" box. The properties page will look like Figure 1-25.

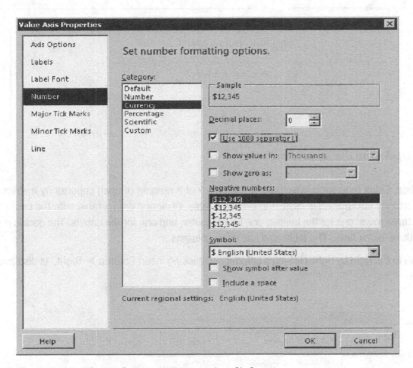

Figure 1-25. *The Value Axis Properties dialog*

22. Drag a text box on to the canvas. Click the text box, and type **Sales Report**. Make the text box larger, and move it to the top of the canvas, as shown in the upper left-hand corner of Figure 1-26.

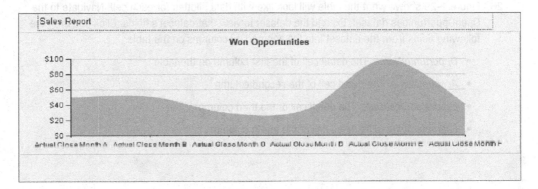

Figure 1-26. *Adding a text box*

23. Click the text box, and use the toolbar shown in Figure 1-27 to set the font to Calibri and font size to 24pt and to center the text.

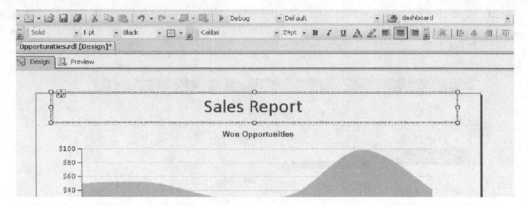

Figure 1-27. *Updating the report font*

24. Open the toolbox. Sales representatives need to keep track of a number of open opportunity metrics, and open opportunity information is easiest to view in a table. Click and drag a table onto the canvas. The table has three rows: one for the header, one for the footer, and one for the details. The details row is marked by three black lines. The table also has three columns.

25. Insert a column to the right by right-clicking a column and clicking Insert Column ➤ Right, as displayed in Figure 1-28.

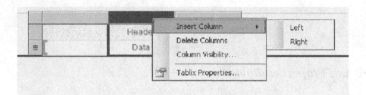

Figure 1-28. *Inserting a column*

26. Figure 1-29 shows what the table will look like with data allotted for each cell. Navigate to the OpenOpportunities dataset. Expand the dataset to view that dataset's fields. Click and drag the following fields from the dataset into the appropriate columns on the table:

   - *OpportunityName*: The detail cell of the first column on the table
   - *AccountName*: The detail cell of the second column
   - *EstimatedCloseDate*: The detail cell of the third column
   - *EstimatedValue*: The detail cell of the fourth column

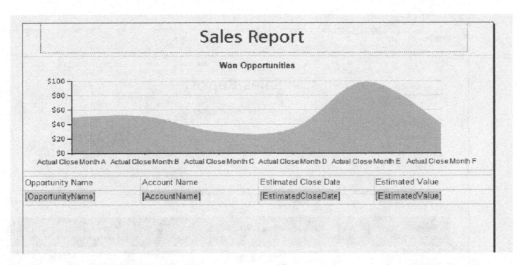

Figure 1-29. *The updated report*

27. Highlight the table, and use the toolbar to change the font to Calibri.

28. Highlight the top row, and change the background to MediumSeaGreen by clicking the background color button on the toolbar.

29. Right-click the header row, and click Insert row ➤ Above. Highlight the new row and right-click. Choose Merge Cells. Use the properties window to change the background color to SeaGreen, text color to White, font size to 14pt, and text alignment to Center. Type **Open Opportunities** into the new row.

30. To create a totals row at the bottom of the table, right-click the details row, and click Insert Row ➤ Outside Group—Below. Navigate to the totals row. Mouse over the cell where the totals row and the Estimated Value column intersect. A table icon will appear. Click the icon, and select EstimatedValue. The new cell will read [Sum(EstimatedValue)]. The result is shown in Figure 1-30.

Opportunity Name	Account Name	Estimated Close Date	Estimated Value
[OpportunityName]	[AccountName]	[EstimatedCloseDate]	[EstimatedValue]
			[Sum(EstimatedValue)]

Figure 1-30. *Adding row totals*

31. Format the dollar values for Estimated Value by highlighting the applicable cells and navigating to Properties. Set the Format cell to $#,###.

32. The report is ready to be deployed to a report server. Navigate to the Preview tab to see how it looks when an individual runs the report. Figure 1-31 provides an example of this.

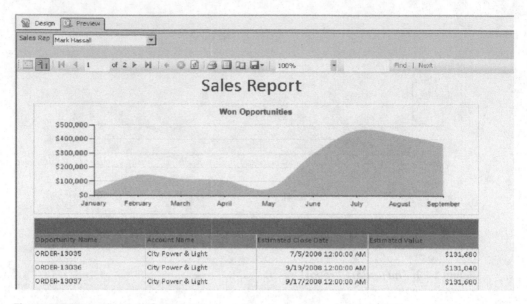

Figure 1-31. *Previewing the report*

33. For extra practice, try to do the following on your own:

a. Add more columns to the open opportunities table for the Owner and Modified On.

b. Alphabetize the names of the sales representatives in the drop-down.

c. Enable sorting on the Opportunity Name, Account Name, and Estimated Value fields.

Summary

This chapter provides a background on analytics and on a number of the tools that will be used throughout this book. The exercises in future chapters will add more detail and complexity to both the product and the analytics system.

In general, most organizations need to go beyond Excel reporting and out-of-the-box application reports but don't understand how to get started and how to plan a long-term strategy. The two upcoming chapters of this book will help in those departments by providing guidelines for successful implementations. These chapters also assist with the most fundamental of tasks, the development of key performance indicators (KPIs).

CHAPTER 2

■ ■ ■

Seven Keys to Successful Reporting Projects

Finding the balance between the functional components of an analytics implementation, like process design, key performance indicator (KPI) development, development, look and feel, and the technical items, like tool selection and complex feature development, is a daunting task. You typically must evaluate the trade-offs associated with spending time in one area vs. another. This chapter will focus on providing you with the key tasks and tools necessary to lay an effective groundwork for any analytics implementation, large or small.

The Seven Keys Approach

Our approach to BI is based on three fundamental beliefs:

- All successful BI projects start with an understanding of the key metrics that drive the business and work through a proven design and implementation approach.

- Cost-effective BI projects focus on leveraging only the components of the BI platform necessary to deliver the key metrics in an accurate and timely manner. There is no one-size-fits-all solution when selecting the right components of the BI platform. A large part of defining the technical solution has to be driven by selecting the right tool for the skill level and preferences of the user community.

- Integrity of the business processes and underlying data will ultimately define the success or failure of any created reports, dashboards, and scorecards.

With these beliefs in mind, we recognize that successful business intelligence initiatives will require different tools from the Microsoft BI platform for different organizations, but we use a set of seven common key tasks that allow our clients to select the right technologies and to make the appropriate implementation choices to achieve their desired outcomes.

Key 1: Developing Executive Sponsorship

The first key of a successful business intelligence project begins at the top. Ensuring that the management team and key managers are aligned with the goals of the project will allow these individuals to take a more active role in designing and implementing an analytics solution. This executive sponsorship can take two forms: department managers and senior executives.

Department Managers

As we mention briefly in Chapter 1, a number of factors contribute to failed business intelligence initiatives, including a lack of trust. Oftentimes, when senior executives use analytics to quantify the success or failure of a specific group or department, managers will immediately dismiss the quality of the data or will challenge the availability of the displayed information. In addition to posing an employee-management challenge, this lack of trust creates other issues throughout the team.

Paramount among the additional issues created is proliferation of distrust throughout the rest of the employees in the business unit. Once managers distrust the analytics presented to them, members of their teams will not only follow suit but may begin to use critical business applications less frequently.

Senior Executives

From a senior executive perspective, there are two distinct values to having a great reporting solution. First, it is important to have metrics to point to when gauging the health of a business. Second, analytical information is invaluable when managing employees and providing feedback during evaluations.

To ensure adoption of the delivered solution, senior executives can choose between the carrot and the stick approaches. While both of these approaches have merit, the decision on direction depends on management style and the existing adoption situation within an organization. Based on our experience, few managers have the stomach to make the stick work in the absence of carrots, so keep that in mind as your planning process progresses.

Regardless of their positions in the organization, the executive sponsors' roles in the process are to drive requirements, facilitate the key performance indicator and deliverable prioritization process, and drive the overall process to completion. Ultimately, the sponsor should ensure that the organization seeks outside help where needed but owns the overall implementation.

Key 2: Identifying Organizational Key Performance Indicators

The second key step to effectively leverage the Microsoft BI tools is to identify the key organizational metrics that drive business performance; such metrics are called key performance indicators (KPIs). This may sound obvious, but it's critical to have a clear business-oriented target when selecting the appropriate components of the platform to use. In addition, it's important to not only identify the metrics that stakeholders find interesting but to focus on identifying and clearly defining the metrics that serve as leading indicators for where the business is headed for each key stakeholder group.

This process can be as simple as creating a list of the important metrics and may result in the identification of 10 to 20 key metrics for each stakeholder group and 10 to 20 key metrics for the executive team and board. Once the list is generated, each metric can be evaluated against a number of criteria, including these:

- Is the data that it takes to evaluate this KPI trustworthy and readily available?

- Is the metric well defined, and will it make sense to those who evaluate it?

- Does the identified metric align with the goals of the organization?

Figure 2-1 provides a high-level example of what makes a good metric. Significantly more information on developing KPIs can be found in Chapter 3.

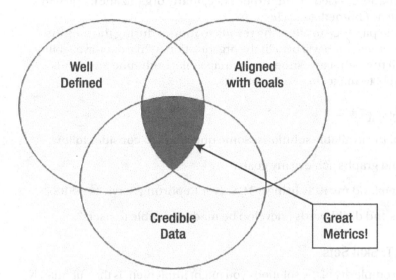

Figure 2-1. *Ideal KPIs*

Key 3: Delivering Structured, Ad Hoc Reports

Once you have secured executive sponsorship and reviewed and developed the KPIs that are pertinent to the business, it is appropriate to move into the evaluation and solution design process. Keep in mind that, in phase one at least, you should deliver only the most necessary solution components. Your solution and evaluation process should include selecting the appropriate technologies, reviewing the appropriate Microsoft BI tools for various user roles, and identifying and prioritizing final phase-one solution components.

Selecting Appropriate Technologies

Evaluating the technologies to use for phase one of the implementation is an important process. This evaluation should include the high-level decision points and questions described in the following subsections.

Assessing Existing Technology Investments

Take stock of the organizations' existing BI tools. Understanding what is available will allow better-informed decisions to be made, in terms of both additional product purchases and investments in consulting assistance during the analytics implementation. Here are some questions to consider:

- What technologies does my organization currently own?

- Do I need to purchase additional technologies?

- If so, what is the associated cost?

Leveraging products that are already part of the organization, and thereby reducing the phase-one investment, may also enable the business to be more patient when evaluating the results of the initial implementation. Based on our experience, many organizations rush to judgment when the results are not immediately clear.

Taking time and having the patience to allow the results to morph during the months immediately following the implementation will benefit the organization. While data-availability and quality issues may arise, if the initial investment is manageable, both time and funds (if needed) will then be available to make these adjustments.

Assessing Technology Complexity

Think about the complexity of the available solutions. Some questions to consider follow:

- Do Excel pivot tables and graphs achieve my goals?

- Can I develop and understand my KPIs using SQL Server Reporting Services (SSRS)?

- How should the reports and dashboards I develop be made available to users?

Assessing Power User and I.T. Skill Sets

One reason to think about the complexity of the solutions you might implement is that, ultimately, people have to use and apply those solutions. A sure road to failure is to pick a solution that is too complex for the users in question. So consider these questions:

- Do I have data or reporting analysts as part of the business units consuming the reports?

- With what technologies are my IT and development staff members comfortable working?

Leveraging functional expertise as needed is important. However, you should ultimately own your analytics implementation. This notion of ownership is also true when it comes to building and supporting the tools developed. Like most business applications, if reports aren't consistently tweaked and updated, the information they present will become stale and hold less value for the organization. Table 3-1 provides a high-level overview of the development and administration capabilities needed to work with many of the available Microsoft tools.

At every stage in the functional deployment process, these technology items should be considered. Working through these items makes straightforward tasks of evaluating the Microsoft BI platform and targeting the appropriate tools to get business users on their way to making better-informed decisions aligned with their KPIs.

Table 3-1. *Microsoft Product Development Skills*

Microsoft Product	Development Skills and Environment	Data Access
Excel	Business users can develop reports through knowledge of pivot tables and Excel functions.	Users will have built-in access to online analytical processing (OLAP) cubes and SQL Server data. Access is most frequently accomplished through pivot tables.
SQL Server Reporting Services (SSRS)	Reports are developed via the Microsoft BI Studio (Visual Studio) using SQL and Multidimensional Expressions (MDX).	SSRS provides built-in access to OLAP cubes and authoring for SQL Server data sets.
SQL Server Analysis Services (SSAS)	Cubes are developed via the Microsoft BI studio (Visual Studio) using MDX.	Cubes can consume SQL queries or access SQL tables directly.

Reviewing the Appropriate Microsoft BI Tools for Various User Roles

From a technology perspective, evaluating tools relative to those needing to use them is likely the most important factor in selecting which components belong in phase one. Specifically, when provided with tools that don't meet their daily or reporting needs, business users may begin to utilize data and tools that are not part of the organization-wide strategy for business intelligence.

The following roles should be considered when reviewing the appropriateness of users' tools:

- *Reporting and data analysts*: Employees who are responsible for generating reports and evaluating the success of KPIs developed for the business

- *Business application users*: Users like sales or service representatives who are the source of much of the organization's valuable data and who spend most of their time within lines of business applications or Microsoft Outlook

- *Senior executives and managers*: Individuals within the organization who need to see quick, often graphical representations of information and statistics

Reports available for analysts, such as the example in Figure 2-2, typically offer options allowing analysts to see both the data and associated graphical representations. Additionally, those reports often offer tools that analysts can use to slice, dice, and filter the data as needed to accomplish the desired results and answer the analyst's questions. Finally, many analyst-focused reports and dashboards emphasize the way in which data is trending.

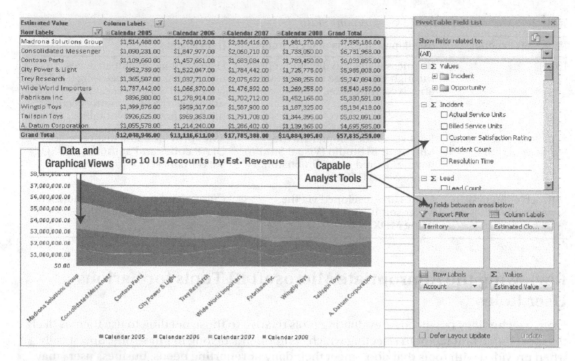

Figure 2-2. *An analyst-focused tool example*

Reporting tools used by a more typical user within the business, such as sales or service representatives, need to be available quickly. They also need to be aligned with those users' regular activities, as shown by the example in Figure 2-3. This example shows how a user can open a specific CRM account and find detailed, contextually relevant information inside the Account window. Users of ERP or accounting applications often use quick views or lists to manage information or metrics that are important. Similarly, users of CRM applications benefit from analytics that are embedded in various places throughout the tool that provide information at a glance.

Because of their level of responsibility, executives and managers within the organization typically require the ability to view information quickly and without having to manipulate or change the view or data. For this reason, executives benefit from highly data-dense reporting tools. Data-dense displays can be developed in many tool sets, but one solution is provided by SharePoint leveraging PerformancePoint services, where all information is available on one screen with the ability to filter and drill down intuitively. Figure 2-4 shows an example of one of these types of dashboards.

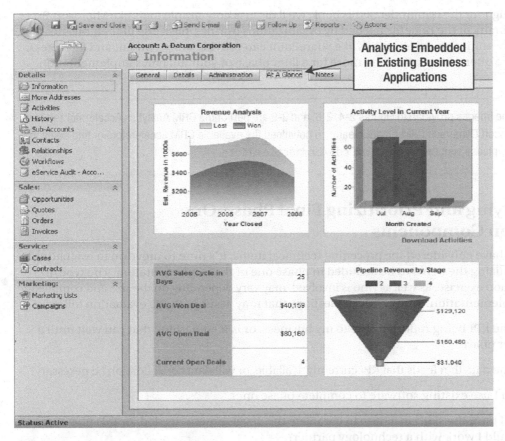

Figure 2-3. *An example of embedded analytics for business application users*

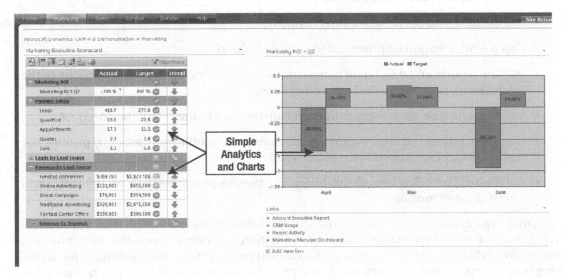

Figure 2-4. *A SharePoint-delivered executive dashboard*

Throughout the remainder of this book, we'll discuss how simple tools like Microsoft Excel can offer many of the benefits needed by organizations during phase one of their business intelligence initiative. Applications like SharePoint can provide more content and flashiness, but you are often better off saving those for a later phase of your analytics implementation.

Note The images provided in Figures 2-4, 2-6, and 2-9 are part of the CRM Analytics Accelerator released by the Microsoft Dynamics CRM product team. To download the available CRM accelerators or find additional information, please visit www.codeplex.com/crmaccelerators.

Identifying and Prioritizing Final Phase-One Solution Components

Once you have considered the preceding technical items, it's time to move on to evaluating and prioritizing the items to be included in phase one of the implementation. The type of prioritization exercise, as well as who is involved, may vary depending on the size and complexity of the implementation. Some typical questions that may assist with the evaluation follow:

- Is the KPI being reported core to my business, or is it something that can wait until a later phase?

- Is the data that feeds that KPI currently available, or will data consolidation be necessary?

- Can I use existing software to complete phase one?

- Do I have the skills in-house to complete the development needed for this phase, or should I work with a technology partner?

- Can I compare the metrics I defined?

- Are the data sources needed clearly defined?

- Can the information be presented in a timely fashion?

- Will the reports and dashboard being considered allow me to draw user attention to the information, rather than the bells and whistles?

- Will the structure allow users to interact with the data to the extent they need to?

- Can users interact with the reports online, offline, on mobile devices, or by printing the reports, whichever format is the most useful?

- Are the displays being considered data dense, thereby providing the most information in a consolidated format?

Once organizations select the technology tools based on their ability to achieve the effective delivery of the prioritized KPIs, the implementation generally is most effective if it focuses on iterative delivery of reports for specific functional groups, pulling data from multiple underlying business applications simultaneously and providing the most value to end users. Figure 2-5 shows how an iterative approach allows business users to start with a general understanding of the metrics they would like to see and subsequently clarify their requirements within the context of the actual data with each new version of reports. In this scenario, no detailed design document is generated. Instead, the development team builds iteratively toward a solution.

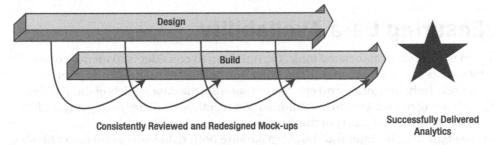

Figure 2-5. *Iteratively designing and building an analytics solution*

The solution is actively developed with the business users; business owners see a quick return on their investments, and the project has built-in flexibility to adapt to meet the business needs as they evolve. The final solution, which could end up as shown in Figure 2-6, provides for robust, effective operational reporting.

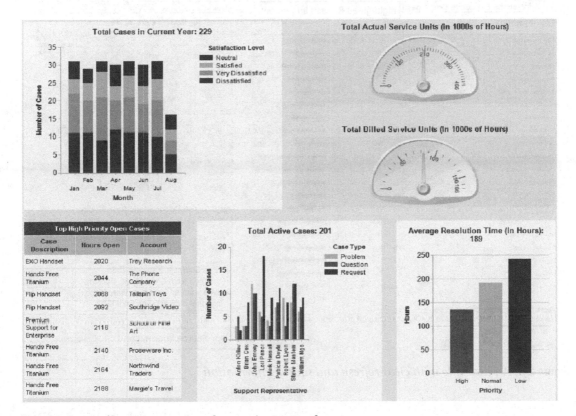

Figure 2-6. *An effective operational reporting example*

With functional and technical components of the implementation evaluated, it becomes practical to manage the relevant attributes from the core systems that will serve as the source data for the business intelligence initiative. At this stage in the process, the next two key steps, which both focus on data, become important.

Key 4: Ensuring Data Availability

After deciding on the KPIs and associated tools, the next step to consider is to identify where the relevant data exists and how it relates to the other attributes that make up any given KPI. This is normally a relatively straightforward exercise of reviewing the data models of the affected applications, identifying related keys to link information together, and identifying any underlying inconsistencies in the granularity of the data.

Once you've identified the data, you should make sure both data source and data refresh information is available on all the reports that you generate. That source and refresh information will quickly answer questions about the source of the data should inconsistencies arise and will allow users to compare apples to apples when viewing multiple versions of a report.

Figure 2-7 provides an example of how refresh information can be provided and where source information can be displayed on a complex, data-rich report.

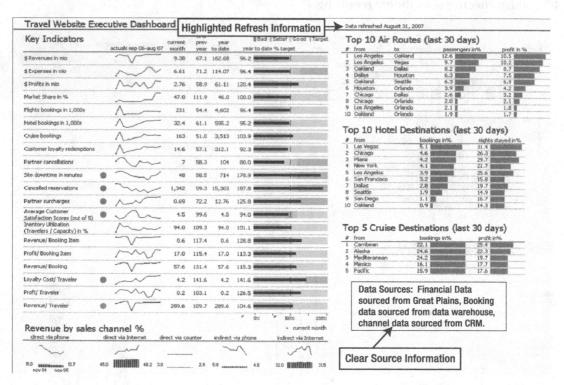

Figure 2-7. *An example with clear refresh and source information*

Key 5: Proactively Reviewing Data Quality

Conduct a proactive, thorough review of the quality of the underlying data. By ensuring the data is of good quality and up to date, you can avoid confusion about report accuracy and ensure that your project does not fail due to business stakeholders' inability to trust the data.

In many instances, data quality can be reviewed within the lines of business applications themselves. By performing advanced searches and reviewing simple lists of information, many data issues will become apparent. Additionally, many applications contain algorithms that help to identify issues that exist with the data.

Figure 2-8 illustrates a simple CRM application query that can identify sales opportunities that would otherwise corrupt pipeline reports. Most business applications will provide the same functionality, and organizations must be able to rely on power users of key applications to complete this analysis. A simple review of this type of operational and ad hoc report will identify any data irregularities that exist.

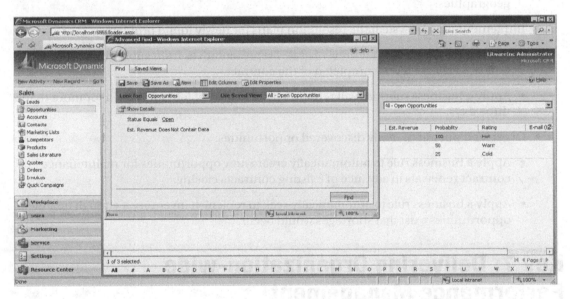

Figure 2-8. *A data-quality search example*

Key 6: Adjusting Core System Business Rules

Many organizations get through the first five steps in this process successfully. They are able to roll out the phase-one version of operational and ad hoc reports for executives and managers and see some short-term value in the data displayed. Unfortunately, often the insight gathered from adoption of these tools is never fully realized, because time is not allocated after deployment to update business rules in the underlying applications based on the initial learning.

Based on our implementation experience, the most effective way to get improved return on any BI initiative is to allocate 15–20 percent of the total project time to support the business and associated applications after the initial reporting rollout has gone into production. This level of planning allows the team to improve the business performance by combining the insights from the reporting systems with their underlying business applications' ability to manage business rules. Here are some enhancements that may happen during this postdeployment phase:

- Development of improved accuracy and consistency within reports:

  - Modify field values available in pick lists to ensure all individuals are using common terms.

  - Modify the attributes that are required in underlying business systems to ensure reporting is complete.

  - Deliver ad hoc training to resolve data inconsistencies among users in different geographies.

- Implementation of systematic resolution plans for newly found problems:

  - Apply a business rule that prevents sales representatives from submitting orders unless a legal review is completed of the contract.

  - Apply a business rule that will reroute assigned leads if left untouched for more than three days.

- Organized pursuit of newly discovered opportunities:

  - Apply a business rule to automatically create new opportunities for maintenance contract renewals in advance of existing contracts closing.

  - Apply a business rule to automatically seek to replenish inventory if enough qualified opportunities exist that shortages would occur.

Key 7: Delivering Organization-wide Performance Management

Following the completion of the preceding steps, and more importantly, delivery of an operational, ad hoc, phase-one reporting solution, organizations are ready to commit additional time and project cycles to report enhancement and growth of their existing analytics solution.

The development of a report commonly used for organization-wide performance management, such as the example in Figure 2-9, is generally undertaken as a second and ongoing phase of a business intelligence rollout. Implementing performance management is the logical next step from a fully functioning reporting solution, as it combines the insight from operational and ad hoc reports with dynamic scorecarding, planning, and budgeting tools. The resulting application systematically manages and displays KPIs in the context of performance targets with the ability to drill down to granular details of how each component of the business is performing to its target. To achieve this goal, Microsoft provides the PerformancePoint application that consolidates access to all other reporting tools and allows for extremely robust and visual analysis of the business.

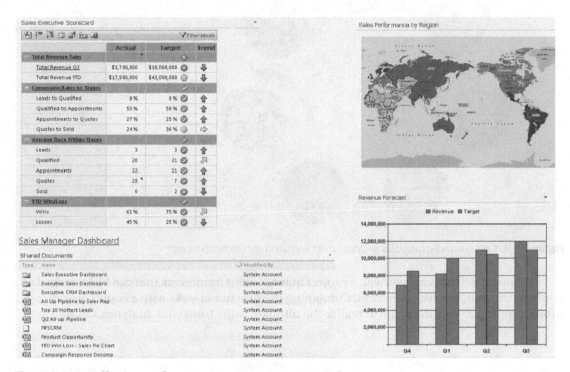

Figure 2-9. *An effective performance management example*

Implementing organization-wide performance management is the goal for many organizations undertaking BI initiatives, but it is critical to take a step-by-step approach toward achieving this goal.

Summary

By working through the key steps in this chapter in small, manageable stages, you will ultimately provide for a more successful analytics implementation. These keys to implementation also allow you to avoid some of the primary pitfalls associated with implementations discussed in Chapter 1, especially:

- Differing Priorities
- Data Explosion
- Lack of Trust.

Consistently performing the tasks highlighted in Figure 2-10 will not only allow for continued growth of an analytics solution, but also will prevent existing operation and ad hoc reports and dashboards from becoming stale and less valuable.

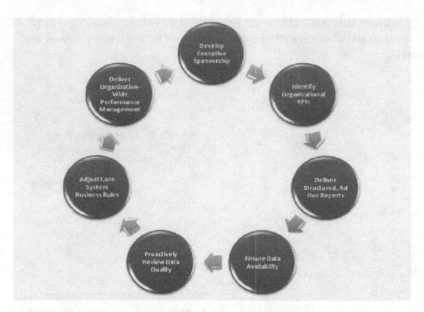

Figure 2-10. *Continued analytics process and technology improvement*

Chapter 8 will provide you with a project management framework that can be leveraged as you move through these seven keys. Combining the functional tasks with a sound overall project approach will allow you to realize the ultimate value from your analytics solution.

CHAPTER 3

■ ■ ■

Key Performance Indicators

This chapter outlines key considerations in defining key performance indicators (KPIs) that will be meaningful when rolled out in scorecards across the organization. This is not intended to be a comprehensive presentation on KPIs (a topic that could itself span the length of an entire book), but it will outline core principles that we have seen leveraged by organizations as they have set up their first few versions of dashboards and scorecards. In addition, we will attempt to provide a practical example of how a company might apply these principles to develop a list of meaningful KPIs.

Keeping KPIs Forward Looking

Analytics initiatives often begin with organizations requesting that business users document their requirements for dashboards and reports. Users will work as individuals or in small teams to list a set of metrics that they believe are used to quantitatively evaluate their performance. The technical team will follow up with a proposed approach for rendering these metrics in a dashboard or set of reports while deprecating any metrics for which they cannot effectively capture the data. At first glance, this approach is a common-sense way to begin to deliver dashboards to the organization, but it does miss a larger truth.

The larger truth is that, in many organizations, the metrics currently in place for evaluating sales and marketing performance are strictly backward looking and reflect performance of past periods. For example, a typical request for a sales manager dashboard might include the following components:

- *Sales forecast*: Show all the deals set to close within the current quarter weighted by probability or sales stage.

- *Sales pipeline*: Show the value of all the open deals in my pipeline and the trend over time.

- *Performance*: Show the performance of my sales team to date (e.g., win value and win rate).

Figure 3-1 shows an example of what a simple sales manager dashboard might look like.

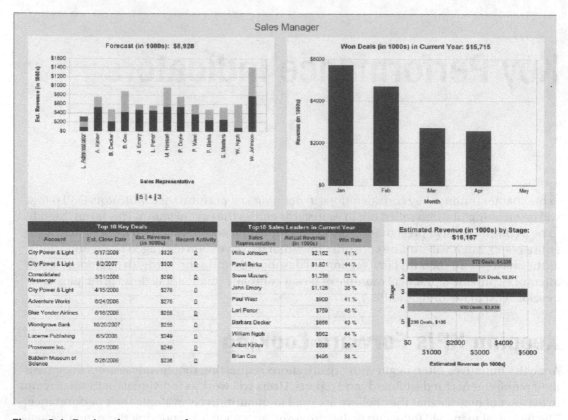

Figure 3-1. *Basic sales scorecard*

Figure 3-1 might appear to represent a comprehensive solution for a sales dashboard. In reality, this dashboard is almost entirely focused on tracking performance using metrics that look backward. By this, I mean that each measure on this dashboard shows you the sales organization from a different perspective based on where it is today (and historical context of where it has been), but it does not provide insight into where it is going to be one, two, or three quarters from now.

A fully functioning analytical solution will combine critical metrics that show performance to date with metrics that are indicative of future performance. The difference is that one set of metrics tells you where you are. The other provides strong evidence for where you will be.

Organizations have a tendency to fall back on the metrics that demonstrate where they are right now, because those metrics generally mirror the way that peoples' job performances are evaluated (i.e., the sales manager is measured on total revenue, so a sales forecast seems like the best metric to review on a routine basis), and these metrics are easier for technical teams to capture and reproduce in repeatable reports and dashboards. The power of a complete set of KPIs is that they can not only illuminate where the organization is today but project where the organization will be and provide visibility into where key individuals can engage to correct the course for the organization if the forward-looking KPIs are off track.

With this in mind, this chapter will focus on one process an organization can use to develop a set of KPIs that are not only balanced between forward and backward metrics but also take into account a broader set of core principles that can help ensure that the metrics selected will be effective in leading the organization toward achieving its overall goals.

Understanding the Core Principles for KPIs

The set of core principles outlined in this section can be used by any organization to validate a set of foundational KPIs that can serve as the core business metrics for a comprehensive sales and marketing analytics program. For deeper information on the development of KPIs and their role in organizational strategy the following are excellent resources, see *Key Performance Indicators* by David Paramenter (Wiley, 2007) and *Balanced Scorecard Step-By-Step* by Paul Niven (Wiley, 2006).

In order for KPIs to be useful in driving business performance, you need to have a standard for what constitutes a good KPI. Further, you need to have an awareness of this standard in order to be active participants in managing the KPIs and refining them over time. Core principles that we encourage clients to follow include the following:

- The metric is specific.

- The metric is clearly owned by a given department or group.

- The metric is measurable.

- The metric can be produced in a timely manner.

- The quantity of KPIs must be limited to a manageable few items for a given scorecard.

- KPIs must have targets.

- KPIs must be aligned with overall organizational goals.

Let's examine each of these principles in detail.

Using Specific Metrics

Using specific metrics means that each metric has a precise definition that can be easily explained and will be understood by any reasonable person within the organization. The most common example of a sales and marketing metric that fails the specificity test is forecasted revenue. We're not saying that having a measure for forecasted revenue isn't important, but we do mean to say that this metric must be completely clear and must be well understood across the organization. For many organizations that we work with, when we ask what forecast revenue is, the response will be that obviously this is revenue associated with open deals that our sales team currently has in progress. This definition may be true, but it lacks a great deal of specificity.

A good, specific forecast revenue metric definition might be as follows: forecast revenue is the weighted value for all deals recorded in Microsoft Dynamics CRM that have been qualified and are expected to close this quarter. The value for all deals has been converted to US dollars based on current exchange rates. This calculation can be completed by summing the forecast value and multiplying this amount by the close probability field in Dynamics CRM.

This metric definition is good, because it is unambiguous and detailed enough that any person familiar with the business and the key business systems can clearly understand what the value means once it is being produced at an aggregate level. Without a detailed definition like this, management meetings where these KPIs are being reviewed can easily devolve into questions about what the metric is intending to show (Does this include leads or only late-stage deals? Is this weighted based on close probability?). And valuable time that should be placed on the overall direction of the firm is lost making sense of the numbers.

Ensuring Clear Metric Ownership

Ownership takes a metric from being merely interesting into something that will be acted upon. The key here is that, in order for a metric to be useful in driving the organization forward, some individual or department must be accountable for keeping it on track. Knowing the rate at which maintenance is attached to product sales may be interesting, but that knowledge is unlikely to be relevant enough to be a KPI if no individual is clearly accountable for this attachment. By holding your metrics to a standard that there must be someone clearly accountable for them in order to spend time measuring and displaying them, you are performing one key filtering activity that will help to maintain your focus on a critical few metrics that truly drive the business.

Keeping Metrics Measurable

All elements that are displayed in a scorecard must be quantifiable. Measuring employee satisfaction is a great concept. However, without a business process and system in place to track both current and ongoing satisfaction, it is not a relevant KPI, because you simply can't use the metric in decision making without guessing. Perhaps you will identify a metric as critical, and this will lead you to define the process and systems around it in order to include it in your scorecard. Making a metric measurable can be an excellent use of time and resources, but we would strongly recommend against referring to metrics as KPIs unless you have in place the ability to measure them. Making a metric measurable includes not only the systems to capture the metric but also the business processes that create consistency, audit tracking, and oversight.

Using Timely Metrics

One other seemingly small detail in the management of KPIs is paying attention to the time interval within which a metric can be tracked. If you have a weekly scorecard where two of the seven metrics are only reported monthly, those metrics are of questionable value. We do realize that not all measures will follow the same cadence, but we assert that, in order for your KPIs to be useful in decision making, you must be able to repeatedly produce each metric in a routine, consistent time interval so that it can be used in conjunction with the other KPIs to get an overall picture of the current state of the organization.

Limiting the Quantity of KPIs for a Given Scorecard

One key client of ours asked us to review its management reporting. The company called us in and, with great pride, displayed a 50-page manual that was produced monthly and included metrics for virtually every operation in a 200-person department. The executives explained that the book took too long to assemble (about 20 days) and that, unfortunately, was not widely reviewed. Their conclusions were that the current reports needed to be more automated and that a big rollout of the new book was needed, so people would know that they should refer to it to improve their performance.

We asked the general manager who owned the document if he referred to it on a regular basis. He said, "No, it's really just too much information for me to make sense of it. I don't have a full day to devote to figuring out what it all means."

We agreed and recommended that we work toward a situation in which each management tier in the organization has a scorecard relevant for its role that captures and displays metrics that it can control and influence. Each of these scorecards should display five to ten key metrics, because we believed that was about the capacity of items on which any individual role could truly focus and impact.

The key to this structure is that, as you move up the organizational ladder, the metrics in the scorecards are linked and directly aligned with the organization's strategy. Many organizations assume that measuring as many business processes as possible makes for better performance, but we've found that the reality is almost the opposite. Organizations that carefully choose what to measure and selectively track only a relatively few metrics tend to have the most widely adopted and longest lasting scorecard projects.

Assigning Targets to KPIs

One of the areas where KPIs tend to break down is in moving from the theoretical measures that are developed at a strategy session to the practical management and tracking that occurs on a day-to-day basis. A key to success with KPIs is effectively moving from developing KPIs to setting and managing to targets based on the established KPIs. The keys to target setting follow:

- The designed target metric is captured within a set of existing business processes that are backed by systems where quantitative results are stored and accessible to a dashboard system.

- Achieving, or failing to achieve, the target is within control of the department or person being measured by the scorecard.

- Targets are clearly time bound in a way that is aligned with the realities of the business and fits the organizational strategy. Many times, we've seen good targets undermined by poorly designed software that either leaves the timeline unbounded for achieving a goal, or evenly spreads a target across a series of months without taking into account seasonality that may affect many measures.

Aligning the KPI with Organizational Goals

Recognize that the metrics can only have a positive, long-term impact if you have a clear organizational destination in mind (i.e., you'll have significantly different KPIs if your goal is to grow the organization by 50 percent annually and expand into new geographies than you will if your goal is to maintain 10 percent growth and maximize profitability).

Teams that are developing KPIs must take great care to ensure that the selected metrics that are forward looking will actually lead toward the organization's projected destination. This statement may at first seem obvious, but it is a common failure for a team developing KPIs to become so enthralled with the process of developing creative metrics that it loses track of the need to deliver simple, unambiguous metrics that are clearly linked with the organization arriving at a destination.

Developing a KPI Step By Step

Keeping in mind the principals outlined already, let's step through an example of how an engineering company might work through the development of its KPIs. Our engineering company, Dyno Technologies, has two primary lines of business: mechanical engineering systems for building projects and maintenance on existing systems. The organization has a ten-year history of successful business operations and has recently decided that it would like to expand its operations beyond Boise—by opening an office in Seattle, it hopes to double revenue for the overall business within the next five years. The executives at Dyno have decided that they would like to formally start a scorecard project to both improve the performance of their existing sales and marketing teams and better manage the initiative to expand the business to Seattle. These are the steps they are going through to deliver an effective scorecard:

1. Assemble a small team to define KPIs.

2. Categorize potential metrics.

3. Brainstorm possible metrics.

4. Prioritize draft metrics.

5. Perform a final filter on metrics.

6. Set targets for selected metrics.

Assembling a Team to Define KPIs

Dyno Technologie's combined sales and marketing departments total 65 employees. There is a clear recognition that, for this project to work, all the staff must be committed to capturing the data required for the dashboard but not every team member needs to be a part of defining the KPIs. As a result, Dyno has established a team made up of an executive sponsor (the chief financial officer), the sales vice president, one key sales manager, one leading sales representative, the marketing manager, and the IT director. This team of seven is small enough to meet regularly but includes relevant resources from each key department that must sign off that the KPIs established are the right metrics to measure and that the end scorecard is technically feasible.

The key takeaway here is that, in order for the team to get off the ground, it must have executive support; have representative support from sales, marketing, and IT; and be nimble enough to actually hold multiple working sessions within a relatively short period of time (e.g., four to six weeks).

Categorizing Potential Metrics

To look at the business from perspectives other than strictly financial metrics, each scorecard will differ. Recall the idea of the balanced scorecard: making sure your metrics are not overly weighted on financial measures will be extremely valuable; that is, make sure you focus on other core perspectives that drive the long-term health of the business.

With this in mind, Dyno has established that it will make a first pass at metrics by dividing them into the following perspectives, which the KPI team members believe they must satisfy in order for the business to be effective:

- *Financial*: Metrics that capture the overall fiscal health of the sales and marketing organization

- *Customer*: Metrics that capture both how the organization is performing from a customer's perspective and how effectively the organization is generating interest and demand from customers

- *Employee*: Metrics that capture how the organization is performing with respect to meeting the needs of employees

- *Current initiative*: Any unique metrics explicitly associated with a current critical initiative, which in the case of Dyno, are metrics associated with the business expansion into a new market

Brainstorming Possible Metrics

Hold an initial team working session where the overall objectives of the project will be reviewed and an initial draft of five to ten metrics in each category will be established. For each organization, this list will be unique, but the key takeaway is that this task should be a high-level brainstorming activity where many possible measures can be discussed and captured without deciding on a final list. Then, the metrics will be critically reviewed by the team members as individuals and in a joint session where the team applies the core principles to determine just how appropriate each metric may be.

Table 3-1 provides our list of draft metrics for Dyno Technologies. In this table, each department's metrics are displayed in columns, and you will notice that some departments have identified more metrics than others.

Table 3-1. *Initial Brainstorming of Potential KPIs by Department*

Marketing	Sales	Customer	Employee	Current Initiative
New leads	Forecast revenue	Customer satisfaction	Regrettable turnover	New customers
Campaign return on investment	Total pipeline value over time	Customer renewals	Percentage of representatives hitting quota	Booked revenue
Product market share	Cost of goods sold	Win ratio	Employee satisfaction	Introductory calls
Buzz	Sales representative win rate	Referrals		Value of deals proposed in the new market
Brand awareness	Year-over-year revenue			Customer satisfaction
Cost per lead	Activity level			
	Number of qualified prospects			
	Number of initial prospect meetings			
	Average sales cycle			

Prioritizing Draft Metrics

At this point, most organizations will adjourn the working session with a full list of draft metrics (some realistic, other less so). The organization will then pass this list around to allow feedback from the KPI team and perhaps the larger organization. After that, the KPI team will reconvene about a week later.

In our case, Dyno Technologies has set up the team to hold weekly meetings, and the team follows up the initial session with a facilitated discussion that will go through metrics on the original list and narrow down that list. This prioritization of metrics will be done with the goal of reducing the list of potential KPIs to 10 to 12 of the most meaningful possible metrics, determined by how well they satisfy the following key questions:

- What is the precise definition of this metric?

- Is this a leading or lagging metric (the goal is to have an even split of leading and lagging metrics)?

- Does this metric indicate a key causal event in taking us toward our destination?

- Can we use this metric to rally employee action and impact behavior?

- Is this metric linked to a specific set of business processes that we can drill into if it goes off target?

- Do we have representation of at least one to two metrics for each key category?

After reviewing the draft metrics based on these questions, Dyno Technologies has generated the list of prioritized KPIs outlined in Table 3-2.

Table 3-2. *The Second Revision, a Prioritized List of Potential KPIs*

Metric	Definition	Category	Leading or Lagging?
New leads	Each opportunity record created in Dynamics CRM represents one new lead. An opportunity record will be created for any potential deal where a prospect or customer has expressed interest in new or additional products or services.	Marketing	Leading
Cost per lead	This metric refers to the total marketing expenditure directly related to lead-generation activities (advertising, trade shows, and campaigns) divided by the quantity of new leads during a specific interval of time.	Marketing	Lagging
Forecast revenue	This is the weighted value for all deals recorded in Dynamics CRM that have been qualified and are expected to close this quarter. The value for all deals has been converted to US dollars based on current exchange rates. This calculation can be completed by summing the forecast value and multiplying this amount by the close probability field in Dynamics CRM.	Sales	Leading

Table 3-2. *The Second Revision, a Prioritized List of Potential KPIs (Continued)*

Metric	Definition	Category	Leading or Lagging?
Qualified prospects	This counts opportunities in Dynamics CRM that have moved from stage one (new lead) to stage two (qualified) within a defined time period. This change in stage should be based on the prospects having clearly indicated that they have a specific timeframe within which they will purchase and have allocated budget for the project, and the sales representative clearly understands who the ultimate decision maker is.	Sales	Leading
Activity level	This is the total quantity of e-mails, meetings, and phone calls logged in Dynamics CRM associated with a given sales representative within a defined time period.	Sales	Leading
Won deals (year-over-year)	This tracks the total value, converted to US dollars, of all Dynamics CRM opportunities marked as won. This metric will be presented with visibility into year-over-year comparisons.	Sales	Lagging
Average sales cycle	This metric calculates the average duration, in days, between the time an opportunity is created in Dynamics CRM and the date on which the opportunity is closed as won or lost.	Sales	Lagging
Regrettable turnover	The quantity of employees who terminate their employment and who the firm intended to continue to retain within a given time period is tracked in this metric.	Employee	Leading
Percentage of representatives hitting quota	This is the percentage of total sales representatives that achieve their quota in a given year.	Employee	Lagging
Referrals	Here, the company will count opportunities created in Dynamics CRM where the referral check box is marked on the opportunity form within a given time interval.	Customer	Leading
Win ratio	This is the quantity of CRM opportunities marked as won in CRM divided by the total quantity of opportunities closed in the system within a given time interval.	Customer	Lagging
Introductory calls (new market)	This counts the total quantity of phone calls logged in Dynamics CRM by sales representatives focused on the Seattle market where the recipient is a new prospect within a given time interval.	New initiative	Leading
Value of deals proposed (new market)	Sum all opportunities in Dynamics CRM for deals where the prospect is in the Seattle market that is at stage three or better in the sales cycle.	New initiative	Leading

Table 3-2. *The Second Revision, a Prioritized List of Potential KPIs (Continued)*

Metric	Definition	Category	Leading or Lagging?
Booked revenue (new market)	Sum all won opportunities in Dynamics CRM where the prospect is in the Seattle market within a given time interval.	New initiative	Lagging
Customer satisfaction (new market)	Track the overall satisfaction level of customers in the Seattle market.	New initiative	Lagging

Performing a Final Filter on Metrics

The last step is to perform a final filter on the metrics to validate that you have credible data that supports a metric tightly aligned with key strategic goals. With the list of metrics from the previous step in hand, the KPI team will typically meet one final time to drill into an additional set of qualifying questions to help refine the list to a final set of the five to ten most meaningful metrics to track on the overall scorecard.

In the case of Dyno Technologies, the team adjourned after developing a list in step four and is now reconvening to take up a last review. While these review sessions could be completed in one longer working session, in essence making for a longer step four, our experience shows that breaking the review process into shorter sessions leads to greater focus on the task at hand and allows time for team members to reflect on their choices between meetings. This time for reflection can facilitate making adjustments to the list during the planning process, as opposed to making the change later in the program when it may be more difficult to convene all the stakeholders. The key questions that will be reviewed at this stage follow:

Is the metric definition not only unambiguous but also clear to people not on the core team? Quite a bit of focus has been placed on developing metrics that cannot be construed differently by different audiences. This review provides the opportunity to do a final check and validate that not only is the definition clear but that any member of the organization will be able to have an understanding of the metric when they interact with it even if they aren't intimately aware of the precise definition.

Do we have credible data on which to base the metric? Now is the time to validate a clear understanding of the business process that drives the data capture for the metric and to verify that a solid data-capture infrastructure is in place to support that business process. Many scorecard initiatives never make it beyond the white board stage, because even though the metrics are important and thoughtful, no particular attention was paid during planning to determine the practicality of gathering and assembling the data into a scorecard. One of the key roles of the IT director at Dyno will be to provide supporting evidence in this meeting that identifies which data systems are the sources of record in support of the business processes that drive our key metrics. In addition, our IT director will take the responsibility for assessing the data quality in these systems and suggesting a remediation strategy, if necessary, to ensure that our business systems are capable of accurately managing the data that drives the KPIs.

Will achieving the metrics lead to achieving your goals? Perform a final check that each metric is actually aligned with the goals you care about most. The Dyno Technologies team members will take the time during this session to ask themselves, "If we measure these metrics on a regular basis, and we hit our targets, do we believe we will get to our goal?" It may seem redundant to ask such a simple question upon conclusion of a time-consuming process, but it is valuable for the entire team to always keep the focus on the fact that the reason the KPIs exist is to provide tangible evidence about whether the organization is on track to hit its goals. Thus, take a step back and make sure that, during the complicated process of prioritizing and refining metrics, the metrics themselves are still closely aligned with the organizational strategy.

Dyno Technologies has used the filtering questions to refine the list of KPIs one additional time and has now established the metrics in Table 3-3 as the baseline set for their scorecard.

Table 3-3. *Final Revision of the Refined List of Potential KPIs*

Metric	Pass the Current Review?	Why?
New leads	Yes	A clear definition exists, and the data can be directly sourced from the existing CRM system. The business process to create leads is well defined and consistently understood. Most importantly, there is believed to be a direct causal linkage between lead volume and revenue growth.
Cost per lead	Yes	This metric is well defined, and the marketing expenditures are well classified and thoroughly tracked in the existing ERP system. The metric is perceived to represent a clear indicator of the effectiveness of the overall suite of marketing programs.
Forecast revenue	Yes	The definition for this metric is not universally agreed on today, but this metric is perceived as so important to the stability of the business that that sales vice president has committed to refining the definition and rolling out systematic effort to explain the forecast and enforce the accurate data upkeep in Dynamics CRM. With this additional commitment from the sales department, this metric was included as a core KPI.
Qualified prospects	No	The definition is somewhat ambiguous, with each sales representative applying unique informal rules to define "qualified." In addition, the capture of this data in Dynamics CRM is somewhat haphazard. With these points in mind, the team has decided it is more important to focus on getting accurate forecast data and will revisit this metric at a later date.

Table 3-3. *Final Revision of the Refined List of Potential KPIs (Continued)*

Metric	Pass the Current Review?	Why?
Activity level	Yes	The definition is clear and includes any meeting, e-mail, or phone call between a sales representative and a prospect. The data is cleanly tracked in Dynamics CRM. Also, just last year, the IT director rolled out reporting that specifically audited the level of usage of Dynamics CRM for activity tracking, so the systems fully support the management of this business process. In addition, this metric is perceived as a strong leading indicator of how aggressively and actively sale representatives are able to convert new leads into clients.
Won deals (year-over-year)	Yes	The definition is clear, and the data is tracked in the CRM system and readily available. The metric is viewed as lagging but as a very important symbolic measure that the whole organization can comprehend. It is believed that including this makes the scorecard very tangible and likely allows many people in the department to see the links between the other metrics and overall financial performance of the organization.
Average sales cycle	No	The definition is clear, and the data is readily available, but there are questions as to whether this metric truly is an indicator of how effectively Dyno is executing on its primary goal of revenue growth. Clearly, the number is interesting, but it's not currently viewed as critical enough to be considered a KPI.
Regrettable turnover	No	The metric is well understood but too subjective to be a KPI. In addition, no data-driven system distinguishes between good attrition and bad attrition. The team members view this metric as potentially very valuable but do not believe they have the process and systems in place today to track this.
Percentage of representatives hitting quota	Yes	The metric is well understood, and the business processes and systems exist today. The metric is viewed as being an adequate proxy for employee satisfaction and is being included in the KPI for that reason, but the team would like to later replace this metric with a more meaningful measure of employee fulfillment once business processes and systems are in place to facilitate quantifiable measurement of that metric.
Referrals	Yes	The metric is well understood, and data tracking exists in the existing CRM system to capture whether a particular deal or lead was based on a referral. This is seen as a very valuable metric in terms of demonstrating the extent to which customers are truly pleased with the experience they have had with Dyno.
Win ratio	No	This metric is well understood and captured effectively today, but it is another metric that is not perceived to truly be strongly indicative of the revenue growth of the firm.

Table 3-3. *Final Revision of the Refined List of Potential KPIs (Continued)*

Metric	Pass the Current Review?	Why?
Introductory calls (new market)	Yes	The metric is well defined and effectively tracked in existing CRM systems. Further, it is believed to be one of the best leading indicators of whether the new sales force is effectively engaging the new market and carrying out the brand message for Dyno.
Value of deals proposed (new market)	Yes	The metric is well defined and well tracked. This is another sales-centric measure that is perceived to be a simple, tangible measure of how effectively the sales team is moving beyond general conversation about Dyno and toward closing deals that are the first measure of success in the firm's expansion into a new geographical market.
Booked revenue (new market)	Yes	The metric is clearly defined and tracked in the ERP system with categorization that makes it easy to separate the new market. This measure is also viewed as very tangible and likely allows many people in the department to gauge success of the expansion into the new market.
Customer satisfaction (new market)	No	No business process is in place to capture this data consistently, and there is a concern that there will be limited data points at this time, which makes this metric more likely to be manipulated by the local sales and service representatives. Also, during the initial expansion period, the core team believes the most relevant KPIs are sales related but that a metric for customer satisfaction may be merited in future versions of the scorecard.

Setting Targets for Selected Metrics

Perhaps the greatest challenge in establishing KPIs is to set realistic targets for each metric. Target setting is a combination of art and science. During the initial phases of a project, compiling historical data for each KPI dating back as far as is realistically possible may be useful. This broad historical context can allow the core team to make good choices in establishing baseline targets for each of the metrics. Using this historical information does not mean that it will be the only influence on the targets, but it can serve as a useful guide against which the core team can look at industry benchmarks, economic conditions, and any unique elements of the current business to determine an appropriate value. The end goal should be that the target can serve as both a yardstick for progress and a rallying point for the organization.

At Dyno Technologies, the core team looked at historical data from the CRM system for sales metrics, historical data from the human resources database for employee metrics, and marketing metrics from past executive presentations to use to develop the following set of targets. The team seeks to ensure that the targets outlined can be seen as both achievable and challenging for the whole organization.

As Table 3-4 shows, Dyno Technologies has arrived at a set of beta KPIs. We say "beta" because Dyno Technologies has yet to implement them and test whether they actually do drive business performance, and it is critical to realize that you will never really be finished with refining and adjusting the set of KPIs you use; you'll always need to tune them to impact business performance.

Table 3-4. *KPIs and Their Associated Targets*

Metric	Target	How Was the Target Established?
New leads	5,000 leads in the 2009 calendar year	This prior-year total was 3,500 leads. The team expects to expand that total by 15 percent and contribute an additional 1,000 leads from investments in the new market.
Cost per lead	$50/lead	The prior year amount was $65. The team expects to shift resources from high-cost mediums like radio advertising to more targeted web advertising on both trade periodical sites and search engines.
Forecast revenue	Q1 = $2,300,000 Q2 = $2,600,000 Q3 = $2,600,000 Q4 = $3,100,000	The forecast amounts represent 15 percent growth from the prior year.
Activity level	8,000 activities per month, increasing by 2 percent each month of the year	The activity level represents 15 percent growth from the prior year.
Won deals (year-over-year)	25 percent year-over-year growth	Revenue growth is based on 15 percent growth in core markets and on having the new market contribute an additional 10 percent.
Referrals	150 referrals	In the prior year, 85 referrals were generated. The expected 150 referrals are based on duplicating the prior year's performance and assumes significant growth based on the rollout of a peer-to-peer program that matches each client executive with a Dyno executive. This peer-to-peer program is intended to improve customer satisfaction and deepen personal relationships leading to increased referrals.
Percentage of sales representatives hitting quota	80 percent	In the prior year, this measure was 78 percent. The team would like to see this performance improve more significantly, but there are no direct programs focused on achieving this, and the team currently leads an industry average of 70 percent.
Introductory calls (new market)	500 per month	This number is largely an educated guess based on the assumption that there will be two representatives in place, making 8 to 12 calls per day.
Value of deals proposed (new market)	Q1 = $40,000 Q2 = $150,000 Q3 = $250,000 Q4 = $350,000	This number is largely an educated guess.
Booked revenue (new market)	Q1 = $20,000 Q2 = $80,000 Q3 = $170,000 Q4 = $230,000	This number is largely an educated guess.

Combining the KPIs into a Scorecard

The next step is to take the KPIs that you've developed and integrate them into a system that provides good visibility for all relevant individuals within the organization. In subsequent chapters, we will delve into the different technical options for bringing scorecards to life depending on your audience, infrastructure, and the level of sophistication in your adoption of analytics.

For now, Figure 3-2 shows a mock-up of the scorecard Dyno Technologies first deployed to bring the KPIs to life leveraging a simple web-based UI built on top of SQL Server 2008. You can see the differences between the example shown in Figure 3-2 and our initial example in Figure 3-1: the scorecard developed after following our key principles is balanced between leading and lagging metrics and is highly focused on the metrics that Dyno's team believes are truly paramount to achieving the core strategic objectives.

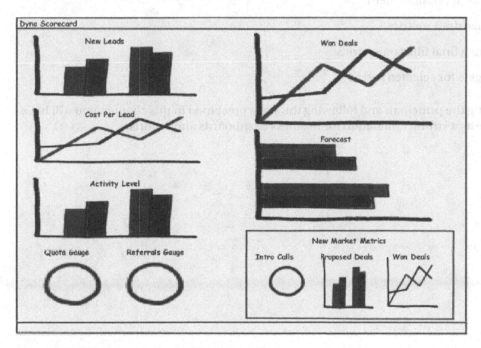

Figure 3-2. *KPI-driven sales dashboard mock-up*

Summary

To define KPIs that will help in decision making, we've found the following key principles to be good guidelines for whether a metric will be useful:

- The metric is specific.

- The metric is clearly owned by a given department or group.

- The metric is measurable.

- The metric can be produced in a timely manner.

- The quantity of KPIs is limited to only the most critical metrics for a given audience.

- The metric has a target.

- The metric is specifically aligned with the overall organizational goals.

In addition, we frequently follow a specific set of steps when developing our KPIs in order to develop consensus around the KPIs and ensure that the results are consistent with the core principals:

1. Assemble a small team to define KPIs.

2. Categorize potential metrics.

3. Brainstorm possible metrics.

4. Prioritize draft metrics.

5. Perform a final filter on metrics.

6. Set targets for selected metrics.

By applying the principals and following the steps presented in this chapter, you will have KPIs that serve as a strong foundation for business dashboards and reports.

CHAPTER 4

■ ■ ■

Microsoft Platform Components for Dashboards

In past chapters, we've outlined some key considerations for the overall management of your dashboard project, and we've detailed some principles for selecting your KPIs. At this point, we turn to execution, which includes a discussion of both the tools available and an approach to successfully deliver on the initiative.

The Microsoft business intelligence platform is broad and deep, but it can be confusing to determine which components you need to deliver your KPIs in a compelling format that will be extensible to meet business demands and scale as adoption grows. If there is one thing you take away from this chapter, it should be that the foundation of the BI platform is SQL Server, and gaining skills with the core elements, that is, SQL Server Integration Services (SSIS), SQL Reporting Services (SSRS), and the SQL Language, will serve you extremely well in delivering analytics. A second key takeaway is that organizations that are starting or restarting analytics initiatives are almost always best served by treating their analytics program as if they are building a pyramid and incrementally developing and releasing tools based on progressing through a set of steps up the pyramid.

Understanding the Analytics Pyramid

The levels of the pyramid for incrementally adding complexity to your analytics solution are as follows:

- *Basic*: Solidify core SQL skills and develop comprehensive abilities with SSRS. Combine these technical capabilities with good design principles and a clear understanding of key sales and marketing needs to deliver compelling dashboards and reporting solutions.

- *Intermediate*: Develop skills with SSAS and SSIS in order to enhance the user experience by providing robust ad hoc tools.

- *Advanced*: Assemble end-to-end performance management solutions by integrating the tools developed at the basic and intermediate levels deep into the day-to-day workflows of sales and marketing users.

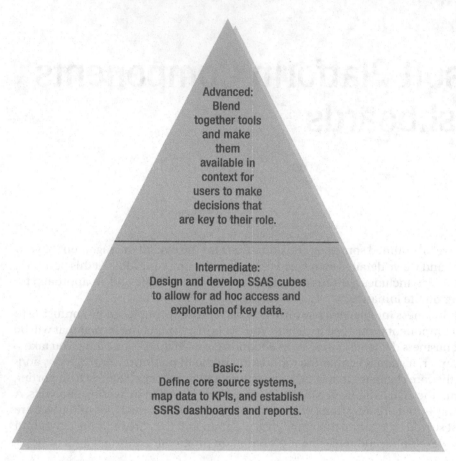

Figure 4-1. *The analytics pyramid*

Creating Basic Analytics

The basic stage of analytics with the Microsoft BI platform involves using all of the core database services and SSRS as well. This may sound like an elementary step, but it provides a solid foundation from which to build, and it is critical to put in place a quality data architecture before attempting to layer on top OLAP cubes or performance management applications. We have consistently found that by starting with the basics of good data practices and layering on SSRS, organizations realize a quick return on investment in a short time frame. In addition, the quick implementation time for basic reporting helps to ensure clarity on business requirements, because the key stakeholders can rapidly see their initial thoughts come to life. This allows them to refine their thinking about which KPIs are most critical and to refine the precise definition for each KPI.

At the basic stage, an organization is looking to answer the following questions:

- What is a fast and cost-effective way to deliver my KPIs to key business users?

- What are the key threats to data quality that must be addressed for the system to be trusted?

- What are the key skills that are necessary to put in place a foundation for effective analytics?

At this stage, organizations should be taking the following actions:

1. Map KPIs to source systems and look for data weaknesses.

2. Identify specific analytics stakeholders and segment based on how they will consume data.

3. Define a roadmap that prioritizes the scorecards and reports necessary to deliver on KPIs for each constituency.

4. Develop initial reports and dashboards.

Step 1: Mapping KPIs to Source Systems

Analytics projects depend on quality data, and quality data is largely a function of effective business processes. The most important step you can take at this stage in the development of an analytics program is to begin mapping out the core business systems and working to achieve consensus on which applications are, in fact, the system of record for key customer, order, campaign, quota, and product data. This mapping process may not be completely necessary to develop your initial dashboards, but it is highly beneficial to set a standard for these systems. Going through the process now will likely help you to identify weaknesses in data quality that might not otherwise become evident until after the initial reports have been released. Identifying these weaknesses early is beneficial in that it allows you to proactively notify business stakeholders about the expected limitations in their reports. You may also be able to have them begin the process of cleaning up bad data so that, by the time dashboards are released, the resulting picture is both an accurate depiction of the business and a clear success for the group that built it.

Let's take a look at the process of developing a data map and the resulting output for our example company, Dyno. In Chapter 3, we focused on setting up KPIs across the organization, and in our data map example, we will focus in specifically on sales and marketing in order to provide a deeper analysis of bringing analytics to these departments. The development of the data map should follow the business processes as they exist in the organization. With this in mind, identify the top tier sales and marketing business processes about which data exists. In the case of Dyno, the analytics team began by asking key business stakeholders these questions and used their answers to drive the development of the data map:

- Sales

  - Is there a common system for tracking all customers and key sales interactions?

  - What is the system of record for orders?

  - Where is quota and commission data stored?

  - What processes are in place to manage data quality for customer data?

  - Does an initial scan of the customer system reveal any duplicate records?

- Marketing

  - Is there a common system for tracking marketing campaigns and responses?

  - How are web statistics used as a measure of marketing success?

  - How are web leads tracked?

  - Where is marketing spending tracked?

  - Are marketing invoices associated with specific campaigns and activities?

  - How is conversion from lead to opportunity to closed deal tracked?

At Dyno Technologies, these questions were reviewed by our marketing, sales, and IT teams. The sales and marketing teams are the primary owners of answers to these questions, but IT is a critical stakeholder as those team members typically bring the deep domain knowledge about how the data is stored and have the ability to bring insight into the current data quality.

Table 4-1 represents a map of data assets that resulted from the discussion around our key questions. In this map, we've focused on identifying the key logical categories of data related to sales and marketing. We refer to these logical categories as business entities and then track, in detail, where they are stored as well as how they are linked to our KPIs. In addition, we complete the map by providing a textual overview of the typical flow of information through the sales and marketing process so that everyone involved in the BI project gets the general understanding of how the business operates.

Table 4-1. *Sample Data Map*

Business Entity	System of Record	Data Quality/Linked to KPI?	Comments
Campaigns	CRM	High/Yes, directly linked to new leads and cost per lead	Basic information is tracked about campaigns including the budget, name, and goals.
Campaign responses	CRM	Medium/Yes, directly linked to new leads	Basic information is captured in responses, but data is imprecise, as many duplicates exist.
Web site visitors	Google Analytics	Medium/No	Web site visitors don't leave a complete trail of activity, so this cannot be directly linked to leads.
Web site leads	CRM via a custom database	Medium/Yes, directly linked to new leads	People who register via the web site have leads automatically created for them in the CRM system. This data is moderately clean but can include duplicates.
Events	Custom web application that pushes into CRM	High/Yes, directly linked to new leads	The event-tracking application is a custom tool that manages both summary information about events and detailed information on registrants and attendees.

Table 4-1. *Sample Data Map*

Business Entity	System of Record	Data Quality/Linked to KPI?	Comments
Event participants	Custom web application that pushes data into CRM	Medium/Yes, directly linked to new leads	Event participants are tracked by our lead application, and they are loaded as leads into the CRM system. The challenge is to make sure that there is no double counting between this group and individuals loaded for other activities.
Prospect records	CRM	Medium/Yes	These records are recorded as leads in the CRM system. They are fed by direct entry, event participants, and campaign responses. There is already a process in place to prevent duplication, but this data element is challenging to maintain without duplicates.
Customer records	CRM	High/No	These records are maintained as account records in the CRM system, and a business process is in place to have the order entry team manage the maintenance of key fields on these records.
Sales activity records	CRM	Low/Yes	These records are activities in the CRM system and are created and maintained by sales representatives. However, data quality is considered poor, as many sales representatives do not record all of their activities in the CRM system.
Sales opportunities	CRM	Medium/Yes	These records are opportunities in the CRM system and are created and managed by sales representatives. Data quality around the value and close date is high, but many other fields are not well maintained.
Sales orders	Dynamics GP	High/Yes	Orders are tightly managed based on a structured business process defined and maintained by the order entry team, and the data is high quality.
Sales quotas	Excel spreadsheet	High/Yes	Quotas are maintained on a spreadsheet by the chief financial officer. It is critical to incorporate this data to allow for tracking of KPIs.
Sales commissions	Access database	High/No	Sales commissions are tracked in an Access database by the controller. This data is not considered critical for tracking KPIs but does provide good context for the sales team.

Here's a typical scenario: A prospect is engaged at a trade show. The prospect leaves a business card with a Dyno sales representative, and that information is scanned into the Dyno Microsoft Dynamics CRM application. The prospect then has an individual record in the CRM system, a company record for that organization, as well as an automatically generated sales opportunity. The prospect then automatically receives a follow-up e-mail, which is recorded in the CRM system as a sales activity. This e-mail points that prospect to the web site for more information on our products. The prospect views the information on the web site and registers for a web seminar. After the web seminar, the telesales team makes a follow-up phone call, and interest is expressed in getting a quote to purchase the Dyno product. At this point, the sales representative moves the sales opportunity from the lead stage to the qualified stage and sends the prospect a quote. After a series of negotiations, the prospect purchases the product; the sales opportunity is closed as won, and an order is submitted in Great Plains by the fulfillment team. Quotas are tracked in an Excel spreadsheet, and the Great Plains data is compared to this spreadsheet for the purposes of paying out commissions.

With this data map, we now have a powerful tool that connects the business process with the existing data systems. This link helps us to begin planning and estimating the development effort associated with key reports. The information also allows us to have precise conversations with business owners about how their reporting needs map to our existing infrastructure and will highlight any lack of consensus about which system truly is the system of record for specific business data.

Step 2: Identifying Specific Analytics Stakeholders

At this point in the project, you must begin to think specifically about how the users would like to interact with the data. It is critical for the BI team to think from the perspective of the intended audience to select the right tools from the BI platform so that the result is a compelling tool that fits within the users' typical daily processes.

An initial approach is to break out the roles of targeted users and to define the level of interactivity they are expecting with the data. This segmentation allows us to map precisely which audiences will use SSRS dashboards and which will use SSAS cubes. It also provides a guideline for planning the release cycle and serves as a source of documentation that can demonstrate how the BI budget is relating specifically back to different functional areas of the business.

Table 4-2 shows the initial stakeholder segmentation developed by Dyno Technologies.

Table 4-2. *Sample Stakeholder Map*

Role	Primary Need	Secondary Need	Overall Goal
Chief executive officer	Dashboard view of overall performance in the context of targets and trends	The ability to drill down to see the performance and trends in individual metrics	Obtain an at-a-glance view of business performance and identification of key successes and risks.
Marketing vice president	Dashboard view of specific marketing commitments with the ability to look at individual campaigns and the associated return on investment (ROI)		Obtain an at-a-glance view of business performance and identification of underperforming and overperforming campaigns.

Table 4-2. *Sample Stakeholder Map*

Role	Primary Need	Secondary Need	Overall Goal
Sales vice president	Dashboard view of critical pipeline and forecast metrics	The ability to drill down to understand which sales representatives and products are performing well or are underperforming and why	Accurately forecast revenue for the period and take corrective action where possible to maximize revenue.
Marketing manager	View campaign performance and ROI on a campaign-by-campaign basis and look at sales conversion on campaign-generated leads	The ability to drill down to view the performance of individual campaign tactics	Maximize the performance of individual campaigns by focusing resources on campaigns and tactics that are the most effective.
Sales manager	View the pipeline, forecast for the sales team, and drive accurate sales projections	The ability to drill down to view individual sales representative performance at each stage in the sales cycle	Accurately predict revenue and focus team's effort effectively on the opportunities most likely to close.
Marketing analyst	The ability to generate detailed, ad hoc analysis for the marketing vice president	The ability to review trends on KPIs in depth	Spend minimal time assembling data, but use data to answer key questions about how the business is performing.
Sales analyst	The ability to generate detailed, ad hoc analysis for the sales vice president	The ability to review trends on KPIs in depth	Spend minimal time assembling data, but use data to answer key questions about how the business is performing.
Sales representative	Insight into performance against quota	A simple tool for updating and managing pipeline and forecast information	Understand performance and easily manage the rollup of forecast information.

Step 3: Prioritizing Scorecards and Reports

Your next job is to prioritize scorecards and reports needed to deliver on your KPIs. Be sure to consider each of your critical audiences, such as executive management, sales, and so forth. The road map in Table 4-3 brings together the key metrics, with the audience's preferred approach for consuming the data, and identifies the technologies required to deliver the solution. The road map does this in a way that is focused on building incrementally more sophisticated tools so that the software and hardware costs associated with the BI initiative are only incurred as the increased sophistication is necessary to meet users' needs. This road map can then serve as a living document as the organization moves from the basic stage through intermediate analytics and onto advanced tools.

In the case of Dyno Technologies, a priority of 1 indicates that the item is critical to execute on as soon as possible. A priority of 2 indicates that the team believes these items are important and part of a comprehensive solution that should be developed as soon as the priority 1 items are complete. Items with a priority of 3 represent deliverables that fulfill the vision the team has for analytics, but these are not tied to a specific time line today.

Table 4-3. *Sample Road Map*

Deliverable	Audience	Priority	Key BI Platform Components Utilized
Executive KPIs	Chief executive officer, marketing vice president, sales vice president	1	Initial release in SSRS with the ability to extract data to Excel for ad hoc analysis, and subsequent releases to leverage SharePoint
Sales manager dashboard	Sales vice president and sales management	1	Initial release in SSRS with the ability to extract detailed data to Excel for ad hoc analysis, and subsequent releases to leverage SharePoint
Campaign dashboard	Marketing vice president and marketing manager	1	Initial release in SSRS with the ability to extract detailed data to Excel for ad hoc analysis, and subsequent releases to leverage SharePoint
Sales representative dashboard	Sales representatives	2	SSRS
Sales pipeline trending	Sales manager, sales analysts, and sales vice president	2	Initial release in SSRS, though future releases may include the ability to navigate this data through Excel connected to an OLAP cube and ultimately include display in SharePoint
Lead trending	Marketing vice president, marketing manager, and marketing analysts	2	Initial release in SSRS, though future releases may include the ability to navigate this data through Excel connected to an OLAP cube and ultimately include display in SharePoint
Ad hoc sales reporting toolkit	Sales analysts	2	Initial release in an OLAP cube accessed via Excel, though future releases may include the ability to interact with this data via SharePoint
Ad hoc marketing reporting toolkit	Marketing Analysts	2	Initial release in an OLAP cube accessed via Excel, though future releases may include the ability to interact with this data via SharePoint
Customer data mining	Sales analysts	3	Initial release in data mining models accessed via Excel, though future releases may incorporate mining model display in SSRS or SharePoint

Table 4-3. *Sample Road Map*

Deliverable	Audience	Priority	Key BI Platform Components Utilized
Prospect data mining	Marketing analysts	3	Initial release in data mining models accessed via Excel, though future releases may incorporate mining model display in SSRS or SharePoint
Comprehensive performance management dashboard	Chief executive officer, sales vice president, marketing vice president, marketing analysts, and sales analysts	3	SharePoint Server

Note that many of the high-priority items describe using SSRS initially with subsequent development to occur in SharePoint. It is our experience that most organizations benefit from heavily leveraging reporting services in conjunction with Excel to deliver their initial analytics solutions. These projects provide for a quick turnaround, and they allow for the fastest way to get the business up and working in a structured way with the Microsoft BI platform. This quick implementation time frame both creates momentum for analytics and allows the team good logical break points between which priorities can be reevaluated and any changing requirements can be accommodated.

Step 4: Developing Initial Reports and Dashboards

Finally! Having laid some solid plans, you can begin to generate useful results by creating reports and dashboards. A baseline competency with SQL and SSRS is critical. It serves as the foundation for all advanced analytics, and it allows the organization to begin to deliver the business value of analytics while making a minimal investment in software and hardware. Chapter 5 will focus in detail on leveraging SQL Server 2008 to step through the development of a set of key reports that leverage the new analytical tools built into SQL 2008, as well as stepping through specific examples of how SQL 2008 can serve as a central repository that allows you to consolidate data between multiple core business systems. Right now, in Exercise 4-1, we'll build on the earlier SSRS exercises and the road map outlined in Table 4-3 by developing the initial release of the Dyno Technologies executive KPIs.

Exercise 4-1. Building an Executive KPI Dashboard with SSRS 2008

We will build on the SQL Server Reporting Services exercise in Chapter 1 by creating a new reporting project to deliver the Executive Dashboard mock-up designed in Chapter 3. Begin by opening Microsoft BI Development Studio. Then execute the following steps:

1. Navigate to File ➤ New ➤ Project. Select the Report Server Project, as shown in Figure 4-2.

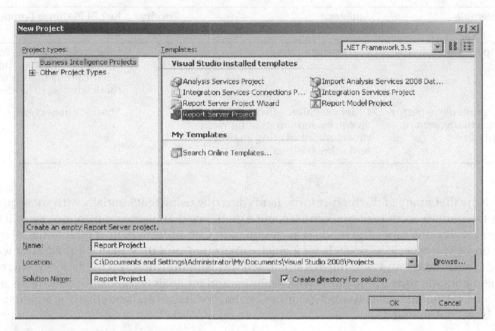

Figure 4-2. *Creating a new reporting project*

2. Give the Report a name, and click OK.

3. When the Solution Explorer window in Figure 4-3 comes up, right-click Reports, and click Add.

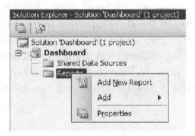

Figure 4-3. *Adding a report*

4. Click Add New Item. Select Report. Type **Dashboard.rdl** for the name of the report, and click OK. The report will open to the design page. On the toolbar, click View, and select Toolbox to get a list of all of the available charts. Figure 4-4 displays the View menu expanded with Toolbox as an available option.

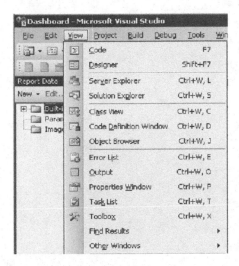

Figure 4-4. *Accessing the toolbox*

5. We will begin our design of the report by setting the page dimensions so that the report can easily be printed or exported. Open the Properties tab on the far right-hand side, and select Body in the drop-down menu. Type **6.75in, 5.75in** for the Size, as shown in Figure 4-5.

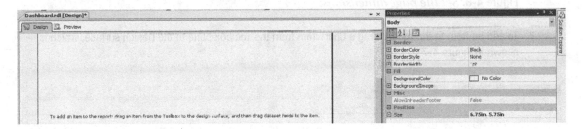

Figure 4-5. *Accessing report Body properties*

6. Select Report in the drop-down menu. Type **11in, 8.5in** for the InteractiveSize and PageSize of the Report, and type **0in, 0in, 0in, 0in** for Margins, as shown in Figure 4-6.

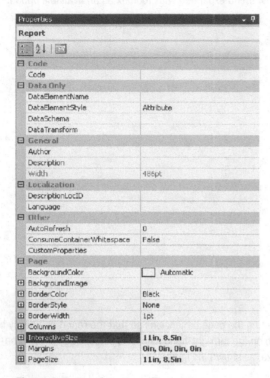

Figure 4-6. *Set the page dimensions.*

7. To add an item to the report, drag a Chart item from the Toolbox pane to the Design surface, which is shown in Figure 4-7.

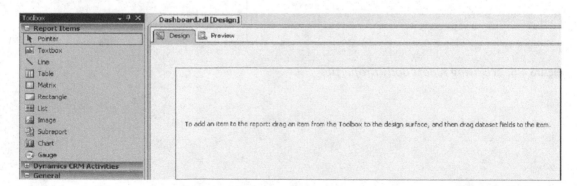

Figure 4-7. *To add a chart, select Chart from the Report Items menu and drag it to the Design surface.*

8. The next dialog box will prompt for a chart type, as shown in Figure 4-8. You'll notice that the dialog box includes a wide selection of charts that are new for SQL 2008. Specifically, the funnel shapes are newly added and provide a set of visualizations that are frequently asked for as part of executive dashboards. Select the Stacked Column chart type, and click OK.

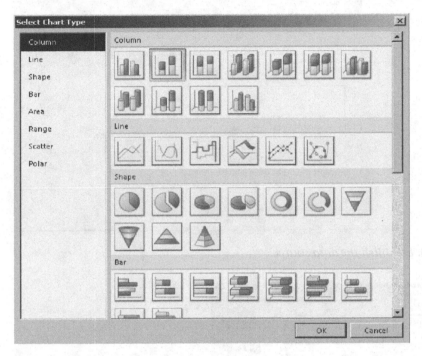

Figure 4-8. *Select the chart type.*

9. The next screen, shown in Figure 4-9, will prompt you for a data source. This screen will only appear when the report does not yet have a data source.

10. Click the Edit button to configure the data source.

11. In this example, the report will be built on information from the sample database. Since the database is located on the same server as the report being built, the server is localhost. The database is called Contoso_MSCRM. Set the "Server name" to "localhost" and the database name to Contoso_MSCRM, as shown in Figure 4-10. Then click OK.

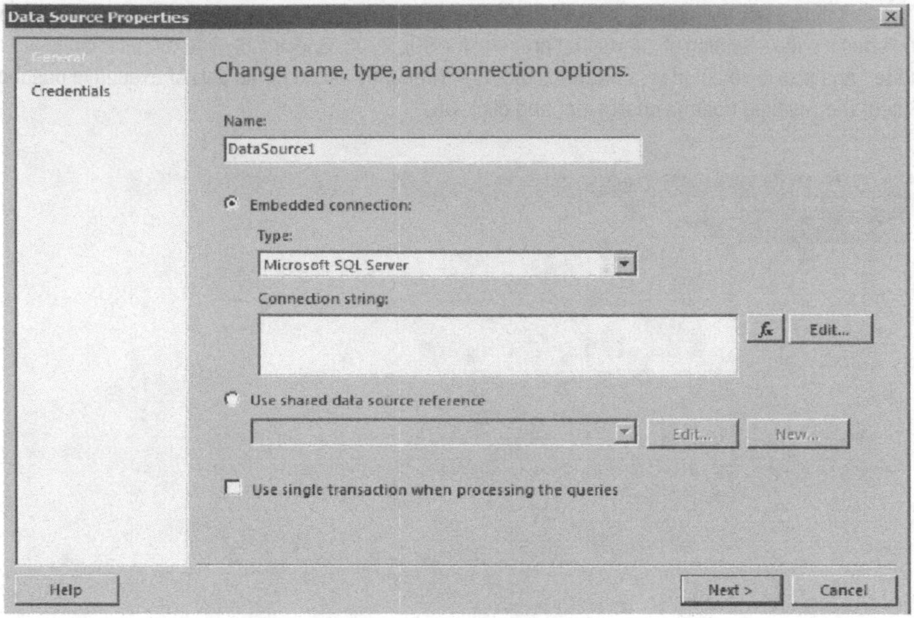

Figure 4-9. *Establish the data source.*

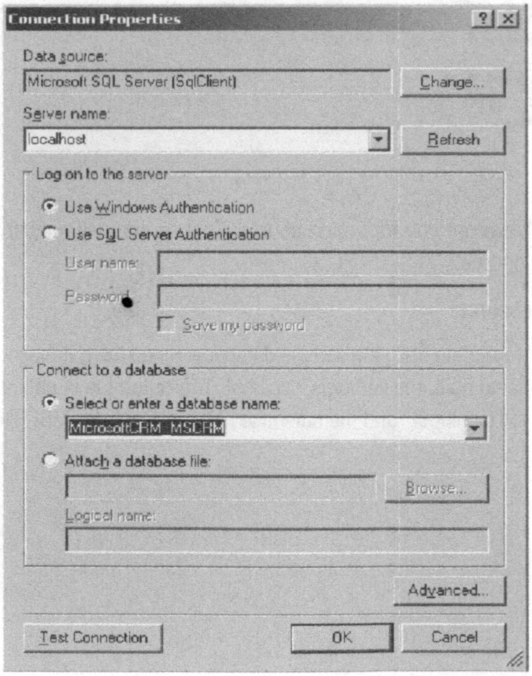

Figure 4-10. *Define the dataset.*

12. Click Next, shown in Figure 4-11, to create a new dataset.

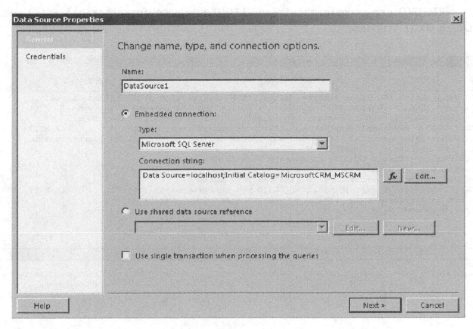

Figure 4-11. *Dataset connection properties*

13. In the Query Designer, which is shown in Figure 4-12, type the following code, and click Finish:

```
SELECT    O.owneridname AS 'Sales Representative'
    ,LEFT(S.firstname,1) AS 'First Initial'
    ,S.lastname AS 'Last Name'
    ,LEFT(S.firstname,1) + '. ' + S.lastname AS 'Name Label'
    ,SUM(O.estimatedvalue)/1000 AS 'Revenue in 1000s'
    ,LEFT (O.stepname,1) AS 'Stage'
,SUBSTRING(RIGHT(O.crm_moneyformatstring, LEN(O.crm_moneyformatstring) - 1),
    1,CHARINDEX('"', RIGHT(O.crm_moneyformatstring,
    LEN(O.crm_moneyformatstring) -
    1)) - 1) AS 'Currency Symbol'
FROM    FilteredOpportunity O
INNER JOIN FilteredSystemUser S ON O.owneridname = S.fullname
WHERE    O.stepname != 'NULL'
    AND O.stepname >= '3'
GROUP BY O.stepname
    ,O.owneridname
    ,S.firstname
    ,S.lastname
```

```
   ,SUBSTRING(RIGHT(O.crm_moneyformatstring, LEN(O.crm_moneyformatstring) -
      1), 1, CHARINDEX('"',
   RIGHT(O.crm_moneyformatstring, LEN(O.crm_moneyformatstring) - 1)) - 1)
ORDER BY O.stepname
```

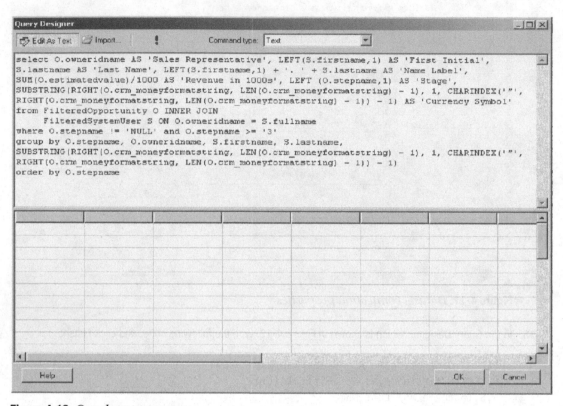

Figure 4-12. *Our dataset query*

14. Create a new dataset called WonDeals by right-clicking DataSource1 in the Report Data tab and selecting Add Dataset, which is shown in Figure 4-13. Figure 4-14 shows the window that will display once you click Add Dataset.

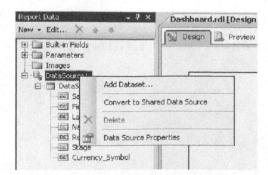

Figure 4-13. *Add an additional dataset.*

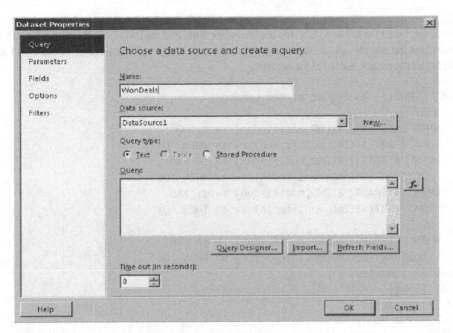

Figure 4-14. *Establish the dataset's details.*

15. Insert the following SQL into the Query box, and then click OK:

```
SELECT      DATEPART(MONTH, actualclosedate) AS Month
      , DATEPART(YEAR, actualclosedate) AS Year
      , SUM(actualvalue) / 1000 AS [Revenue in 1000s]
      , CASE

      WHEN DATEPART(MONTH, actualclosedate) >= 1
        AND DATEPART(MONTH, actualclosedate) <= 3 THEN 'Q1'
      WHEN DATEPART(MONTH, actualclosedate) >= 4
        AND DATEPART(MONTH, actualclosedate) <= 6 THEN 'Q2'
      WHEN DATEPART(MONTH, actualclosedate) >= 7
        AND (MONTH, actualclosedate) <= 9 THEN 'Q3'
      WHEN DATEPART(MONTH, actualclosedate) >= 10
        AND DATEPART(MONTH, actualclosedate) <= 12 THEN 'Q4' END
      AS Quarter
FROM        FilteredOpportunity
WHERE       (DATEPART(YEAR, actualclosedate) >= YEAR(GETDATE()) - 2)

      AND (actualclosedate <= GETDATE())
      GROUP BY DATEPART(MONTH, actualclosedate),
        DATEPART(YEAR, actualclosedate), DATENAME(MONTH, actualclosedate)
ORDER BY Year DESC
```

16. Create a new dataset called NewDeals by right-clicking DataSource1 in the Report Data tab and selecting Add Dataset. Insert the following SQL into the Query box. Note that the DATEPART function is being used to insure that the sample data displays correctly in this report, but in a production setting, the DATEPART would be on the month instead of the second.

```
SELECT COUNT(*) AS [Count of New Leads]
    ,CASE
      WHEN DATEPART(SECOND,modifiedon) >= 1 AND
        DATEPART(SECOND,modifiedon) <= 15 THEN 'Q1'
      WHEN DATEPART(SECOND,modifiedon) >= 16 AND
        DATEPART(SECOND,modifiedon) <= 30 THEN 'Q2'
      WHEN DATEPART(SECOND,modifiedon) >= 31 AND
        DATEPART(SECOND,modifiedon) <= 45 THEN 'Q3'

      WHEN DATEPART(SECOND,modifiedon) >= 46 AND
        DATEPART(SECOND,modifiedon) <= 60 THEN 'Q4'
    END AS [Quarter]
,60 AS [Goal]
FROM FilteredLead

    GROUP BY  DATEPART(SECOND,modifiedon)
    ORDER BY DATEPART(SECOND,modifiedon)
```

17. Create a new dataset called ActivityLevel as you did in the previous two instances. This time, insert the following SQL into the Query box:

```
SELECT COUNT(*) AS [Activity]
    ,CASE
      WHEN DATEPART(SECOND,modifiedon) >= 1 AND
        DATEPART(SECOND,modifiedon) <= 15 THEN 'Q1'
      WHEN DATEPART(SECOND,modifiedon) >= 16 AND
        DATEPART(SECOND,modifiedon) <= 30 THEN 'Q2'
      WHEN DATEPART(SECOND,modifiedon) >= 31 AND
        DATEPART(SECOND,modifiedon) <= 45 THEN 'Q3'
      WHEN DATEPART(SECOND,modifiedon) >= 46 AND
        DATEPART(SECOND,modifiedon) <= 60 THEN 'Q4'
    END AS [Quarter]
    ,60 AS [Goal]
FROM FilteredActivityPointer
GROUP BY DATEPART(SECOND,modifiedon)
ORDER BY  DATEPART(SECOND,modifiedon)
```

18. Create a new dataset called Referrals, and insert the following SQL into the Query box:

```
SELECT COUNT(*)  AS [Referrals]
FROM FilteredAccount
```

19. Create a new dataset called Quota, and insert the following SQL into the Query box:

```
SELECT COUNT(*)  AS [Quota]
FROM FilteredLead
```

20. One informative and visually appealing way to display revenue by sales representatives grouped by stage is to chart the information in a graph. Earlier, in step 9, a stacked column chart was created. The results are shown in Figure 4-15.

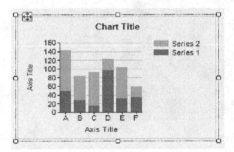

Figure 4-15. *Our stacked column chart*

21. Right-click Chart Title, and select Title Properties. Input the following text in the "Title text" field shown in Figure 4-16, and click OK:

```
="Forecast (000):  " & Fields!Currency_Symbol.Value &
FormatNumber(Sum(Fields!Revenue_in_1000s.Value),0)
```

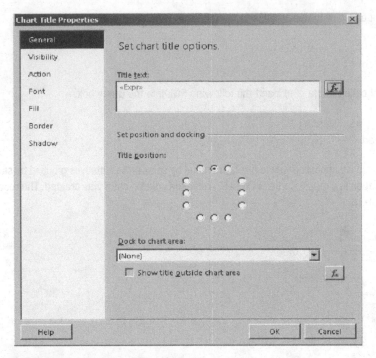

Figure 4-16. *The Chart Title Properties dialog*

22. Drag Revenue_in_1000s into the "Drop data fields here" box. Drag Stage into the "Drop series fields here" box. Drag Name_Label into the "Drop category fields here" box. Refer to Figures 4-17 and 4-18 as an example.

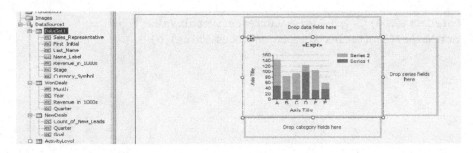

Figure 4-17. *The chart in design mode*

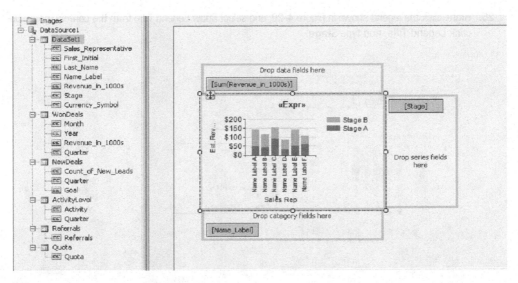

Figure 4-18. *The chart with data attributes*

23. Double-click the y axis title, and type **Est. Rev. (000)** for the name, denoting "Estimated Revenue in 1000s". Double-click the x axis title, and type **Sales Rep**.

24. Right-click the y axis, and select Axis Properties. Select Number ➤ Currency, and set "Decimal places" to 0. Check the "Use 1000 separator" box. Click OK. Refer to Figure 4-19 as an example.

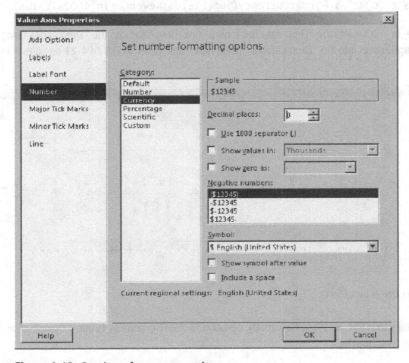

Figure 4-19. *Setting chart properties*

25. Right-click the legend shown in Figure 4-20, and select Show Legend Title from the context menu. Double-click Legend Title, and type **Stage**.

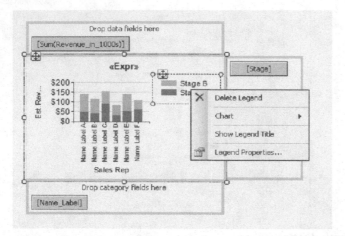

Figure 4-20. *Formatting the chart's legend*

26. Open the toolbox. Drag another chart onto the body of the report. This time, select the Smooth Line chart type to create a graph displaying "Revenue (000)" for won deals by quarter over the last two years.

27. Input the following text for the chart title:

```
="Won Deals (000): " & FormatCurrency(Sum(Fields!Revenue_in_1000s.Value),0)
```

28. Drag Revenue_in_1000s into the "Drop data fields here" box. Drag Year into the "Drop series fields here" box. Drag Quarter into the "Drop category fields here" box. Refer to Figure 4-21 as an example.

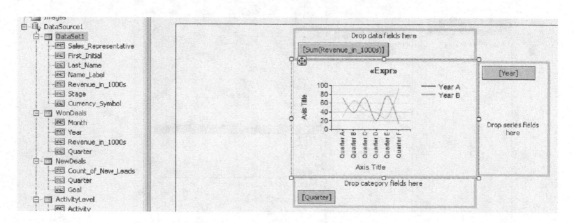

Figure 4-21. *Creating the line chart*

29. Double-click the y axis title, and type **Rev. (000)**, denoting "Actual Revenue in 1000s". Double-click the x axis title, and type **Quarter**.

30. Right-click the y axis, and select Axis Properties. Select Number ➤ Currency, and set "Decimal places" to 0. Check the "Use 1000 separator" box. Click OK.

31. Right-click the legend, and select Show Legend Title. Double-click the Legend Title, and type **Year** for the name.

32. Open the toolbox. Drag a gauge onto the body of the report. Select the Radial gauge type to create a gauge displaying referrals.

33. Drag Referrals into the "Drop data fields here" box, as shown in Figure 4-22.

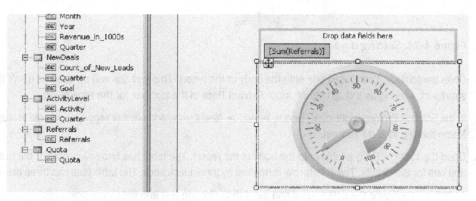

Figure 4-22. *The Referrals gauge*

34. Right-click the scale of the gauge, and select Scale Properties, which is as shown in Figure 4-23, to set the scale. Input preferred minimum and maximum values, and click OK.

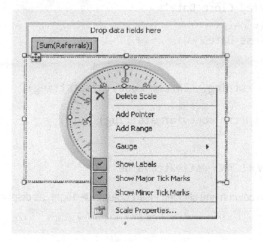

Figure 4-23. *Gauge Scale Properties*

35. Right-click the red target range of the gauge, and select Range Properties to set the target range, as shown in Figure 4-24. Input preferred start and end values for the range.

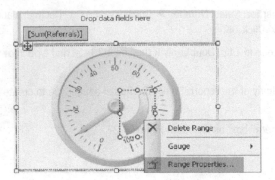

Figure 4-24. *Setting a gauge's range*

36. Open the toolbox. Drag a text box onto the body of the report. This text box will be used as a link to a subreport, serving as a data extract. Input **Extract Data** in the text box for the time being.

37. In the Solution Explorer, right-click Reports ➤ Add ➤ New Item to add another report, as you did in step 4. Name the report **Data Extract**.

38. Open the toolbox. Drag a table onto the body of the report. The table has two rows, one for the header and one for the details. The details row is marked by three black lines. The table also has three columns.

39. As before, configure the data source and input the following text into the Query box:

```
SELECT  opportunityid
    ,name AS 'Deal Title'
    ,accountidname AS 'Account Name'
    ,estimatedvalue AS 'Estimated Revenue'
    ,estimatedclosedate AS 'Estimated Close Date'
    ,actualvalue AS 'Actual Revenue'
    ,actualclosedate AS 'Actual Close Date'
    ,owneridname AS 'Owner Name'
    ,statecodename AS 'State'
    ,SUBSTRING(RIGHT(crm_moneyformatstring, LEN(crm_moneyformatstring)
        - 1), 1, CHARINDEX('"',
    RIGHT(crm_moneyformatstring, LEN(crm_moneyformatstring) - 1))
        - 1) AS 'Currency Symbol'
FROM FilteredOpportunity
WHERE estimatedclosedate IS NOT NULL AND estimatedvalue > 0
```

40. Insert a column to the right by right-clicking a column and clicking Insert Column ➤ Right, as displayed in Figure 4-25.

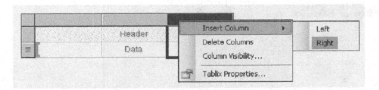

Figure 4-25. *Adding a column to a table*

41. On the Report Data tab, drag the fields into the details row, as shown in Figure 4-26.

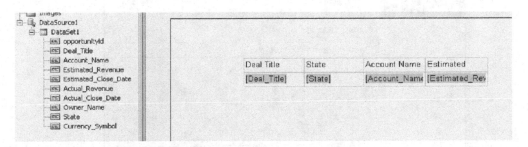

Figure 4-26. *The table in design mode*

42. Back in the main dashboard report, right-click the text box previously created, and select Text Box Properties, as shown in Figure 4-27.

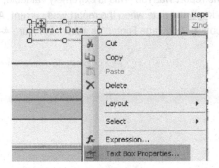

Figure 4-27. *Access text box properties.*

43. In the Text Box Properties window, select Action ➤ "Go to report," and select the subreport Data Extract in the drop-down menu, as shown in Figure 4-28. Click OK.

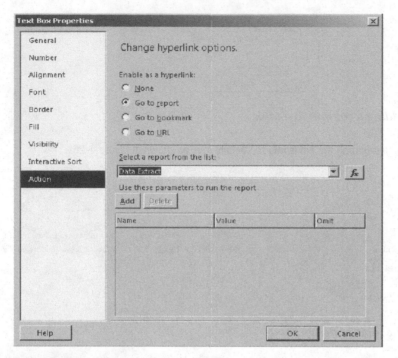

Figure 4-28. *Setting text box properties*

44. Insert a page footer in the report to display the time the report was run. This is extremely valuable, as the report may be printed, and it is critical for users to know the date when the report was current. Add the footer by navigating from the menu toolbar to Report ➤ Add Page Footer, as shown in Figure 4-29.

Figure 4-29. *Adding a report footer*

45. In the page footer, add a text box, and input the following text to display the current date and time of when the report was run:

```
="Current as of " & Now()
```

The main report dashboard has now been started with examples of a column chart, line chart, and radial gauge. A text box has been added to allow navigation to a subreport, serving as a data extract that contains a table of raw data.

For extra practice on your own, try to do the following to the dashboard report:

1. Add two more column charts to include the datasets ActivityLevel and NewLeads.

2. Add another radial gauge to include the dataset Quota.

3. Also, to the Data Extract report, add additional columns to the table to accommodate all of the fields created in the query provided in step 39.

Figures 4-30 and 4-31 are examples of complete dashboard and data extract reports. The power of this dashboard is that it provides a simple visual interface for executives to use to understand the business from multiple perspectives and it provides the raw data in a format that can be exported to Excel with one click in order to engage in deeper analysis.

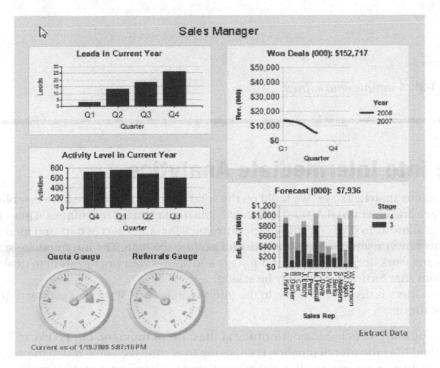

Figure 4-30. *A sample sales manager dashboard*

Raw Data

Deal Title	State	Account Name	Estimated Revenue	Est. Close Date	Actual Revenue	Actual Close Date	Owner Name
Looking seriously at new provider	Open	Wingtip Toys	$603,052	06/25/2007	$432,522	05/10/2007	Mark Hassall
Looking seriously at new provider	Open	Humongous Insurance	$331,264	05/23/2006	$312,400	05/26/2006	Mark Hassall
Interested in Some Options	Open	The Phone Company	$390,601	06/25/2006	$224,390	03/26/2007	Anton Kirilov
Looking seriously at new provider	Open	Tailspin Toys	$536,102	05/23/2007	$276,417	05/27/2007	Mark Hassall
Looking seriously at new provider	Open	Northwind Traders	$611,663	06/29/2007	$426,093	05/29/2006	Mark Hassall
Interested in Some Options	Open	Wide World Importers	$309,689	06/28/2006	$351,461	03/23/2006	Anton Kirilov
Interested in Some Options	Open	Fabrikam Inc.	$449,596	05/30/2006	$250,984	05/26/2007	Anton Kirilov
Looking seriously at new provider	Open	School of Fine Art	$548,033	06/20/2006	$24,105	03/20/2007	Mark Hassall
Looking seriously at new provider	Open	Tailspin Toys	$623,277	06/22/2007	$28,199	05/04/2007	Mark Hassall
Looking seriously at new provider	Open	Northwind Traders	$54,798	05/25/2007	$469,486	05/27/2007	Mark Hassall
Interested in Some Options	Open	Adventure Works	$82,073	05/22/2006	$301,470	03/08/2007	Anton Kirilov

Figure 4-31. *A sample data extract*

Moving into Intermediate Analytics

At the intermediate analytics stage, we build on the solid data foundation we have established in the basic stage and layer on OLAP and enhanced data management techniques. These tools and techniques allow us to deliver improved performance for larger sets of data and increased options for how power users may interact with and explore the data. The intermediate stage fully leverages the work done at the beginning stage and allows your organization to deal with deeper questions that business users may be asking.

You'll know there is demand to move to the intermediate stage if you are getting requests from users like these:

- I can see how my sales team is performing at the current moment, but I'd like to better understand how the overall pipeline is changing over time (i.e., how much money in proposals do we have outstanding today compared to last quarter at this time?).

- I have good visibility into my marketing spending on online ads because of the data automatically extracted from Yahoo and Google, but I need to look at this as one overall program by keyword without having to run two separate reports.

- These SSRS reports are great, but they just take too long to run. Is there any way to speed this up?

- I like having access to my data in pivot tables. Can we open up the data behind this report for one of our analysts to really look through for hidden patterns?

At this stage, organizations should be taking the following actions:

1. Develop basic SSAS cubes to allow business users to explore the data running behind key dashboards in an easy-to-use, high-performance environment.

2. Think through a design approach to determine how to best deliver trend-based data via a data mart and SSAS cube.

3. Develop the data mart and SSAS cube based on the SSIS toolkit and analysis services tools bundled with SQL Server 2008.

4. Evaluate the limitations of the overall BI platform you've established to determine if your next initiative should involve revisions to your existing SQL Server–based solution or a migration to a more comprehensive solution based on PerformancePoint.

In Chapter 6, we will address these steps in detail, but at this stage, we'll walk through the development of one sample cube and touch on the high-level concepts that must be addressed to deliver on the actions outlined in this section.

Step 1: Developing a Basic Analysis Services Cube

Your first step is to develop an analysis services cube. That cube forms the basis for everything else that you do in this intermediate stage. Exercise 4-2 walks you through the creation of an initial cube for Dyno Technologies. Later, you'll see that cube extended to deliver tools that analysts can use to explore their sales and marketing data in an ad hoc fashion.

Exercise 4-2. Developing a Simple Cube Using SSAS

Cubes can come in many shapes and sizes, ranging from the all-encompassing data warehouse to a small cube an analyst uses on a desktop to run reports. What is the difference? The difference is in the type of cube. A small, or simple, cube contains information from only one point in time. It is what is known as a transactional cube.

In a transactional cube, there are no updates, either to the fact row or to the dimension. This type of cube is useful for a few reasons. One reason is speed. It is much faster to query a cube than it is to query a transactional database. The second reason is reduced stress on the production database. Without a cube, any reporting must be done against the same database people are using to access and update records. This puts the server under unnecessary strain.

Execute the following steps to build a simple Analysis Services cube:

1. Navigate to Start ➤ Programs ➤ Microsoft Visual Studio 2005. Create a new project by navigating to File ➤ New ➤ Project, as shown in Figure 4-32.

Figure 4-32. *Initiate a project.*

2. Click Business Intelligence Projects. The templates section on the right will display a number of Visual Studio installed templates. Click Analysis Services Project. Give the project a name. The completed new project attributes will look like Figure 4-33. Click OK to complete the new project.

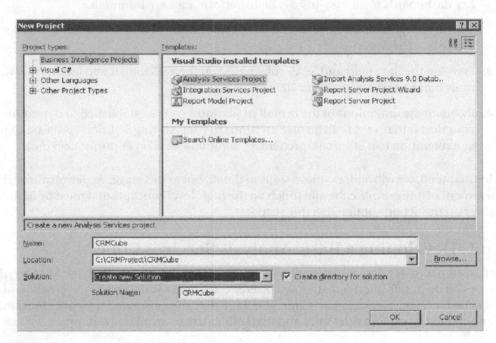

Figure 4-33. *Create an Analysis Services project.*

3. In the Solution Explorer, right-click the Data Sources folder, and select New Data Source. Click Next to get past the wizard introduction page.

4. Select "Create a data source based on an existing or new connection" to create a new data source. Click New to define the data source. Since the database is located on this computer, the server name is localhost, which can also be denoted as a period, as shown in Figure 4-34. Set the connection to log on with Windows authentication. Connect the database Contoso_MSCRM. Click the Test Connection button to make sure the connection succeeds. Click OK.

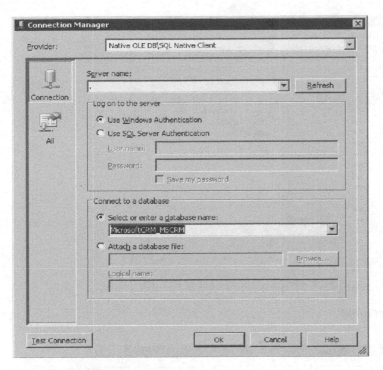

Figure 4-34. *Define the data source.*

5. Click Next. Select "Use a specific user name and password." Set the user name to "administrator" and the password to "pass@word1." Click Next again.

6. Give the data source a name, and click Finish.

7. Right-click Data Source Views, and select New Data Source View. Click Next to get past the introduction page.

8. Select the previously created data source, and click Next.

9. Select FilteredOpportunity, FilteredAccount, and FilteredSystemUser. Move them into the Included Objects section. Figure 4-35 provides an example of the completed table selection. Click Next and then Finish.

10. Right-click the FilteredSystemUser table, and select Replace Table ➤ With New Named Query.

11. Edit the FilteredSystemUser table to include the system user's manager. Add this SQL: `ISNULL(parentsystemuserid, systemuserid) AS Manager`. An example of the edited query is in Figure 4-36.

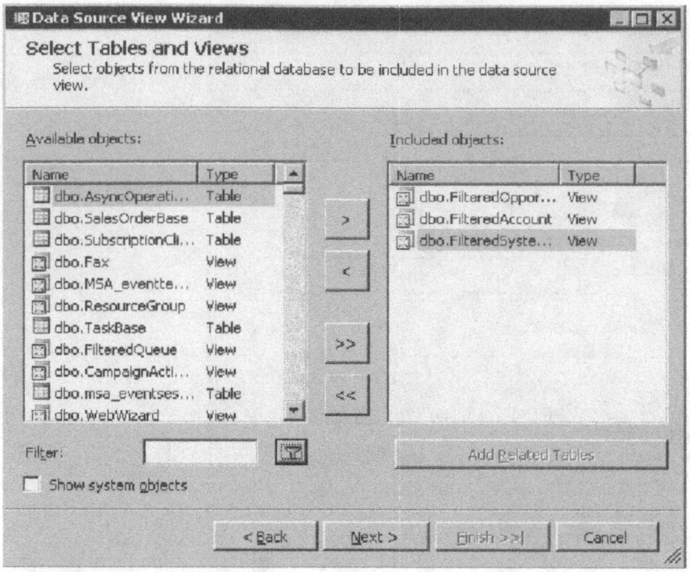

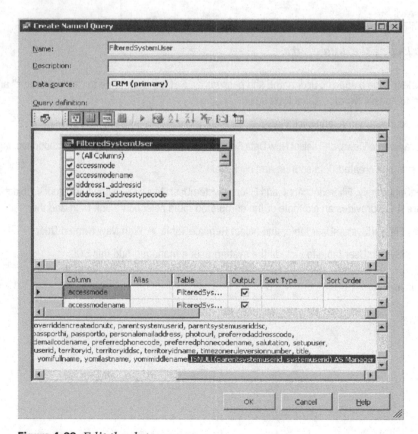

Figure 4-35. *Select tables.*

Figure 4-36. *Edit the data source.*

12. Click OK to exit the Create Named Query dialog. On FilteredSystemUser, find SystemUserId. Right-click SystemUserId, and select Set Logical Primary Key. Right-click SystemUserId again, and select New Relationship. Set the Source to FilteredSystemUser and the Source Column to Manager. Set the Destination table to FilteredSystemUser and Destination Columns to SystemUserId. The relationship displayed in Figure 4-37 allows people to use a managerial hierarchy when browsing the cube. Click OK to close the Create Relationship dialog box.

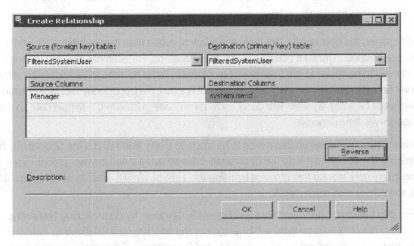

Figure 4-37. *Establish key relationships.*

13. Right-click Data Source View, and select New Named Query. Name the query OpportunityFact, and type the following code into the Query box:

```
SELECT  O.opportunityid AS OpportunityId,
    O.campaignid AS CampaignId,
    O.accountid AS AccountId,

    ISNULL(ISNULL(A.city, 'NA_') + ISNULL(A.stateorprovince, 'NA_')
    + ISNULL(A.country, 'NA_'),     'NA_NA_NA_') AS
    CityCode,
    O.originatingleadid AS OriginatingLeadId,
    CONVERT(DATETIME, CONVERT(VARCHAR(10),
    ISNULL(O.estimatedclosedate, '1/1/1990'), 120))
     AS EstimatedCloseDateKey,
    CONVERT(DATETIME, CONVERT(VARCHAR(10),
      ISNULL(O.actualclosedate, DATEADD(day, 90, O.createdon)), 120))
      AS ActualCloseDateKey,
    CONVERT(DATETIME, CONVERT(VARCHAR(10), O.createdon, 120))  AS
      CreatedOnDateKey,
    CONVERT(DATETIME, CONVERT(VARCHAR(10), O.modifiedon, 120)) AS
      ModifiedOnDateKey,
    O.closeprobability AS CloseProbability,
    O.estimatedvalue AS EstimatedValue,
```

```
        O.actualvalue AS ActualValue,
        O.ownerid AS OwnerId,
        CASE WHEN statecode = 1 THEN 1 ELSE O END AS OpportunityWon
        , CASE WHEN statecode = 2 THEN 1 ELSE O END AS OpportunityLost

FROM      FilteredOpportunity AS O LEFT OUTER JOIN
                FilteredCustomerAddress AS A ON O.accountid = A.parentid
WHERE     (A.addressnumber = 1)
```

The query that creates the Opportunity fact table has a few of subtle data manipulations. The data manipulations are created to make it possible to link to dimensions. For example, the server time dimension will need to be linked to the Opportunity fact table in order for time to be kept accurately. Since the server time dimension's smallest time increment is a day, the Opportunity fact table's smallest time increment must be a day, as well. The query converts any time metric into a simple date so it can be joined to the server time dimension.

Null removal is another manipulation that needs to be made to many fields within the Opportunity fact table. Any dimension that tries to join to the Opportunity table by using a null key will produce an error. The preceding query gets around this problem by using the ISNULL() SQL statement to replace any null row with something else, such as NA.

14. Make a relationship between OpportunityFact and FilteredSystemUser by right-clicking OwnerId on OpportunityFact from the Tables menu in the left-hand column and selecting New Relationship. Configure the relationship to have OpportunityFact as a Source table and OwnerId as a Source column. Set the Destination table to FilteredSystemUser and Destination column to SystemUserId. Click OK.

15. In FilteredAccount, make AccountId the logical primary key by right-clicking AccountId from the Tables menu in the left-hand column and selecting set logical primary key.

16. In FilteredAccount, edit the query. Give the name attribute alias AccountName.

17. In FilteredOpportunity, make OpportunityId the logical primary key.

18. In FilteredOpportunity, edit the query. Give the name attribute alias OpportunityName.

19. Repeat step 14. This time, however, create a relationship between OpportunityFact and FilteredOpportunity. Do this by setting the Source table to OpportunityFact, Source column to OpportunityId, Destination table to FilteredOpportunity, and Destination column to OpportunityId.

20. Repeat step 14 to create a relationship between OpportunityFact and FilteredAccount. To do this, set the Source table to OpportunityFact, Source column to AccountId, Destination table to FilteredAccount, and Destination column to AccountId.

21. Add a new Named Query. Insert the following code into the Named Query window. Call the Named Query LeadFact, and click OK to close the window.

```
SELECT leadid AS LeadId,
    contactid AS ContactId,
     accountid AS AccountId,
    campaignid AS CampaignId,
    ISNULL(ISNULL(address1_city, address2_city) +
      ISNULL(address1_stateorprovince,
```

```
    address2_stateorprovince) + ISNULL(address1_country, address2_country),
        N'NA_NA_NA_') AS CityCode,
        ownerid AS OwnerId,
    CONVERT(DATETIME, CONVERT(VARCHAR(10),
        estimatedclosedate, 120)) AS EstimatedCloseDate,
    CONVERT(DATETIME, CONVERT(VARCHAR(10),
        createdon, 120)) AS CreatedOn
FROM    FilteredLead
```

22. Set LeadId as the Logical Primary Key on LeadFact. Create a new relationship between LeadFact and FilteredAccount. To do this, set the Source table to LeadFact and Source column to AccountId. Set the Destination table to FilteredAccount and Desitnation column to AccountId. When the relationship is configured, the data source view will resemble Figure 4-38.

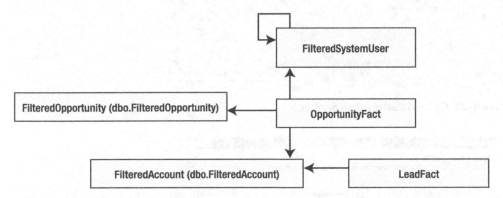

Figure 4-38. *Viewing the data source relationships*

23. With the appropriately configured Data Source View, it is possible to create a cube. Right-click Cubes in the Solution Explorer, and select New Cube. Click Next to get past the welcome screen. Select "Use existing tables". Click Next.

24. Select the default data source. Click Next.

25. Select Opportunity Fact and Lead Fact as measure groups. Click Next. Click Next. Click Next.

26. The final screen on the Cube Wizard should look like the one shown in Figure 4-39. Give the cube a meaningful name, and click Finish.

27. Now that the cube is created, a new dimension must be added for time. Right-click the Dimensions folder in the Solution Explorer, and click New Dimension.

28. Click Next to get past the welcome screen.

29. Select the "Generate a time table on the server" option. Click Next.

30. Extend the Last calendar day to December 31, 2013. Select "Year," "Quarter," "Month," "Week," and "Date" for Time periods as shown in Figure 4-40. Click Next.

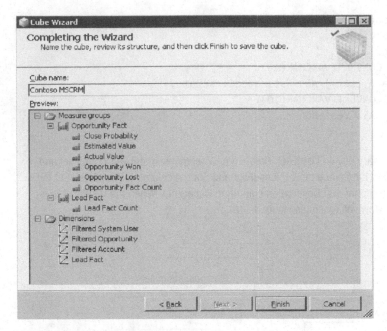

Figure 4-39. *Cube Wizard Final Screen*

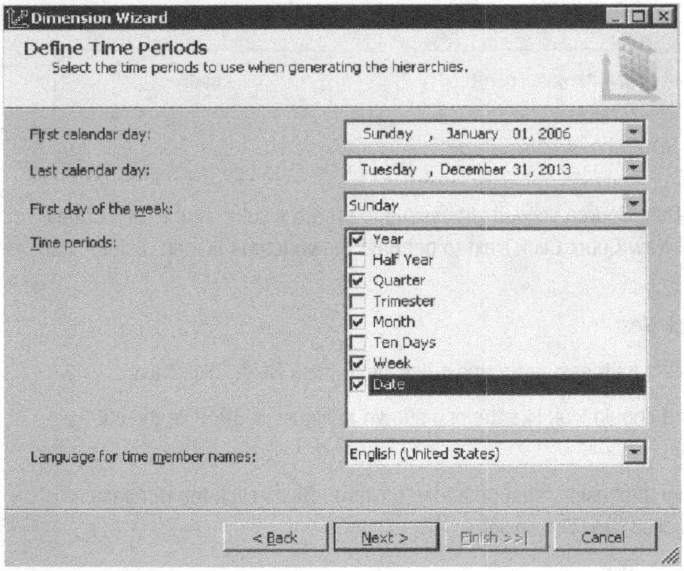

Figure 4-40. *Define time periods.*

31. Select Regular calendar. Click Next.

32. Type **Time** for the name, and click Finish.

33. Once the dimension has been created, return to the Cube Structure tab and right-click the cube name in the dimensions section of the form. Click Add Cube Dimension. Select the Time dimension, and close the window.

34. Now you will add the appropriate attributes for each dimension.

    a. Return to the Cube Structure tab and right-click on FilteredOpportunity and select Edit Dimension.

    b. In the Data Source View section, select the following attributes to add to the dimension: accountidname, closeprobability, OpportunityName, salesstagecodename, statecodename, statuscodename, and stepname.

    c. Right-click and select New Attribute from Column to add the attributes to the dimension as shown below in Figure 4-41.

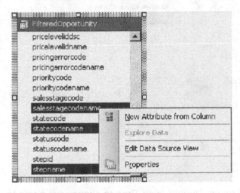

Figure 4-41. *Add attributes to dimensions.*

35. Select the Time dimension, and close the window.

36. Navigate to the Dimensions tab on the top menu of BIDS. As shown in Figure 4-42, Time is displayed as a dimension that can be linked to either fact table.

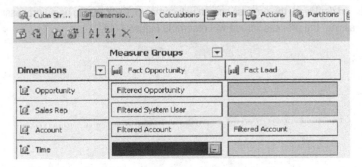

Figure 4-42. *Map the Time dimension.*

37. Open the grey box where Time and Fact Opportunity meet. When the Define Relationship dialog shown in Figure 4-43 opens, set the relationship type to Regular. Set the Granularity attribute to Date. For the measure group columns, select ModifiedOnDateKey. Click OK to close the window.

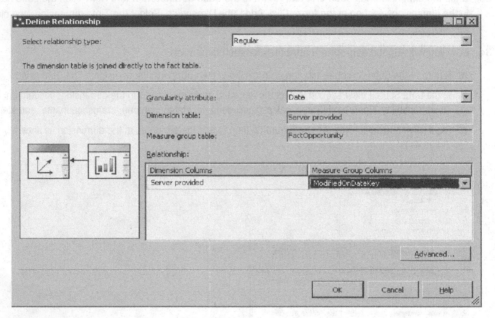

Figure 4-43. *Define the Time relationship.*

38. At this point, your screen will display Figure 4-42 again. Double-click Time to change the name to Modified On.

39. Save the cube to make sure any changes made since the cube's development will be processed.

40. Click the process icon in the upper left-hand corner next to the toolbox. A message will appear stating that the server content appears out of date. It will ask if Visual Studio can build and deploy the project first. Click OK.

41. When the project is built and deployed, the process screen will come up. Click Run to begin processing. When the project is processing, the process screen will resemble Figure 4-44.

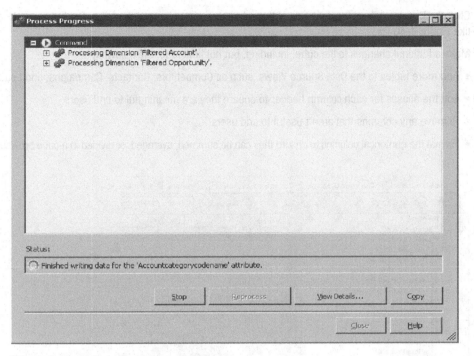

Figure 4-44. *Cube processing*

42. When the process completes, the status will change to "Process succeeded," as shown in Figure 4-45. Click Close to exit the process screen.

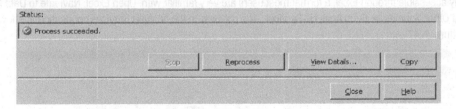

Figure 4-45. *The cube has been processed successfully.*

43. Click the Browser tab on the right side of the cube menu bar to browse the cube. The browser will look like Figure 4-46.

44. Make additional changes to the cube, including, but not limited to, the following:

- Add more tables to the Data Source Views, such as Competitors, Contacts, Campaigns, and Leads.

- Edit the aliases for each column header to ensure they are meaningful to end users.

- Remove any columns that aren't useful to end users.

- Format the numerical columns to ensure they can be summed, averaged, or divided in a cube browser.

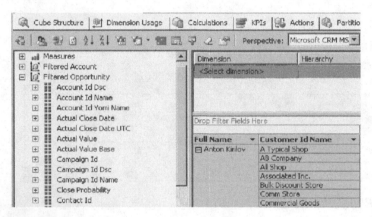

Figure 4-46. *The drag-and-drop cube browser*

45. Now that the cube is complete, you need to help users figure out how to access the cube. The cube is easily accessible through Excel, a format most users are very familiar with. Open Excel. Navigate to Data ➤ From Other Sources ➤ From Analysis Services. The pathway to the Analysis Services connection is shown in Figure 4-47.

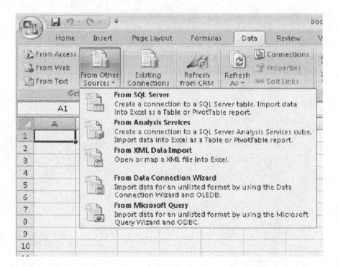

Figure 4-47. *Establish a data connection in Excel.*

46. Click Next. The next page will ask for connection information. For the server name, type a period. The period is another way of saying "localhost" or "this computer." Let the log-on credentials be set to Use Windows Authentication. Click Next.

47. The next page requests more detailed connection information. Specify the names of the database and the cube that was just created. The name of the database is typically whatever the project was named. Click Next.

48. Give the data connection a name, and click Finish. A window like the one shown in Figure 4-48 will pop up asking which way the data should be displayed in Excel. PivotTable Report is typically the best option. Accept the defaults, and click OK.

Figure 4-48. *Select the PivotTable Report destination.*

49. Click some interesting metrics and values. Add them to the pivot table. In Figure 4-49, for example, each sales representative has an actual and an estimated close value for deals.

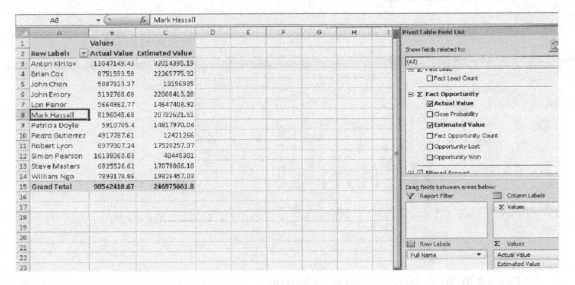

Figure 4-49. *Browse the cube in Excel.*

50. Add a filter by clicking and dragging the field "Is Disabled Name" from the fields list into the report filter on the Pivot menu available in the right-hand frame of Excel. Once created as a report filter, Is Disabled Name will show up above the pivot table. Set the filter to show only enabled, or active, employees. An example of the filter is shown in Figure 4-50.

Is Disabled Name	Enabled	
	Values	
Row Labels	**Actual Value**	**Estimated Value**
Anton Kirilov	13047149.43	32014395.19
Brian Cox	8751593.58	22265775.32
John Chen	5087313.37	13196935
John Emory	9132768.08	22008413.28
Lori Penor	5664982.77	14647403.92
Mark Hassall	8196045.68	20732621.51
Patricia Doyle	5910705.4	14817970.04
Pedro Gutierrez	4917787.61	12421266
Robert Lyon	6977307.24	17520257.37
Simon Pearson	16138060.03	40445801
Steve Masters	6825526.62	17078866.18
William Ngo	7893178.86	19826457.03
Grand Total	**98542418.67**	**246975661.8**

Show fields related to:
(All)

☐ Invite Status Code
☐ Invite Status Code Name
☐ Is Disabled
☑ **Is Disabled Name**
☐ Job Title
☐ Last Name
☐ Middle Name
☐ Mobile Alert Email
☐ Mobile Phone

Drag fields between areas below:
▼ Report Filter   Colum
Is Disabled Name ▼   Σ Value

Figure 4-50. *Adding a filter in Excel*

51. To graph the results, click the PivotChart button located on the Options tab of the PivotTable Tools section. A graph like the one shown in Figure 4-51 will come up to display the information from the pivot table. This graph, for example, shows that sales representatives tend to overestimate how much sales they will bring by a factor of two.

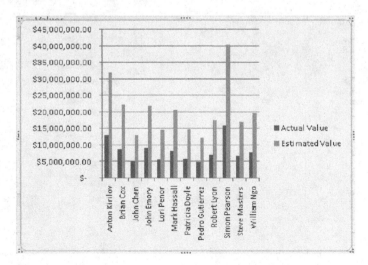

Figure 4-51. *A pivot chart based on cube data*

While this cube provides the viewer with enough information to do some forecasting regarding estimated value and actual value, a more complex cube would give viewers the ability to see each sales representative's actual value vs. estimated value over time, allowing them to do better forecasting with less uncertainty. Viewers would be able to answer questions such as these: Are the sales representatives' estimated values always nearly double? Or is it only during the summer months, when business is at its heaviest? In Chapter 6, you'll see how to create a cube to help answer time-based questions about the business.

Now that you have a functioning cube, spend some time in Excel working with that cube. Try adding a new parameter to limit the Excel table shown in Figure 4-50 to only closed deals. You might also try looking for visible trends in the data by adding additional pivot charts based on the data in Figure 4-50. For example, with a pie chart, you might notice the disproportionate amount of actual revenue generated by Anton and Simon. Cubes help a great deal in allowing you to explore the data collected by the business. This ad hoc exploration is a powerful way to pick up on trends and patterns that can help drive your business forward in the right direction.

Step 2: Designing an Approach to Deliver Trend Data

With a transactional cube in place, you now need to think through an approach to deliver trend data. All BI projects focused on sales and marketing data must deal with the problems that the underlying source data is constantly changing and that there are not always well-defined business rules for how key sales forecasts and pipeline trends should be displayed.

Specifically, many sales managers and vice presidents are eager to know how the pipeline is changing over time, and many marketing vice presidents are eager to know the cycle time at each sales stage of the leads they provide. Both of these problems present a challenge for transactional reporting as it's delivered in either our SSRS examples or our basic OLAP cube, because many transactional CRM systems store the state of these records at only the current point in time. The result is that analytics practitioners must be prepared to work around these transactional system limitations by leveraging the breadth of the SQL Server data platform to deliver tools that can meet these business needs. In Chapter 6, we will explore one approach and discuss alternative options for delivering sales and marketing trending and cycle time data.

Step 3: Developing Your Data Mart and SSAS Cube

Based on the design established in step 2, you will need to establish a persistent data store to capture and maintain the data that is only temporary in the transactional CRM system. Many times, this data store is referred to as a data mart or data warehouse. The primary distinction between a data mart and data warehouse is one of the breadth of data captured. A warehouse captures a full cross section of organizational data (e.g., financial, customer, sales, marketing, support, and operations), whereas a data mart typically is specific to one business domain (e.g., sales and marketing).

For the purposes of this book, we will focus on capturing sales and marketing specific data and will use the term "data mart." The primary tools for development of the data mart will be SSIS and SSAS. These frameworks available in SQL Server 2008 are specifically designed to extract, load, and transform data from transactional systems into data marts and data warehouses and then deliver cubes that allow users to explore the extracted and transformed data.

In Chapter 6, we will step through two specific examples where we are using SSIS and SSAS to build a data mart and deliver an SSAS cube in order to support the ad hoc exploration of sales and marketing data.

Step 4: Evaluating Limitations in Your BI Platform

The delivery of the core intermediate tools including the deployment of trend-based cubes and a data mart marks a great opportunity for an analytics team to stop and reflect on what the next step should be. Many organizations would use reaching the intermediate stage as an immediate call to move toward performance management, but our experience is that taking this next step is not always necessary.

Many organizations that reach this stage will benefit greatly from revising their dashboards and cubes before they take the next step and move into performance management. We'll dig more deeply into the details in Chapter 7, but many organizations find that by effectively deploying and extending solutions built at the basic and intermediate levels, they are delivering the value that their business customers need. They further find that, occasionally, the business has not fully evolved its requirements for performance management, and the result of deployment of project management tools would lead to additional software and hardware costs without delivering the corresponding return on business value. In other situations, the business and technology teams are effectively moving together down this path, and it is a natural step to make the financial and human investment required to move up the analytics pyramid.

Considering Advanced Analytics

At the advanced stage, we look to take advantage of the investments in time and resources we've made at both of the prior stages to deliver broad and deep performance management applications that will be driven by both the data foundation we established in the basic stage and the OLAP cubes we've developed in the intermediate stage.

The key with advanced analytics is in fully integrating the tools built at the basic and intermediate stages so that they fit elegantly into the day-to-day work of all the relevant stakeholders. Many organizations would like to jump directly to advanced analytics, but our experience has been that the organizations that experience the greatest success with BI follow a clear path from focusing on business processes and data infrastructure at the basic stage to development of robust OLAP capabilities at the intermediate stage; only then do they truly have the skills and knowledge necessary to move onto full-fledged performance management. You will know there is demand to move to this stage based on getting requests like these:

- I've managed to create some great insights in my pivot tables from the cubes, but I'd really like to be able to share these more broadly to provide context for our KPIs.

- We've got a great set of analytical capabilities between the cubes and the SSRS reports, but we need some way to put them all together and shift from one environment to the next.

- The SSRS reports and cubes do a great job of pulling together our metrics, but I'm working on my plan for next year and really need a tool that will facilitate setting up budgets, commissions, and goals in an iterative approach.

At the advanced stage, organizations should be taking the following actions:

1. Evaluate the licensing implications of moving from the intermediate solution.

2. Refine OLAP cubes and existing datasets to support scorecard design.

3. Establish a plan for performance management that leverages SharePoint.

4. Define drill-through paths for key sales and marketing KPIs.

5. Deploy SharePoint scorecards and dashboards.

Details regarding these actions will be covered in depth in Chapter 7.

Summary

The material in this chapter has provided insight into our approach toward aligning our KPIs with business systems and beginning to prioritize business requirements. In addition, we've introduced the analytics pyramid as a way to break your analytics program into specific incremental steps. These key stages are as follows:

- *Basic*: The organization is new to analytics or is restarting an analytics initiative. The basic stage focuses on defining a clear road map and executing on key dashboards with SQL Server and SQL Server Reporting Services (SSRS).

- *Intermediate*: The intermediate stage builds on the core infrastructure and skills developed at the basic level and focuses on providing users ad hoc analytics via OLAP cubes built with SQL Server Analysis Services (SSAS).

- *Advanced*: The final stage focuses on enhancing all of the tools built at earlier stages and embedding them into the workflow of users to provide end-to-end performance management.

CHAPTER 5

∎∎∎

Core Components of SQL Server 2008

In Chapter 4, we walked through the development of our executive KPI dashboard using SQL Server 2008 with a focus on SSRS. The combination of SQL Server's database services and SSRS is the technical foundation for the basic level of our analytics platform as described in our analytics pyramid, shown again for reference in Figure 5-1.

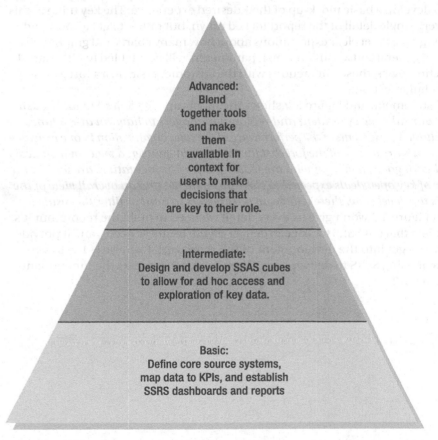

Figure 5-1. *The analytics pyramid*

This chapter will cover these core components in greater depth, and weave in examples from our fictional company, Dyno Technologies, to show these components in action. In our deep dive into SQL Server 2008, we will focus on both a set of enhancements in SQL Server 2008 that bring out a richer user experience as well as on leveraging some core functionality that has been in existence in earlier versions of the software.

Let's get started by looking at how SQL Server 2008 can help to deliver on the relevant priority 1 items in our Dyno Technologies road map that was established in Chapter 4. These priority 1 items include:

- *Sales Manager dashboard*: With our Sales Manager dashboard, we will develop an SSRS report that will look deeper into the sales-related metrics than is possible at the executive KPI level.

- *Marketing Campaign dashboard*: With our campaign dashboard, we will develop an SSRS report that will focus on delivering analytics specifically for the marketing team.

Developing a Sales Manager Dashboard

Dyno Technologies begins the process of developing a Sales Manager dashboard by working with the key users to develop a basic mock-up of their desired experience. The key thing at this stage is not to get every single detail of the report locked down, but rather to get a good understanding of the users' goals, to set clear expectations about how many charts and graphs will be displayed, and to have general consensus on which parameters will be enabled to filter data. In the case of Dyno Technologies, these interactions with the customer result in a short goal statement and corresponding mock-up.

Here is the goal statement, and Figure 5-2 shows the mock-up: *The Sales Manager dashboard will allow for our sales vice president and regional managers to have an at-a-glance understanding of multiple key elements of the performance of the sales organization in one viewable frame. These key elements are a view of the forecast for the current quarter, a view on won deals to date as compared with goals, a view of who the leading sales representatives are within the organization, a view of key open deals expected to close this quarter, and an overall view of the sales pipeline. At this top-level view, there will be no parameters to limit or filter the results.*

The mock-up in Figure 5-2 won't give us every detail we need to build the report, but it's enough for us to validate that our SSRS toolkit can deliver on the business needs, and it provides a starting point for us to get into the development of the scorecard. Exercise 5-1 walks you through the process of using SSRS to deliver a real-time report that meets the functionality demonstrated in Figure 5-2.

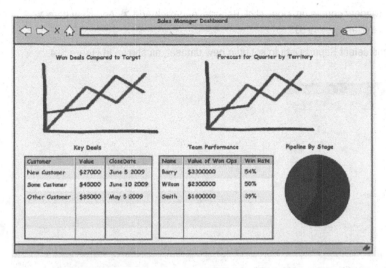

Figure 5-2. *The Sales Manager dashboard mock-up*

Exercise 5-1. Building a Sales Manager SSRS Report

Develop the dashboard mock-up shown in Figure 5-2. Create the report by leveraging SSRS, the built-in reporting tool that comes as part of SQL Server. Here are the steps to follow:

1. Start Microsoft Business Intelligence Development Studio (BIDS), and select the Report Server Project template. Enter the project information as shown in Figure 5-3.

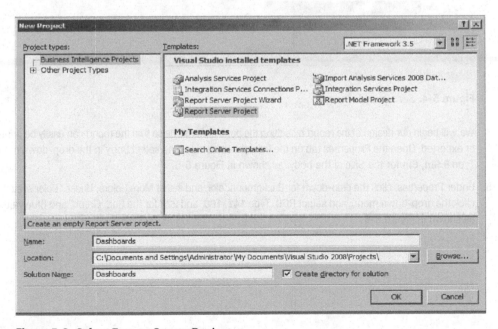

Figure 5-3. *Select Report Server Project.*

2. When the Solution Explorer window comes up, right-click Reports, and click Add ➤ Add New Item ➤ Report. Name the report `SalesManager.rdl`.

3. On the toolbar, click View, and select Report Data to set up a new dataset, as shown in Figure 5-4.

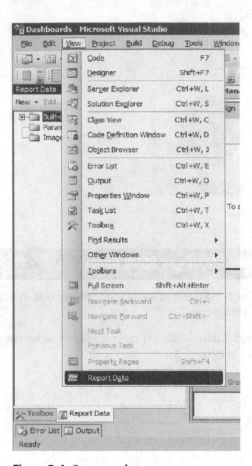

Figure 5-4. *Set up a dataset.*

4. We will begin our design of the report by setting the page dimensions so that the report can easily be printed or exported. Open the Properties tab on the far right-hand side, and select Body in the drop-down menu. Type **9.9in, 8in** for the Size of the body, as shown in Figure 5-5.

5. Under Properties, click the drop-down for BackgroundColor, and select More Colors. Under "Color system," click the drop-down menu, and select RGB. Type **141**, **180**, and **227** for the Red, Green, and Blue values, as shown in Figure 5-6.

Figure 5-5. *Set the page dimensions.*

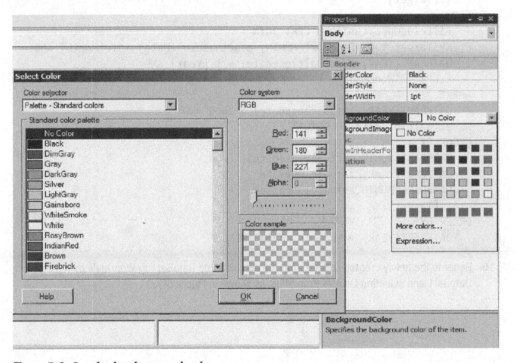

Figure 5-6. *Set the background color.*

6. Under Properties, select Report in the drop-down menu. Type **11in, 8.5in** for the InteractiveSize and PageSize of the report and **0in, 0in, 0in, 0in** for the Margins.

7. To add an item to the report, drag a Chart from the toolbox to the design surface. Select the first line chart in the Select Chart Type dialog, and click OK.

8. The Data Source Properties dialog will pop up and ask you to define your connection. The option to define a data source only appears if there is no data source yet defined for the current report. Under Name, type **Contoso_MSCRM**. Click the Edit button, and type **localhost** in the Server name field. Select Contoso_MSCRM under the "Select or choose database name" label, and then click OK and Next.

9. In the Query Designer, type the following query, and click Finish:

```
SELECT
    DATEPART(MONTH, actualclosedate) AS 'Month',
    LEFT (DATENAME(MONTH,actualclosedate),3) AS 'Month Name',
    DATEPART(YEAR, actualclosedate) AS 'Year',
    SUM(ISNULL(actualvalue, 0))/1000 AS 'Revenue in 1000s',
    t.[Target]
FROM
    FilteredOpportunity o LEFT JOIN
    KPITarget t ON DATEPART(MONTH, o.actualclosedate) = t.[Month] AND
    DATEPART(YEAR, o.actualclosedate) = t.[Year] AND
    t.KPI = 'WonDeals'
WHERE
    DATEPART(YEAR, actualclosedate) > 2006 AND
    actualclosedate <= GETDATE()
GROUP BY
    DATEPART(MONTH, actualclosedate),
    DATEPART(YEAR, actualclosedate),
    DATENAME(MONTH,actualclosedate),
    t.[Target]
ORDER BY
    DATEPART(YEAR, actualclosedate) DESC
```

10. Rename the newly created dataset from the default name DataSet1 to WonDeals by right-clicking DataSet1 and selecting Dataset Properties, as shown in Figure 5-7.

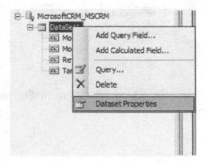

Figure 5-7. *Review the dataset properties.*

11. Change the Name property to WonDeals, and click OK.

12. Click the chart under the Design panel, and then go to the Properties menu to change the DataSetName from the old DataSet1 to WonDeals, as shown in Figure 5-8.

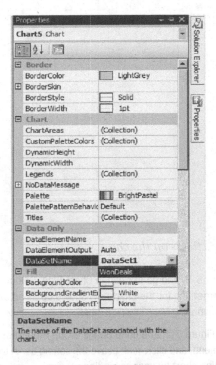

Figure 5-8. *Name the dataset.*

Scroll down in the same Properties box to change the Size to **4.45in, 3.75in**, and press Enter.

Select the Report Data tab on the left of the screen, and drag the Target, Revenue_in_1000s, Year, and Month_Name fields onto the chart, as shown in Figure 5-9.

13. Right-click Chart Title, and select Title Properties ➤ "fx." Put the following in the Set expression for Caption box, and click OK twice:

```
="Forecast (in 1000s) for Specified Quarter:
" & FormatNumber(Sum(Fields!Revenue_in
_1000s.Value),0)
```

14. Right-click the [Sum(Target)] box shown in Figure 5-9, and go to Series Properties ➤ Legend. Click the box next to "Do not show this series in a legend," and click OK.

15. Right-click the [Sum(Target)] box shown in Figure 5-9, and go to Series Properties ➤ Fill. Click "fx" under Color. Type **#d787cefa** in the expression box, and click OK. This changes the color of the area chart to our custom color.

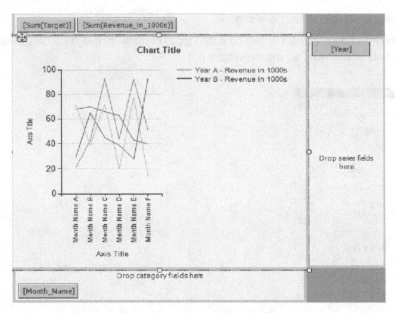

Figure 5-9. *Drop the series, category, and metric fields on the chart.*

16. Again, right-click the [Sum(Target)] box shown in Figure 5-7, and go to Change Chart Type. Select the first chart under the Area section, and click OK. The target line for the chart now shows up as an area chart, while the 2007 and 2008 data remains as a line chart.

17. Right-click the [Year] box in the series fields shown in Figure 5-7, and go to Series Group Properties ➤ Sorting. Click Add; click the "Sort by field" drop-down menu, and click Year. Leave the setting as "A to Z" under the Order column. Click OK. This will order the line chart by year ascending.

18. Type **Revenue (in 1000s)** in bold for the y axis title and **Month** in bold for the x axis title.

19. Right-click the x axis (month labels), and select Axis Properties. Under "Set axis scale and style," set the Minimum, Interval, and "Cross at" fields to 1, 3, and 1, as shown in Figure 5-10. This will stretch the chart to cover the entire x axis.

20. Right-click the x axis (month labels) again, and select Axis Properties ➤ Line. Click the "fx" button under "Line color"; type **#c0c0c0** in the expression box, and click OK. Repeat this step for the y axis to change both axes to a grey color. Repeat for the "Line color" property under Major Tick Marks for both the x and y axes.

21. Right-click the y axis (dollars), and select Axis Properties ➤ Number. Under Category, select Currency, and under Decimal places, type **0**. Click OK.

22. Right-click the legend, and select Legend Properties ➤ General, and adjust the "Legend position" to center right, as shown in Figure 5-11. Click OK.

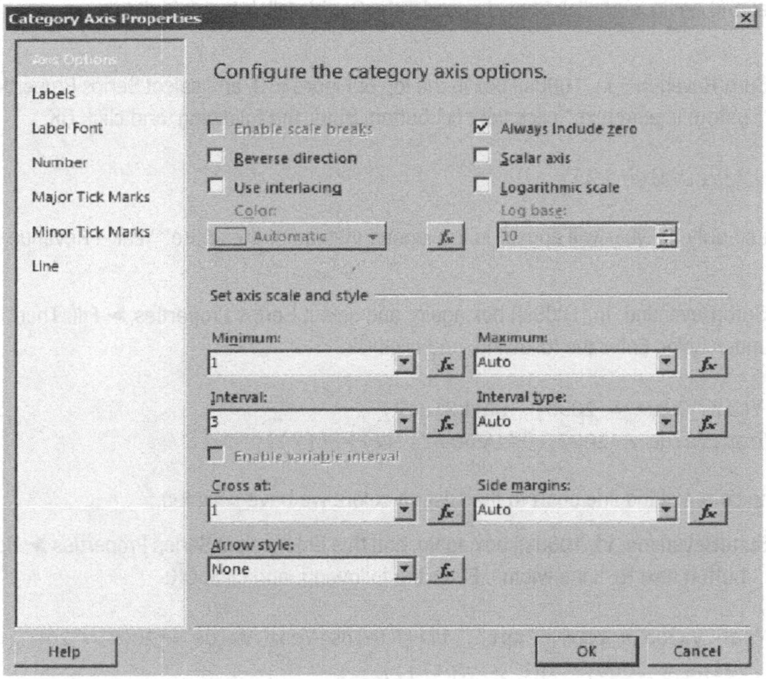

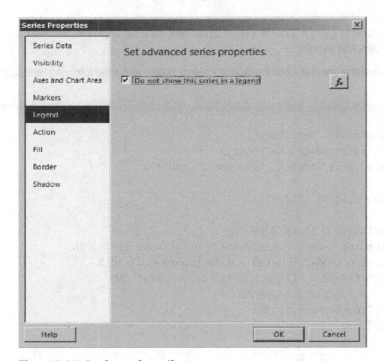

Figure 5-10. *Configure the category axis.*

Figure 5-11. *Set legend attributes.*

23. Right-click the legend again, and click Show Legend Title. Double-click the default title, and rename it to **Year**.

24. Right-click the [Sum(Revenune_in_1000s)] box in the top of Figure 5-9, and select Series Properties ➤ Legend. Under "Custom legend text," click the "fx" button. Enter the following, and click OK:

```
=Left(Fields!Year.Value, 4)
```

This will make it so only the year will appear in the legend instead of the entire "Year – Revenue in 1000s" label.

25. Right-click the [Sum(Revenune_in_1000s)] box again, and select Series Properties ➤ Fill. Then, click the "fx" button under Color. Enter the following, and click OK:

```
=iif(Fields!Year.Value = 2008, "DarkBlue",
iif(Fields!Year.Value = 2007, "#AAAAAA","#FFFFFF"))
```

This will force the colors of the line chart to the custom colors we have selected.

26. Right-click the [Sum(Revenune_in_1000s)] box again, and this time, select Series Properties ➤ Border, and click the "fx" button next to "Line width". Enter the following, and click OK:

```
=iif(Fields!Year.Value = 2008, "4pt", iif(Fields!Year.Value = 2007, "2pt", iif
(Fields!Year.Value = 2006, "1pt", "0pt")))
```

This statement will change the width of the line depending on what year is represented. The first chart is now complete.

27. Next, add another dataset by going to View ➤ Report Data. Right-click the Microsoft_MSCRM dataset created earlier, and click Add Dataset.

28. Name the Dataset **TerritoryForecast**. Click the Query Designer button; enter the following code, and click OK twice:

```
SELECT
    A.territoryidname AS 'Territory',
    YEAR(O.estimatedclosedate) AS 'Year',
    SUM(O.estimatedvalue)/1000 AS 'Revenue in 1000s',
    K.[Target],
    LEFT (O.stepname,1) AS 'Stage'
FROM
    FilteredOpportunity O INNER JOIN
    FilteredSystemUser S ON O.owneridname = S.fullname LEFT JOIN
    FilteredAccount A ON A.accountid = O.accountid LEFT JOIN
    KPITarget K ON K.Year = YEAR(O.estimatedclosedate) AND
    K.Territory = A.territoryidname AND
    K.Stage = LEFT(O.stepname,1) AND
    K.KPI = 'Territory'
```

```
WHERE
    O.stepname != 'NULL' AND
    O.stepname >= '3' AND
    YEAR(O.estimatedclosedate) = 2008
GROUP BY
    A.territoryidname,
    O.stepname,
    YEAR(O.estimatedclosedate),
    K.[Target]
```

29. Click the toolbox on the left, and drag over a new chart to the right of the existing line/area chart just created. Select the first column chart (the default), and click OK.

30. In the Properties window, type **4.63in, 3.75in** for the chart Size, as shown in Figure 5-12.

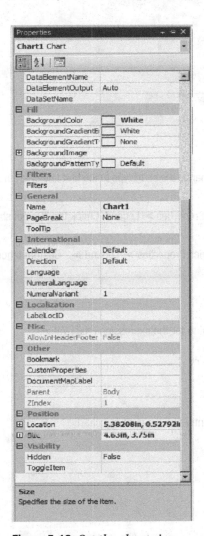

Figure 5-12. *Set the chart size.*

31. Click the chart, and drag the fields from the TerritoryForecast dataset onto the chart, as shown in Figure 5-13.

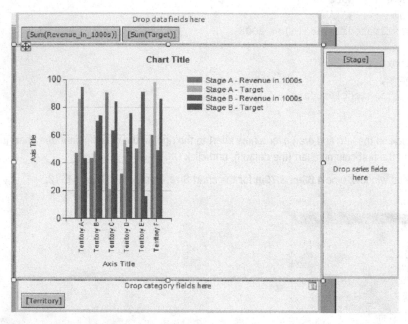

Figure 5-13. *Set up the forecast chart.*

32. Right-click the [Sum(Target)] box in the data fields, and change the chart type to the first line chart under the chart options.

33. Right-click the [Sum(Target)] box again, and go to Series Properties ➤ Legend. Check the "Do not show this series in a legend" box.

34. Right-click the [Sum(Revenue_in_1000s)] box. Go to Series Properties ➤ Legend ➤ "Custom legend text," and enter the following expression:

```
=Left(Fields!Revenue_in_1000s.Value, 1)
```

35. Right-click the default Chart Title, and enter in the following for the expression ("fx") value:

```
="Forecast (in 1000s) for Specified Quarter:
" & FormatNumber(Sum(Fields!Revenue_in
_1000s.Value),0)
```

36. Right-click the legend, and move the position to right-center like the previous chart.

37. Right-click the legend, and enable Show Legend Title. Rename the title to **Stage**.

38. Rename the x axis title to **Territory** in bold.

39. Rename the y axis title to **Est. Rev. (in 1,000s)** in bold.

40. Right-click the x axis value, and go to Axis Properties. Change the Minor Tick Marks values to match Figure 5-14.

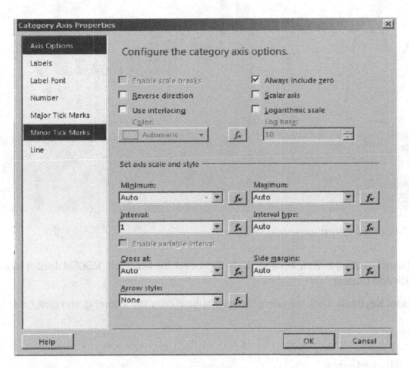

Figure 5-14. *Configure the category axis.*

41. Click Labels, shown on the left of Figure 5-14, and select the "Disable auto-fit" radio button. Type **90** for the Label rotation angle. Click OK.

42. Right-click the y axis values, and change the number format to currency with "0 decimal places,"

43. Right-click the x axis (territory labels), and select Axis Properties ➤ Line. Click the "fx" button under "Line color"; enter **#c0c0c0** in the expression box, and click OK. Repeat this step for the y axis to change both axes to a grey color. Repeat for the "Line color" property under Major Tick Marks for both the x and y axes.

44. Preview your report, and arrange it to resemble Figure 5-15.

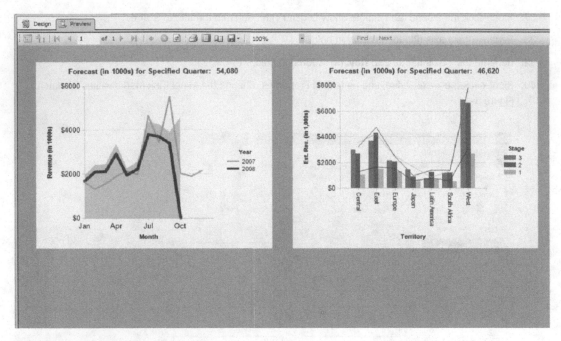

Figure 5-15. *The dashboard in preview mode*

45. Add another dataset by going to View ➤ Report Data. Right-click the Microsoft_MSCRM dataset created earlier, and click Add Dataset.

46. Name the Dataset **KeyDeals**. Click the Query Designer button; enter the following, and click OK twice:

```
SELECT TOP 10
   opportunityid,
   FA.regardingobjectid,
   accountidname AS 'Account',
   estimatedclosedate AS 'Est. Close Date',
   estimatedvalue/1000 AS 'Est Revenue in 1000s',
   ISNULL(FA.[Recent Activity],0) AS 'Recent Activity'
FROM FilteredOpportunity FO
LEFT OUTER JOIN
   (SELECT regardingobjectid, ISNULL(COUNT(*), 0) AS 'Recent Activity'
    FROM FilteredActivityPointer
    WHERE DATEDIFF(MONTH, modifiedon, GETDATE()) <= 30
    AND activitytypecodename != 'Opportunity Close'
    GROUP BY regardingobjectid) FA ON FO.opportunityid = FA.regardingobjectid
WHERE statecode = 0
ORDER BY estimatedvalue DESC
```

47. Go to the toolbox, and drag over a Table under the left-hand chart, as shown in Figure 5-16.

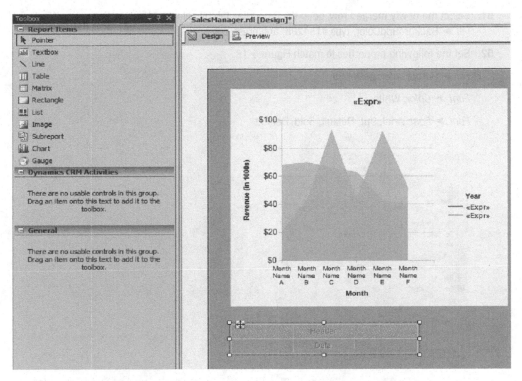

Figure 5-16. *Create the key deals table.*

48. Select the table, and go to Properties. Set the DataSetName to **KeyDeals**.

49. Right-click the header row in the table, and click Insert Row ➤ Above. Right-click any column, and insert a column to the left.

50. Highlight the newly inserted four-column row, right-click to open the context menu shown in Figure 5-17, and click Merge Cells.

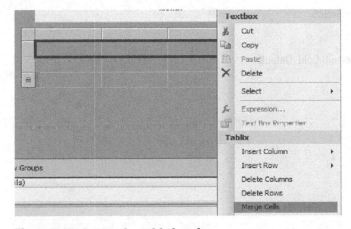

Figure 5-17. *Set up the table header.*

51. Select the newly merged row, go to the Properties tab by selecting View ➤ Properties Window. Under Fill ➤ BackgroundColor, type **#15428b**, and press Enter.

52. Set the following properties to match Figure 5-18:

Fill ➤ *BorderColor*: **#e9e9e9**

Font ➤ *Color*: White

Font ➤ *Font*: Arial, 9pt, Default, Bold, Default

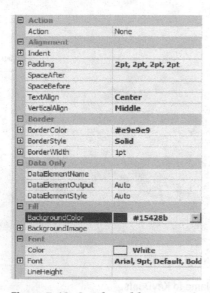

Figure 5-18. *Set the table properties.*

53. Type **Top 10 Key Deals** in the newly formatted merged cell, and center the text.

54. Select the row below the merged cell, and enter in the following properties:

Fill ➤ *BorderColor*: **#e9e9e9**

Fill ➤ *BackgroundColor*: **#c5c5c5**

Font ➤ *Color*: **#15428b**

Font ➤ *Font*: Arial, 8pt, Default, Bold, Default

55. Type the values **Account, Estimated Close Date, Estimated Revenue in (1000s)**, and **Recent Activity** for the titles, as shown in Figure 5-19.

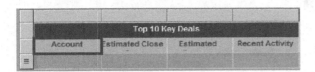

Figure 5-19. *Set table column headings.*

56. Select the last row, and enter the following properties:

Fill ➤ BorderColor. **#e9e9e9**

Fill ➤ BackgroundColor. White

Font ➤ Font Color. Black

57. Hover under the Account header, and click the blue-and-white list box that appears. Select Account to bind the Account data to that column. Repeat for the rest of the columns to match Figure 5-20.

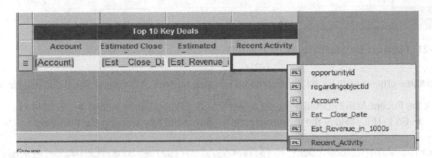

Figure 5-20. *Bind data to the table.*

58. Select the data row, and change the font style and size to Arial and 8pt by selecting these values from the main menu for the report.

59. Right-click the detail line for Estimated Close Date, and select Text Box Properties. Format the number to Date, as shown in Figure 5-21.

60. Center the Estimated Close Date, Estimated Revenue, and Recent Activity detail rows. Also, format the Recent Activity and Account detail boxes to be underlined.

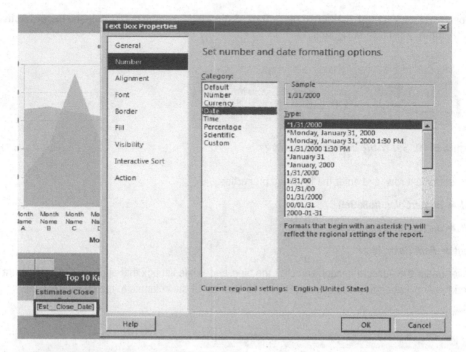

Figure 5-21. *Format the date fields.*

61. Follow the same procedure to format the Estimated Revenue number to Currency with 0 decimal places.

62. Right-click the Recent Activity detail box, and select Text Box Properties ➤ Action ➤ "Enable as a hyperlink" ➤ Go to URL. Modify the expression under "Select URL" by entering the following:

```
="javascript:void(window.open('http://MOSS/reportserver2008?/CRM+Accelerator+
Dashboards/AFRecentActivity&rs:Format=HTML4.0
&rs:Command=Render&rc:Toolbar=False'))"
```

This will allow you to drill through to a more-detailed activity report. Note that the detailed report will only open when the dashboard is published and viewed within a web browser.

63. Right-click the Account detail box, and select Text Box Properties ➤ Action ➤ "Enable as a hyperlink" ➤ Go to URL. Modify the expression under "Select URL" and enter the URL for the CRM system you are using. The following example will take a user to the Opportunity form in Dynamics CRM. If you are using a different CRM system, modify the URL as appropriate:

```
="http://localhost:5555/MicrosoftCRM/sfa/opps/edit.aspx?id=
{" & Fields!opportunityid.
Value.ToString & "}#"
```

This will allow a user to click the company name and open the related opportunity.

64. Add another dataset by going to View ➤ Report Data. Right-click the Microsoft_MSCRM dataset created earlier, and click Add Dataset.

65. Name the dataset **SalesLeaders**. Click the Query Designer button. Enter the following code, and click OK twice:

```
SELECT TOP 10 [Year],
    [Sales Representative],
    sum([Revenue in Dollars])/1000 ASRevenue in 1000s',
    sum([Won Deals]) AS 'Won Deals',
    sum([Total Deals]) AS 'Total Deals' ,
    [Currency Symbol]
FROM
    (SELECT DATEPART(YEAR, actualclosedate) AS 'Year',
     owneridname AS 'Sales Representative',
    sum(ActualValue) AS 'Revenue in Dollars',
    COUNT(opportunityid) AS 'Won Deals',
    0 AS 'Total Deals',
    SUBSTRING(RIGHT(crm_moneyformatstring,
     LEN(crm_moneyformatstring) - 1), 1, CHARINDEX('"', RIGHT(crm_
     moneyformatstring, LEN(crm_moneyformatstring) - 1)) - 1)
    AS 'Currency Symbol'
FROM filteredopportunity
WHERE statecodename = 'won'
    AND DATEPART(YEAR, actualclosedate) = 2008  --    placeholder for dates
GROUP BY owneridname, DATEPART(YEAR, actualclosedate),
    SUBSTRING(RIGHT(crm
    _moneyformatstring, LEN(crm_moneyformatstring) - 1),
    1, CHARINDEX('"',      RIGHT(crm_
moneyformatstring, LEN(crm_moneyformatstring) - 1)) - 1)
UNION
    SELECT DATEPART(YEAR, actualclosedate) AS 'Year',
    owneridname AS 'Sales Representative',
    0,0, COUNT(opportunityid)AS 'Total Deals',
    SUBSTRING(RIGHT(crm_
moneyformatstring, LEN(crm_moneyformatstring) - 1), 1, CHARINDEX('"',
RIGHT(crm_
    moneyformatstring, LEN(crm_moneyformatstring) - 1)) - 1) AS 'Currency Symbol'
    --placeholder for dates
    FROM FilteredOpportunity
    WHERE DATEPART(YEAR, actualclosedate) = 2008
    GROUP BY owneridname, DATEPART(YEAR, actualclosedate),
        SUBSTRING(RIGHT(crm_
    moneyformatstring, LEN(crm_moneyformatstring) - 1), 1, CHARINDEX('"',
RIGHT(crm_
    moneyformatstring, LEN(crm_moneyformatstring) - 1)) - 1)) AllOps
    GROUP BY [Sales Representative], [Year], [Currency Symbol]
    ORDER BY SUM([Revenue in Dollars]) DESC
```

66. Since our next table will be using the same format as the table we just created, make a copy of the existing table, paste the copy next to the existing one, and modify it to appear as in Figure 5-22. Select the newly modified table, and set the DataSetName to **SalesLeaders** in the Properties menu, and set the detail rows accordingly.

Figure 5-22. *Set up the sales leaders table.*

67. Add another dataset by going to View ➤ Report Data. Right-click the Microsoft_MSCRM dataset created earlier, and click Add Dataset.

```
SELECT SUM(estimatedvalue)/1000 AS 'Revenue',
    LEFT (stepname,1) AS 'Stage',
    Count(*) AS 'Deals',
    SUBSTRING(RIGHT(crm_moneyformatstring,
    LEN(crm_moneyformatstring) -
      1), 1, CHARINDEX('"', RIGHT(crm_moneyformatstring,
    LEN(crm_moneyformatstring) - 1))
      - 1) AS 'Currency Symbol'
FROM FilteredOpportunity
WHERE statuscodename = 'In Progress'
    AND stepname != 'NULL'
GROUP BY LEFT (stepname,1) ,
    SUBSTRING(RIGHT(crm_moneyformatstring, LEN(crm_
    moneyformatstring) - 1), 1,
    CHARINDEX('"', RIGHT(crm_moneyformatstring, LEN(crm_
    moneyformatstring) - 1)) - 1)
ORDER BY Stage
```

68. Go to the toolbox, and drag a chart to the bottom-right corner of the dashboard. Select the Funnel chart, as shown in Figure 5-23.

69. Click the chart, and set the Size in the Properties to **2.51in, 3.125in**.

70. Drag the data fields from the dataset onto the chart, as shown in Figure 5-24.

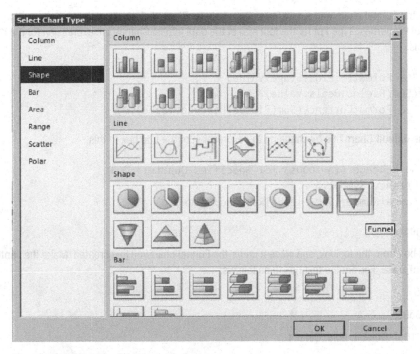

Figure 5-23. *Select the Funnel chart.*

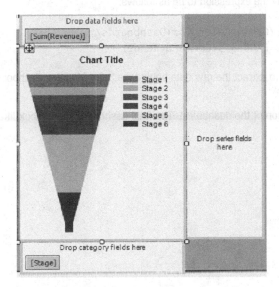

Figure 5-24. *Set up the Funnel chart.*

71. Right-click the Funnel chart, and select Show Data Labels. Right-click the new data labels, and go to Series Label Properties. Type **7pt** for the font size of the data labels. Change the expression for the data labels to this:

```
="Stage " & Format(Fields!Stage.Value) & ", "
& Format(Sum(Fields!Deals.Value)) &
" Opps, " & FormatCurrency(Sum(Fields!Revenue.Value),0)
```

72. Rename the default Chart Title by changing the expression of the title box to this:

```
="Pipeline Revenue (in 1000s) for Specified Quarter: " &
Fields!Currency_Symbol.
Value & FormatNumber(Sum(Fields!Revenue.Value),0)
```

73. Delete the legend.

74. Drag a text box from the toolbox, and place it under the Funnel chart you just created. Make the caption read **Extract Data**. Format the text box to as follows:

Align: Right

Color: **#898c95**

Font: Arial, 10pt, Default, Bold, Default

75. Right-click the Extract Data text box, and go to Textbox Properties ➤ Action. Under "Enable as a hyperlink," choose the "Go to URL" option, and modify the expression to be as follows:

```
="http://MOSS/reportserver2008?/CRM+Accelerator+Dashboards/
AFSalesManagerRawData&rs:Format=EXCEL&rs:Command=Render"
```

This will enable the Extract Data text box to extract the raw data behind the Sales Manager dashboard into an Excel spreadsheet.

76. Type **Sales Manager** for the title at the top of the dashboard. The final dashboard should look like Figure 5-25 when you preview it.

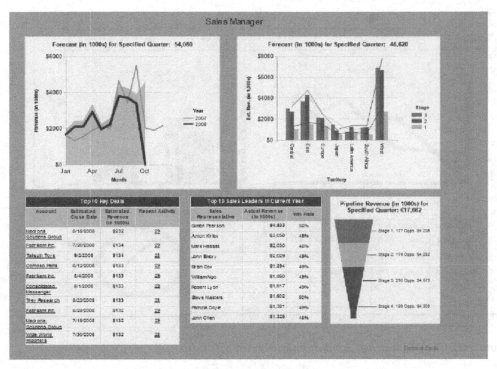

Figure 5-25. *The completed Sales Manager dashboard*

Developing the Marketing Campaign Dashboard

The Marketing Campaign dashboard begins in much the same way as the Sales Manager dashboard. We meet with key stakeholders from the marketing team to understand their primary needs and develop a short goal statement and mock-up. Following is the goal statement, and the mock-up is shown in Figure 5-26: *The marketing organization needs one common interface for the presentation of campaign related metrics. The core metrics to be presented are the volume of leads generated over time, a summary of the key campaigns by the type of campaign, a summary of currently active campaigns, and the average cost of a campaign response. The only associated parameter is that any user should be able to filter on the owner of the campaign to see results associated with a specific owner.*

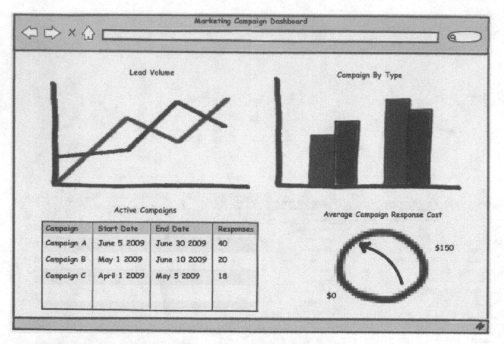

Figure 5-26. *The Marketing Campaign dashboard mock-up*

Exercise 5-2 walks you through the task of creating a real dashboard to correspond to the mock-up.

Exercise 5-2. Delivering a Marketing Campaign Dashboard

Create the dashboard using SSRS to deliver on the functionality described in the goal statement and outlined in the mock-up in Figure 5-26. Here are the steps to follow:

1. Open Microsoft BIDS.

2. Navigate to File ➤ New ➤ Project. Select the Report Server Project, as shown in Figure 5-27.

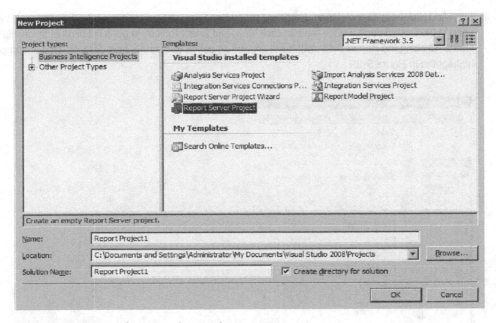

Figure 5-27. *Create the reporting project.*

3. Give the Report a name, and click OK.

4. When the Solution Explorer window shown in Figure 5-28 comes up, right-click Reports, and click Add.

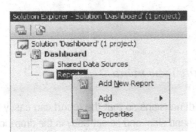

Figure 5-28. *Add the campaign manager report.*

5. Click Add New Item. Select Report. Name the report ManagerCampaign.rdl. Click OK. The report will open to the Design page. On the toolbar, click View, and select Toolbox to get a list of all of the available charts. Clicking the Report Data option will provide an option to create a new dataset. That option is highlighted in Figure 5-29.

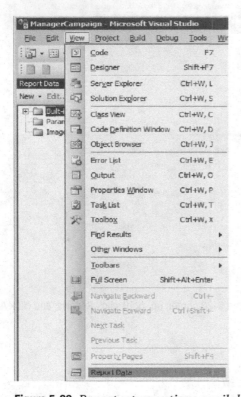

Figure 5-29. *Report setup options available from the View menu*

6. We will begin our design of the report by setting the page dimensions so that the report can easily be printed or exported. Open the Properties tab on the far right-hand side, and select Body in the drop-down menu. Type **6.75in, 5.75in** for the Size of the body, as shown in Figure 5-30.

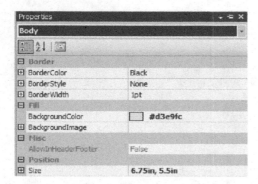

Figure 5-30. *Setting Body properties*

7. Select Report in the drop-down menu. Type **11in, 8.5in** for the InteractiveSize and PageSize of the report and **0in, 0in, 0in, 0in** for the Margins, as shown in Figure 5-31.

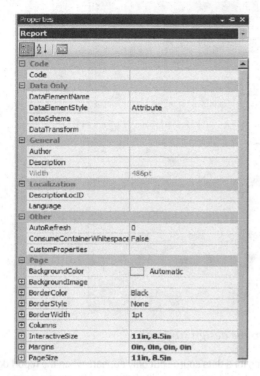

Figure 5-31. *Setting Report properties*

8. To add the first item to our report, drag a Chart from the toolbox to the Design surface, which is shown in Figure 5-32.

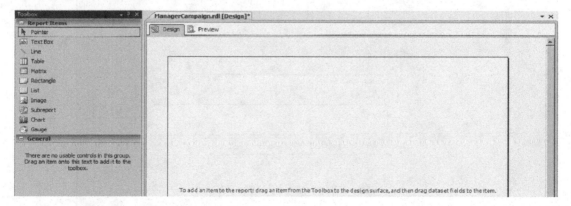

Figure 5-32. *The report's Design surface*

9. The next dialog will prompt for a chart type, as shown in Figure 5-33. Select the first Line type, and click OK.

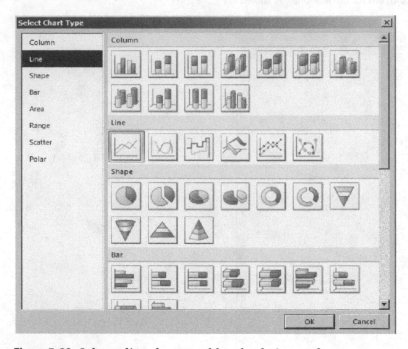

Figure 5-33. *Select a line chart to add to the design surface.*

10. The next dialog, shown in Figure 5-34, prompts for a data source but only appears when the report does not yet have one.

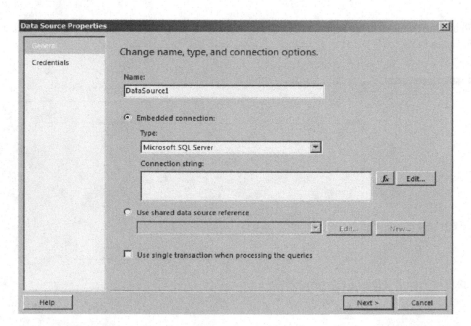

Figure 5-34. *Establish a data source.*

11. Click the Edit button to configure the data source.

12. In this example, the report will be built on information from the sample database. Since the database is located on the same sever the report is being built on, the server is localhost. The database is called Contoso_MSCRM. Set the server name to localhost, and the database name to Contoso_MSCRM, as shown in Figure 5-35. Then, click OK.

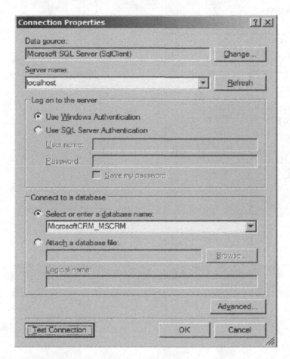

Figure 5-35. *Configure the data source.*

13. Click Next, shown in Figure 5-36, to create a new dataset.

14. Once you click Next, the Query Designer (shown in Figure 5-37) will open.

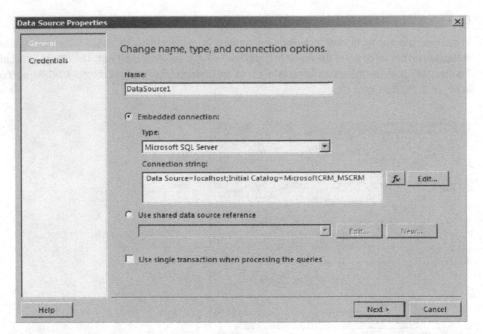

Figure 5-36. *Create a dataset.*

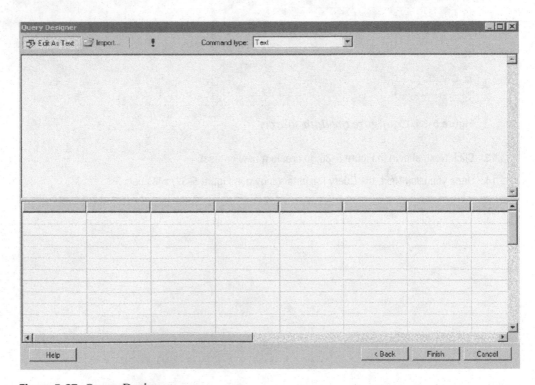

Figure 5-37. *Query Designer*

15. In the Query Designer, type the following SQL code. This code in the Query Designer is pictured in Figure 5-38. Once the code is in place, click Finish on the Query Designer window. Note that the code to capture month and month name are for mock-up purposes only. The date parsing is happening in order to allow for the presentation to work well given the limited dataset. In a production scenario, the DATEPART would be based on month instead of second.

```
SELECT
    SUM([Leads]) AS [Leads]
    ,SUM([Target]) AS [Target]
    ,[Month] AS [Month]
    ,[Month Name] AS [Month Name]
FROM
(SELECT
    COUNT(leadid) AS [Leads]
    ,CASE
WHEN DATEPART(SECOND,modifiedon)
    >= 0 AND DATEPART(SECOND,modifiedon) <= 5 THEN '01'
WHEN DATEPART(SECOND,modifiedon)
    >= 6 AND DATEPART(SECOND,modifiedon) <= 10 THEN '02'
WHEN DATEPART(SECOND,modifiedon)
    >= 11 AND DATEPART(SECOND,modifiedon) <= 15 THEN '03'
WHEN DATEPART(SECOND,modifiedon)
    >= 16 AND DATEPART(SECOND,modifiedon) <= 20 THEN '04'
WHEN DATEPART(SECOND,modifiedon)
    >= 21 AND DATEPART(SECOND,modifiedon) <= 25 THEN '05'
WHEN DATEPART(SECOND,modifiedon)
    >= 26 AND DATEPART(SECOND,modifiedon) <= 30 THEN '06'
WHEN DATEPART(SECOND,modifiedon)
    >= 31 AND DATEPART(SECOND,modifiedon) <= 35 THEN '07'
WHEN DATEPART(SECOND,modifiedon)
    >= 36 AND DATEPART(SECOND,modifiedon) <= 40 THEN '08'
WHEN DATEPART(SECOND,modifiedon)
    >= 41 AND DATEPART(SECOND,modifiedon) <= 45 THEN '09'
WHEN DATEPART(SECOND,modifiedon)
    >= 46 AND DATEPART(SECOND,modifiedon) <= 50 THEN '10'
WHEN DATEPART(SECOND,modifiedon)
    >= 51 AND DATEPART(SECOND,modifiedon) <= 55 THEN '11'
WHEN DATEPART(SECOND,modifiedon)
    >= 56 AND DATEPART(SECOND,modifiedon) <= 60 THEN '12'
    END AS [Month]
    ,CASE
WHEN DATEPART(SECOND,modifiedon)
    >= 0 AND DATEPART(SECOND,modifiedon) <= 5 THEN 'Jan'
WHEN DATEPART(SECOND,modifiedon)
    >= 6 AND DATEPART(SECOND,modifiedon) <= 10 THEN 'Feb'
WHEN DATEPART(SECOND,modifiedon)
    >= 11 AND DATEPART(SECOND,modifiedon) <= 15 THEN 'Mar'
```

```
WHEN DATEPART(SECOND,modifiedon)
    >= 16 AND DATEPART(SECOND,modifiedon) <= 20 THEN 'Apr'
WHEN DATEPART(SECOND,modifiedon)
    >= 21 AND DATEPART(SECOND,modifiedon) <= 25 THEN 'May'
WHEN DATEPART(SECOND,modifiedon)
    >= 26 AND DATEPART(SECOND,modifiedon) <= 30 THEN 'Jun'
WHEN DATEPART(SECOND,modifiedon)
    >= 31 AND DATEPART(SECOND,modifiedon) <= 35 THEN 'Jul'
WHEN DATEPART(SECOND,modifiedon)
    >= 36 AND DATEPART(SECOND,modifiedon) <= 40 THEN 'Aug'
WHEN DATEPART(SECOND,modifiedon)
    >= 41 AND DATEPART(SECOND,modifiedon) <= 45 THEN 'Sep'
WHEN DATEPART(SECOND,modifiedon)
    >= 46 AND DATEPART(SECOND,modifiedon) <= 50 THEN 'Oct'
WHEN DATEPART(SECOND,modifiedon)
    >= 51 AND DATEPART(SECOND,modifiedon) <= 55 THEN 'Nov'
WHEN DATEPART(SECOND,modifiedon)
    >= 56 AND DATEPART(SECOND,modifiedon) <= 60 THEN 'Dec'
    END AS [Month Name]
    ,0 AS [Target]
  FROM FilteredLead
  WHERE ownerid = @Owner
  GROUP BY DATEPART(SECOND,modifiedon)
  UNION
  SELECT
    0 AS [Leads]
    ,CASE
WHEN DATEPART(SECOND,modifiedon)
    >= 0 AND DATEPART(SECOND,modifiedon) <= 4 THEN '01'
WHEN DATEPART(SECOND,modifiedon)
    >= 5 AND DATEPART(SECOND,modifiedon) <= 8 THEN '02'
WHEN DATEPART(SECOND,modifiedon)
    >= 9 AND DATEPART(SECOND,modifiedon) <= 13 THEN '03'
WHEN DATEPART(SECOND,modifiedon)
    >= 14 AND DATEPART(SECOND,modifiedon) <= 21 THEN '04'
WHEN DATEPART(SECOND,modifiedon)
    >= 22 AND DATEPART(SECOND,modifiedon) <= 28 THEN '05'
WHEN DATEPART(SECOND,modifiedon)
    >= 29 AND DATEPART(SECOND,modifiedon) <= 30 THEN '06'
WHEN DATEPART(SECOND,modifiedon)
    >= 31 AND DATEPART(SECOND,modifiedon) <= 35 THEN '07'
WHEN DATEPART(SECOND,modifiedon)
    >= 36 AND DATEPART(SECOND,modifiedon) <= 38 THEN '08'
```

```
WHEN DATEPART(SECOND,modifiedon)
    >= 39 AND DATEPART(SECOND,modifiedon) <= 45 THEN '09'
WHEN DATEPART(SECOND,modifiedon)
    >= 46 AND DATEPART(SECOND,modifiedon) <= 53 THEN '10'
WHEN DATEPART(SECOND,modifiedon)
    >= 54 AND DATEPART(SECOND,modifiedon) <= 55 THEN '11'
WHEN DATEPART(SECOND,modifiedon)
    >= 56 AND DATEPART(SECOND,modifiedon) <= 60 THEN '12'
    END AS [Month]
    ,CASE
WHEN DATEPART(SECOND,modifiedon)
    >= 0 AND DATEPART(SECOND,modifiedon) <= 4 THEN 'Jan'
WHEN DATEPART(SECOND,modifiedon)
    >= 5 AND DATEPART(SECOND,modifiedon) <= 8 THEN 'Feb'
WHEN DATEPART(SECOND,modifiedon)
    >= 9 AND DATEPART(SECOND,modifiedon) <= 13 THEN 'Mar'
WHEN DATEPART(SECOND,modifiedon)
    >= 14 AND DATEPART(SECOND,modifiedon) <= 21 THEN 'Apr'
WHEN DATEPART(SECOND,modifiedon)
    >= 22 AND DATEPART(SECOND,modifiedon) <= 28 THEN 'May'
WHEN DATEPART(SECOND,modifiedon)
    >= 29 AND DATEPART(SECOND,modifiedon) <= 30 THEN 'Jun'
WHEN DATEPART(SECOND,modifiedon)
    >= 31 AND DATEPART(SECOND,modifiedon) <= 35 THEN 'Jul'
WHEN DATEPART(SECOND,modifiedon)
    >= 36 AND DATEPART(SECOND,modifiedon) <= 38 THEN 'Aug'
WHEN DATEPART(SECOND,modifiedon)
    >= 39 AND DATEPART(SECOND,modifiedon) <= 45 THEN 'Sep'
WHEN DATEPART(SECOND,modifiedon)
    >= 46 AND DATEPART(SECOND,modifiedon) <= 53 THEN 'Oct'
WHEN DATEPART(SECOND,modifiedon)
    >= 54 AND DATEPART(SECOND,modifiedon) <= 55 THEN 'Nov'
WHEN DATEPART(SECOND,modifiedon)
    >= 56 AND DATEPART(SECOND,modifiedon) <= 60 THEN 'Dec'
    END AS [Month Name]
    ,COUNT(leadid) AS [Target]
 FROM FilteredLead
 WHERE ownerid = @Owner
    GROUP BY DATEPART(SECOND,modifiedon)) AllLeads
WHERE [Month] IS NOT NULL
    GROUP BY [Month], [Month Name]
    ORDER BY [Month]
```

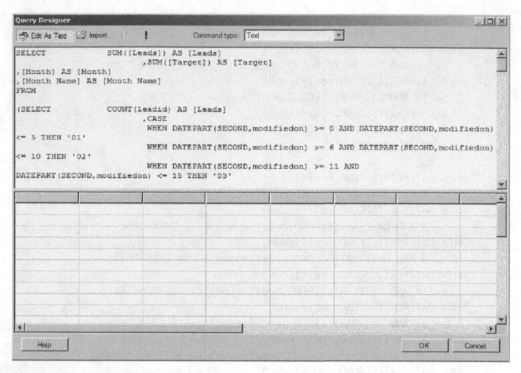

Figure 5-38. *The dataset in the Query Designer window*

16. Create a new dataset called TopPerformingCampaigns by right-clicking DataSource1 in the Report Data tab and selecting Add Dataset from the context menu shown in Figure 5-39. Figure 5-40 shows the Dataset Properties window where the dataset query will be established.

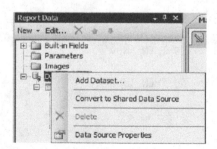

Figure 5-39. *Add a new dataset.*

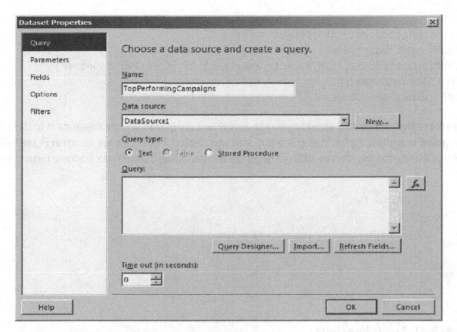

Figure 5-40. *Establish the dataset properties.*

17. Insert the following SQL into the Query box, and click OK twice:

```
SELECT
    typecodename AS [Campaign Type]
    ,expectedrevenue AS [Est. Revenue]
FROM FilteredCampaign
WHERE ownerid = @Owner
```

18. Create a new dataset called ActiveCampaigns by right-clicking DataSource1 in the Report Data tab and selecting Add Dataset. Insert the following SQL into the Query box, and click OK:

```
SELECT
    [name] AS [Campaign]
    ,actualstart AS [Start Date]
    ,actualend AS [End Date]
    ,expectedresponse AS [Expected Responses]
FROM FilteredCampaign
WHERE actualstart < GETDATE()
    AND actualend > GETDATE()
    AND  ownerid = @Owner
```

19. Create a new dataset called BudgetedCostPerResponse by right-clicking DataSource1 in the Report Data tab and selecting Add Dataset. Insert the following SQL into the Query box, and click OK:

```
SELECT
    SUM(budgetedcost) AS [Budgeted Cost]
    ,SUM(expectedresponse) AS [Expected Responses]
    ,SUM(budgetedcost)/SUM(expectedresponse) AS [Cost Per Response]
FROM FilteredCampaign
WHERE  ownerid = @Owner
```

20. One informative and visually appealing way to display and group lead volume over time is to chart the information in a graph. Earlier, in step 9, a line chart was created. The results are shown in Figure 5-41. Now, we'll refine the line chart by adding a target line and formatting based on our business requirements.

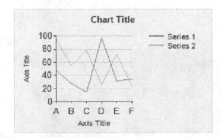

Figure 5-41. *Leads line chart*

21. Right-click the Chart Title, and select Title Properties. Type **Lead Volume** in the "Title text" field, and click OK, as shown in Figure 5-42.

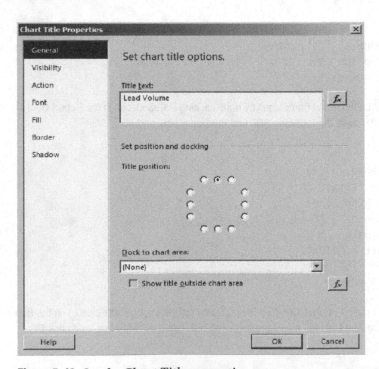

Figure 5-42. *Set the Chart Title properties.*

22. Drag Leads and Target into the "Drop data fields here" box. Drag Month_Name into the "Drop category fields here" box. Refer to Figures 5-42 and 5-43 as examples.

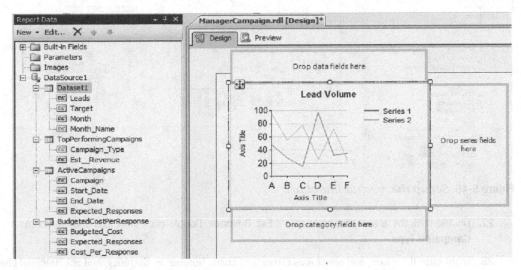

Figure 5-43. *Configure the data in the Leads chart.*

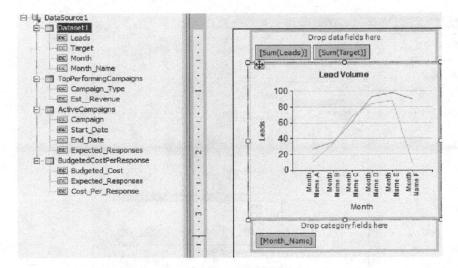

Figure 5-44. *Finished data configuration for the Leads chart*

23. Double-click the y axis title, and name it **Leads**. Double-click the x axis title, and name it **Month**.

24. Open the toolbox. Drag another chart onto the Body of the report. This time, select the Column chart type to create a graph displaying Estimated Revenue by Campaign Type.

25. Type **Estimated Revenue** for the Chart Title.

26. Drag Est_Revenue into the "Drop data fields here" box. Drag Campaign_Type into the "Drop category fields here" box. Refer to Figure 5-45 as an example.

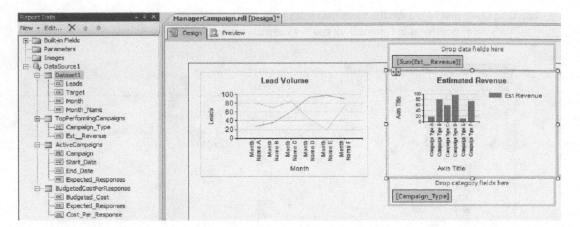

Figure 5-45. *Set up the revenue line chart.*

27. Double-click the y axis title, and name it **Est. Revenue**. Double-click the x axis title, and name it **Campaign Type**.

28. Right-click the y axis, and select Axis Properties. Select Number ➤ Currency, and set "Decimal place" to 0. Check the "Use 1000 separator" box, as illustrated in Figure 5-46. Click OK.

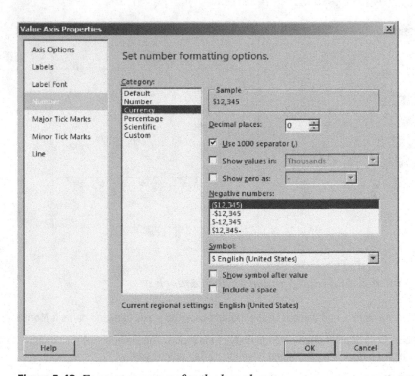

Figure 5-46. *Format currency for the bar chart.*

29. Right-click the legend, and select Delete Legend.

30. Open the toolbox. Drag a gauge onto the Body of the report. Select the Radial gauge type to create a gauge displaying Budget Cost Per Response.

31. Drag Cost_Per_Response into the "Drop data fields here" box. Refer to Figure 5-47 as an example.

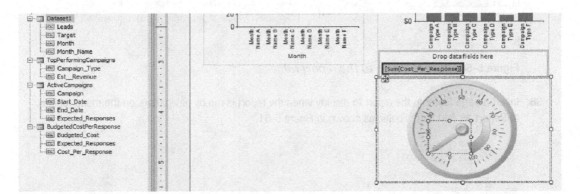

Figure 5-47. *Configure the radial gauge.*

32. Right-click the red target range of the gauge, and select Range Properties, as shown in Figure 5-48, to set the target range. Input the preferred start and end values for the range.

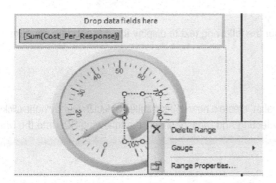

Figure 5-48. *Set the target for the radial gauge.*

33. Open the toolbox. Drag a table onto the Body of the report. The table has two rows, one for the header and one for the details, which are marked by three black lines. The table also has three columns.

34. Insert a column to the right by right-clicking a column and clicking Insert Column ➤ Right (see Figure 5-49).

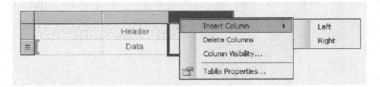

Figure 5-49. *Add a table to the Marketing Campaign dashboard.*

35. On the Report Data tab, drag the fields into the details row as shown in Figure 5-50 to bind the data to the report.

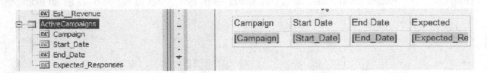

Figure 5-50. *Bind the data to the report table.*

36. Insert a page footer in the report to display when the report is run by navigating, on the menu toolbar, to Report ➤ Add Page Footer, as shown in Figure 5-51.

Figure 5-51. *Add a page footer.*

37. In the page footer, add a text box, and input the following text to display the current date and time of when the report was run:

```
="Current as of " & Now()
```

38. To be able to filter on the owner of the campaign, create a new dataset called SelectOwner by right-clicking DataSource1 in the Report Data tab and selecting Add Dataset. Insert the following SQL into the Query box, and click OK:

```
SELECT DISTINCT  ownerid
    ,owneridname
FROM FilteredCampaign
ORDER BY    owneridname
```

39. On the Report Data tab, click Parameters. Right-click the parameter @Owner, as shown in Figure 5-52, and select Parameter Properties.

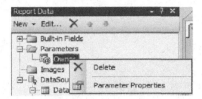

Figure 5-52. *Add a parameter.*

40. In the Report Parameter Properties dialog box, select Available Values and select the following (see Figure 5-53):

"Select from one of the following options": "Get values from a query"

Dataset: SelectOwner

Value field: ownerid

Label field: owneridname

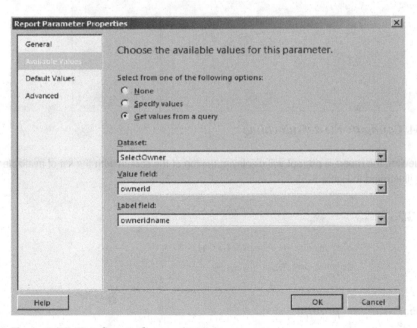

Figure 5-53. *Configure the report parameters.*

41. Select Default Values, and select the following (see Figure 5-54):

"Select from one of the following options": "Get values from a query"

Dataset: SelectOwner

Value field: ownerid

42. Click OK.

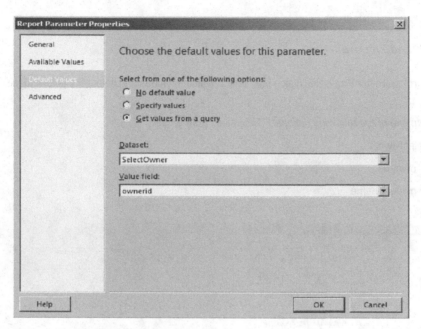

Figure 5-54. *Configure the default values.*

43. When previewing the report, a prompt will display at the top of the screen with the list of available owners, as illustrated in Figure 5-55.

Figure 5-55. *Parameter prompt*

44. The main report ManagerCampaign has been started with examples of a column chart, line chart, radial gauge, and table. Figure 5-56 is an example of our complete Marketing Campaign dashboard.

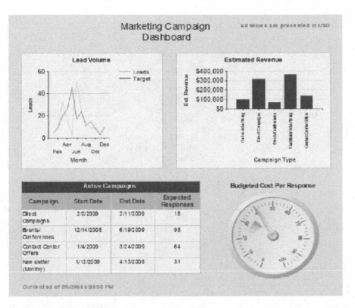

Figure 5-56. *The completed Marketing Campaign dashboard*

Summary

The core components of the Microsoft BI platform, including SQL database services and SSRS, provide the foundation for our analytics pyramid and allow us to deliver compelling dashboards and reports that not only meet the basic analytical needs for sales and marketing but also begin to get the organization thinking rigorously about data and improve our ability to successfully move up the analytics pyramid to more sophisticated tools.

Some key concepts that we covered include:

- Requirements for dashboards do not need to be onerous at the basic level, but it is valuable to have developed some specific goals and a mock-up to ensure that user expectations are aligned with tool capabilities.

- Use of the SQL Server 2008 chart controls provides a significant improvement over using SQL Server 2005 and allows for a much richer user experience for dashboards.

- Effective use of SQL functions can significantly enhance the quality of the user experience with SSRS reports.

- SSRS provides a flexible tool for delivering visually compelling reports and dashboards.

Now, we will move forward with this strong foundation in place and begin to look at how we can explore our data in a more ad hoc fashion.

CHAPTER 6

■ ■ ■

SQL Server Analysis Services

In Chapter 4, we walked through the development of a basic SQL Server Analysis Services (SSAS) cube as a way to allow for increased ad hoc exploration of key business data via Excel. In this chapter, we'll explore a couple of key scenarios that dive deeper into using SSAS to look at how data is changing over time and to look for deeper patterns in the data that are critical for sales and marketing analytical programs. The goal remains to allow key business users to explore the data and answer their own questions. But, the methods get more sophisticated as we use more of the tool set built into SQL Server and look at business questions that go beyond asking, "What is our current state?" Being able to go beyond looking at the current state of the organization represents movement up our analytics pyramid (see Figure 6-1) to the intermediate level, where users engage in more detailed analysis.

Our movement up the pyramid implies not only that the user tools will be more advanced but also that our team's skills will need to grow to leverage additional components of the Microsoft BI platform. To emphasize the new skills, we will look to our example company, Dyno Technologies, and we will specifically explore one set of questions for our sales team and one set of questions for our marketing team.

For our sales team, the dashboards developed in Chapter 5 provided a good view into where the organization is today, but the sales managers' and analysts' goal is to better understand how the business is changing over time and to be able to look for trends and patterns as they affect sales representatives, products, and regions.

The marketing team members have a similar desire to explore the data, but they are interested in looking across business applications and in allowing analysts to engage in ad hoc exploration of the data. The result is that we will dive deeply into how analysts can use Excel as their primary interface to connect to sophisticated SSAS cubes that are powered by our business applications with data transformations provided by SQL Server Integration Services (SSIS). The examples we will walk through in this chapter follow:

- *Sales trends*: Develop a tool set that will allow users to explore not only the current state of sales opportunities but will also offer deeper visibility into how these opportunities are changing over time.

- *Search engine marketing*: Develop a tool set that will leverage search engine marketing results and allow a user to explore this data on an ad hoc basis in Excel.

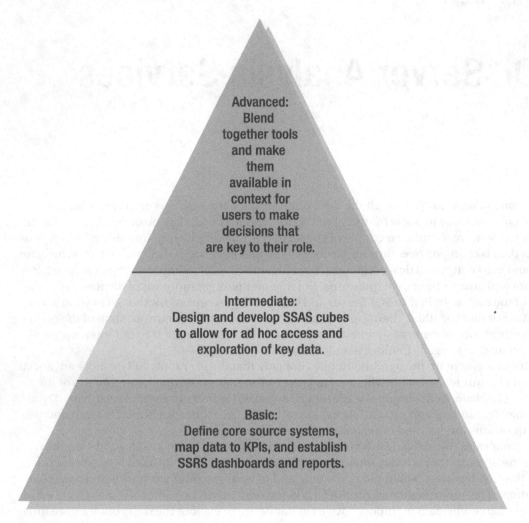

Figure 6-1. *The analytics pyramid*

Understanding Sales Trends

Most sales organizations have a strong desire to not only know how they are performing against key targets but to understand the underlying trends related to their opportunities. Specifically, they are looking to understand the following:

- How has my pipeline changed in the last 30 days?

- What is the trend on a particular sales representative's pipeline?

- How does this quarter compare to last quarter at this point in time?

Answering these questions poses challenges that our basic cube was not designed to solve. The questions require the cube to have an understanding of the state of opportunities at different intervals in time, while many transactional business systems and our basic cube are only aware of the current state of an opportunity. The lack of a snapshot capturing the changing state of our opportunities identifies a challenge we must deal with in providing business users with the information they need to effectively manage the organization. Fortunately, we have tools in SQL Server that will allow us to handle this challenge. This example will take us through our options for tracking changing data and provide the specific steps required to execute on the development of cubes that can answer these questions.

To get started resolving these issues, we will first engage with our business users to outline the specific attributes with which they would like to interact in Excel. It would be possible to pull in all fields from the relevant entities in the transactional system, but that would lead to overly intensive processing and cause end user confusion when interacting with the cubes. The result is that we will map out both the measures (quantifiable fields) and dimensions (attributes that describe our measures) that our business customers are planning to use so that we have a simple blueprint of the data that needs to be included in our design.

Identifying the Sales Trend Measures

Measures represent the core attributes that will be aggregated when an end user interacts with the SSAS cube. The key measures are frequently counts or sums of data. In our case, the measures represent the different ways to assess the value of the sales opportunity and the count of the quantity of sales opportunities. Table 6-1 shows the desired measures for our sales trends example.

Table 6-1. *Measures for Use in Monitoring Sales Trends*

Measure	Comments	Priority
Estimated value	Provides the core measurement for the forecast	1
Actual value	Provides the core measurement for assessing actual success for sales representatives	1
Opportunity count	Useful in gauging individual and group trends	1
Time to qualify	Represents the number of elapsed days between the time the opportunity was created and the time it reached sales stage 2	2
Time to proposal	Represents the number of elapsed days between the time the opportunity was created and the time it reached sales stage 4	2
Open to close	Represents the number of elapsed days between the time the opportunity was created and the time it was closed	2

Identifying the Sales Trend Dimensions

Dimensions represent a set of attributes related to our core measures identified in Table 6-1. The primary use of the dimensions is to provide the capability to filter and group measures. A simple comparison is to think of the dimensions as the rows and columns of an Excel pivot table. One key distinction from a pivot table is that our dimensions can have established hierarchies that we will need to define as we develop the cube. These hierarchies allow a user to look at results for a top-level category (like a calendar month) and expand the category to see details (like a specific date). Table 6-2 shows the desired dimensions and hierarchies for our sales trends example.

Table 6-2. *Sales Trend Dimensions*

Dimension	Comments	Priority
Estimated close date	This provides the ability to slice the data based on when the opportunity is forecast to close. The hierarchy will be the year, quarter, month, week, and date.	1
Actual close date	This provides the ability to slice the data based on when the opportunity actually did close. The hierarchy will be the year, quarter, month, week, and date.	1
Created-on date	This provides the ability to slice the data based on when the opportunity was created. The hierarchy will be the year, quarter, month, week, and date.	1
Extract date	Our end cube will allow a user to look at the data as of a given date, and this attribute represents the date the snapshot was taken. The hierarchy will be the year, quarter, month, week, and date.	1
Opportunity owner	This identifies the sales representative who owns the opportunity. The hierarchy is based on climbing up the management structure of the company.	1
Sales stage	This notes that the deal's sales stage is when the snapshot is taken.	1
Customer name	This is the name of the customer associated with the opportunity.	1
Campaign	This is the campaign associated with the opportunity.	2
Region	This is the sales region associated with the opportunity.	2
Industry	This is the industry associated with the opportunity.	2
Deal source	This is the deal source selected on the opportunity.	2

Now that we have a clear understanding of which attributes our users would like to interact with in the cube, we have the ability to thoughtfully establish a design that will handle their needs. This section is not intended to be a complete discussion on the design of cubes (also known as dimensional modeling), but it is intended to provide you with the foundation of knowledge to deliver a core solution for a sales and marketing team. For more detail on dimensional modeling, you may want to refer to *The Data Warehouse Toolkit: The Complete Guide to Dimensional Modeling* by Ralph Kimball and Margy Ross (Wiley, 2002).

The key design challenge we are looking at with this cube is that our data (the sales opportunity) passes through a series of milestones (sales stage changes and estimated value changes) over an unknowable duration of time before coming to completion. From a business process standpoint, this seems straightforward, and our management team would like to know not just when the key events transpire but also how the overall pipeline (summary of all opportunities) appeared at any given date in time. From a data management standpoint, this is a bit of a tricky problem, because our source system does not track interim milestones or have a way for us to look backward in time.

In Exercise 6-1, we will design a solution that extracts a copy of the data from the opportunity entity on a daily basis and formats the data in the cube so that a user can look at the current state or step backward in time, as well as compare any two dates in time. This approach is commonly referred to as a periodic snapshot design, because it allows us to set a predefined period (typically daily or weekly), and then users can review and compare various snapshots.

The benefits of this approach are that it is well supported by the core Microsoft BI platform tools, and it delivers all of our priority 1 items. The weakness of this approach is that it does not capture metrics around the duration of time passed between milestones within a given opportunity. Specifically, by leveraging this approach alone, we won't be able to easily explore the data associated with the priority 2 metrics of time to qualify and time to proposal.

That said, we have consistently found that the periodic snapshot approach is preferred by most organizations, because it does deliver the most critical data for their analysts and managers. Organizations that find it critical to capture both the information available in a periodic snapshot and data associated with milestones within an opportunity typically deploy the periodic snapshot cube and then leverage workflow within the business application to log the internal milestones. Once these workflows are set up, the cube can easily be modified to pull in the fields related to these milestones.

Exercise 6-1. Using SSIS and SSAS to Deliver Sales Trends Data

Follow the steps in this exercise to develop a simple data mart and SSAS cube that allows users to explore sales trends. Users will interact with this data via Excel connected to an SSAS cube. This cube will likely not meet all of the needs identified in Tables 6-1 and 6-2, but it serves as a foundation for delivering sales trending.

1. Navigate to Start ➤ Programs ➤ Microsoft Visual Studio 2008 ➤ Microsoft Visual Studio 2008. Create a new project by navigating to File ➤ New ➤ Project. Select Business Intelligence Projects under the "Project types" header. Select Integration Services Project from the list of available templates. Type **Data Extract** in the Name field, as shown in Figure 6-2.

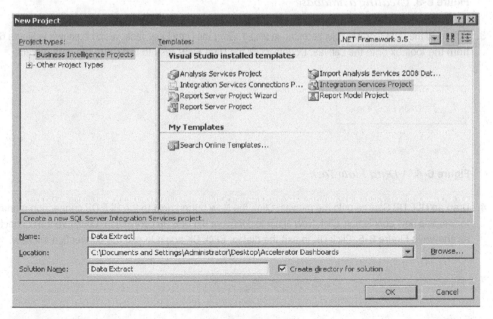

Figure 6-2. *Creating an Integration Services Project*

2. Open Microsoft SQL Server. Right-click Databases, and click New Databases. Figure 6-3 will be displayed. Type to **ExtractDB** in the "Database name" field, and click Add to close the window.

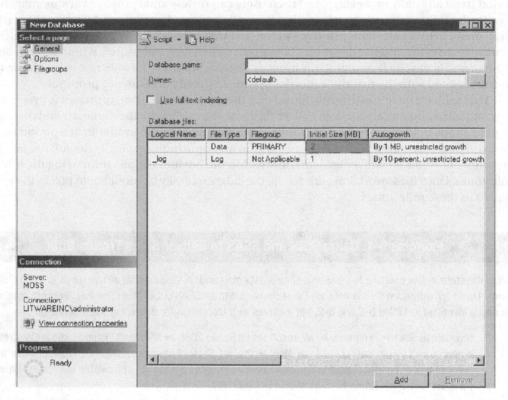

Figure 6-3. *Creating a database*

3. Return to the data extract project created in step 1. Drag the Data Flow Task, which is shown in Figure 6-4, from the toolbox onto the canvas. Double-click the Data Flow Task to configure the data extract.

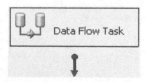

Figure 6-4. *A Data Flow Task*

4. Drag an OLE DB Source onto the canvas. Click the New button next to the OLE DB connection manager to create a new connection. Click New again to configure the OLE DB connection. Configure the connection as shown in Figure 6-5. Click OK to exit the dialog. Click OK again to exit the connection window.

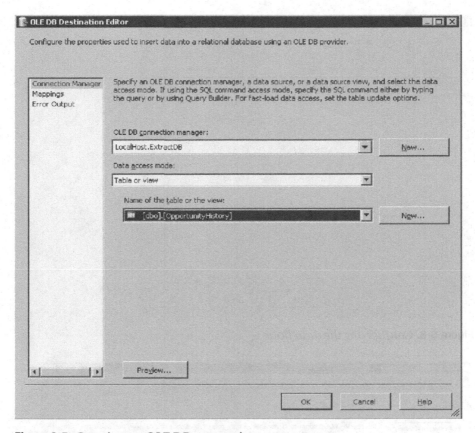

Figure 6-5. *Creating an OLE DB connection*

5. In the OLE DB Source Editor window, make sure the OLE DB connection manager is set to the connection just created. Set the Data Access Mode to "table or view". Set the name of the table or view to FilteredOpportunity. Click OK to close the dialog.

6. Drag the data transformation Audit from the toolbox on the canvas. Drag the green arrow from the OLE DB source to the Audit box. Double-click the Audit box to open the Audit Transformation Editor window. Set the Output Column Name to ExtractDate and the Audit Type to "Execution start time," as shown in Figure 6-6. Click OK.

7. Drag the OLE DB Destination from the toolbox. Drag the green line from the Audit box to the OLE DB Destination. Double-click the OLE DB Destination to open the editor.

8. Click New next to the OLE DB connection manager. Configure a new connection that points to the ExtractDB.

9. Make sure the OLE DB Destination connection is set to the newly created connection. Set the data access mode to "table or view." Click New next to the name of the table or the view. Rename the new table to OpportunityHistory, as shown in Figure 6-7. Click Mappings to ensure the mappings are correct. Click OK to close the window.

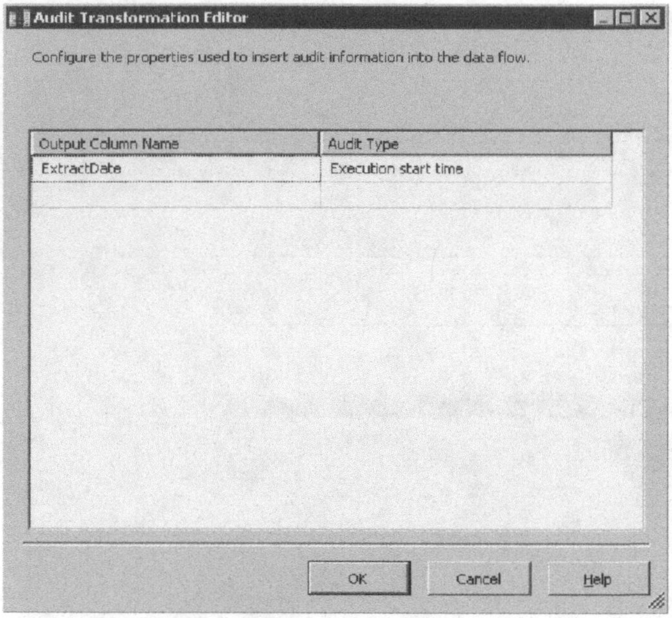

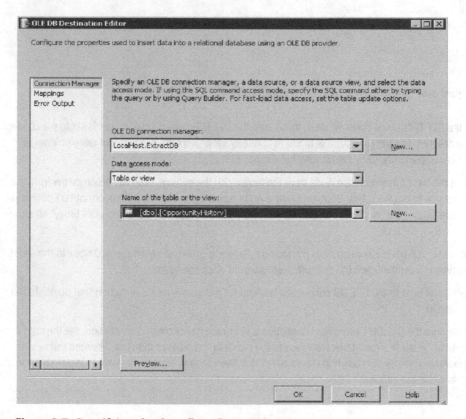

Figure 6-6. *Configuring the data flow*

Figure 6-7. *Specifying the data flow destination*

10. Right-click the canvas, and select Execute Task. The tasks will turn yellow to indicate they are in progress, as shown in Figure 6-8.

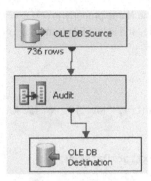

Figure 6-8. *In-progress tasks*

11. When a task completes, that task will turn green, as shown in Figure 6-9. Click the stop button on the menu bar when the project is finished.

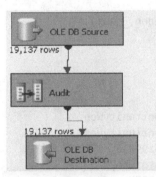

Figure 6-9. *Successfully completed tasks*

12. Save the project. The project can be executed either as a Windows task or from within SQL Server, and each time it runs, it will load a new set of records into our data mart. This item must be scheduled to run at the appropriate business interval (typically daily or weekly) to continuously populate our simple data mart with a record that shows the changing state of sales data. This representation of a data mart is admittedly very simple, but the goal is to establish how easily you can begin to capture data in a consistent fashion with the Microsoft platform. Now, we will turn to connecting a cube to this data. For more detailed information on creating a SQL Server task, visit the following site:

    `http://msdn.microsoft.com/en-us/library/ms137858(sql.90).aspx`

13. Open the cube created in Exercise 4-2 titled CRM Cube. Create a new data source that is directed toward the ExtractDB created in step 2.

14. Open the Data Source View. Click the table with the plus and minus signs in the upper left-hand corner to add a table. Set the data source to the name of the data source recently created. Move the OpportunityHistory table into the included objects section. Click OK.

15. Right-click the OpportunityHistory table, and click Properties. Set the Name property to FactOpportunityHistory. Right-click the FactOpportunityHistory table, and select Edit Named Query. Type the following information into the table:

```
SELECT      O.opportunityid AS OpportunityId,
ISNULL(ISNULL(A.city, 'NA_') +
    ISNULL(A.stateorprovince, 'NA_') + ISNULL(A.country, 'NA_'), 'NA_NA_NA_')
    AS CityCode,
CONVERT(DATETIME, CONVERT(VARCHAR(10),
    ISNULL(O.ExtractDate, '1/1/1990'), 120)) AS ExtractDateKey,
CONVERT(DATETIME, CONVERT(VARCHAR(10),
    ISNULL(O.estimatedclosedate, '1/1/1990'), 120)) AS EstimatedCloseDateKey,
 CONVERT(DATETIME, CONVERT(VARCHAR(10),
    ISNULL(O.actualclosedate, DATEADD(day, 90, O.createdon)), 120)) AS
    ActualCloseDateKey,
CONVERT(DATETIME, CONVERT(VARCHAR(10),
    O.createdon, 120)) AS CreatedOnDateKey,
CONVERT(DATETIME, CONVERT(VARCHAR(10), O.modifiedon, 120)) AS
    ModifiedOnDateKey,
O.closeprobability AS CloseProbability,
O.estimatedvalue AS EstimatedValue,
O.actualvalue AS ActualValue,
O.ownerid AS OwnerId,
CASE WHEN statecode = 1 THEN 1 ELSE 0 END AS OpportunityWon,
CASE WHEN statecode = 2 THEN 1 ELSE 0 END AS OpportunityLost,
CONVERT(VARCHAR(10), ISNULL(O.ExtractDate, '1/1/1990'), 120) +
    CONVERT(varchar(36), O.opportunityid) AS 'HistoryKey'
FROM         OpportunityHistory AS O LEFT OUTER JOIN
Contoso_MSCRM.dbo.FilteredCustomerAddress AS A ON O.accountid =
    A.parentid
```

16. Now, you have your fact table in place, so let's add the corresponding dimension table. Right-click the canvas, and select New Named Query. Type the name **OpportunityHistory**, select the data source Extract DB, and type the following information into the table:

```
SELECT     accountidname,
campaignidname,
closeprobability,
createdbyname,
name,
opportunityid,
owneridname,
stepname,
CONVERT(VARCHAR(10),
ISNULL(ExtractDate, '1/1/1990'), 120) +
    CONVERT(varchar(36), opportunityid) AS HistoryKey
FROM       OpportunityHistory AS o
```

17. Click OK to close the window. Create a relationship between the FactOpportunityHistory table and the OpportunityHistory table. As displayed in Figure 6-10, the "Source (foreign key) table" field should read FactOpportunityHistory, and Source Columns should list HistoryKey The "Destination (primary key) table" field should read OpportunityHistory, and Destination Columns should list HistoryKey. Click OK when the relationship mapping is complete.

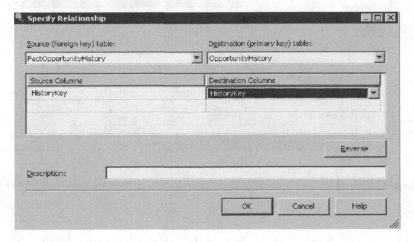

Figure 6-10. *Configuring key relationships*

18. Save the Data Source View. Click the New Measure Group button, which looks like a chart with a star and two brackets around it and is located in the upper left corner. Select the FactOpportunityHistory table. Click OK.

19. When the measure is displayed in the Measures section, it will have a red line underneath it. This is because the measure is not connected to any dimensions. The measure will need to be connected to the date dimension.

    a. Add a new time dimension by right-clicking on the Solution Explorer and selecting New Dimension. Select to "Generate a time table on the Server," and select your preferred time periods.

    b. Upon returning to the Cube Structure tab in BIDS, right click the cube name from the Dimensions frame and select "Add New Dimension." Select the Time dimension and click OK.

20. To map the dimension to the new measure, click the Dimension Usage tab. Click the gray box where the time dimension and the OpportunityHistory dimension overlap to open the Define Relationship window. Set the relationship type to Regular. Set the "Granularity attribute" field to Date. Select ExtractDateKey beneath Measure Group Columns, as shown in Figure 6-11. Click OK.

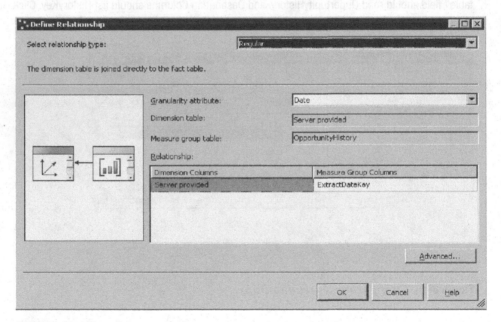

Figure 6-11. *Dimension mapping*

21. Rename the dimension to something more meaningful, such as Extract Date.

22. Now, you will need to add the OpportunityHistory dimension to the cube. Navigate to the Solution Explorer, and right-click Dimensions. Select New Dimension. Select "Use an existing table," and select the OpportunityHistory table. Select the check box next to Attribute Name to make all attributes available for viewing. Click Next and Finish.

23. Navigate to the Solution Explorer, right-click the cube, and select View Designer. Click the Dimension Usage tab, and select the cube icon in the upper left corner. This will open a dialog box that allows you to add a dimension to the set listed in the Dimension Usage tab. From the list of available dimensions, select OpportunityHistory, and click OK. Now, you have the OpportunityHistory dimension linked to FactOpportunityHistory via the HistoryKey.

24. Deploy and reprocess the cube to update the cube definition.

25. Like the cube created in Exercise 4-2, this cube can be viewed within Excel. An example is shown in Figure 6-12.

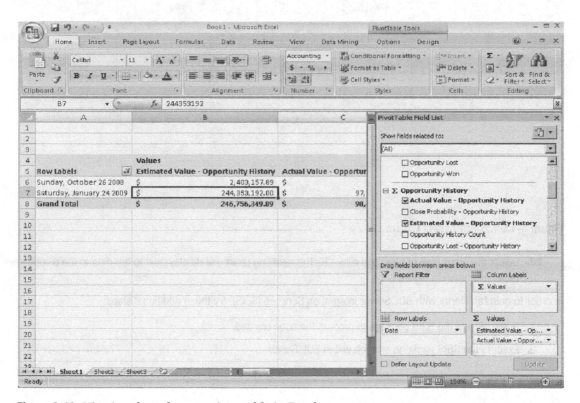

Figure 6-12. *Viewing the cube as a pivot table in Excel*

26. In addition to browsing the data, a user can also create charts from the pivot table in Excel. To do this, highlight the dataset, select the Options tab, and click Pivot Chart. Excel will display your chart options, as shown in Figure 6-13.

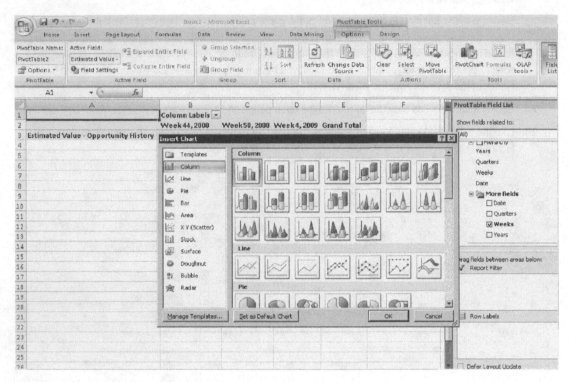

Figure 6-13. *Excel's Insert Chart dialog*

27. Select the chart type of Line, and click OK. The resulting chart will display next to the data in the pivot table, as shown in Figure 6-14.

In order to gain familiarity with SQL Server Integration Services (SSIS), try these additional steps:

1. Add a step to the SSIS package to process the cube created.

2. Execute the SSIS package as a job within SQL Server.

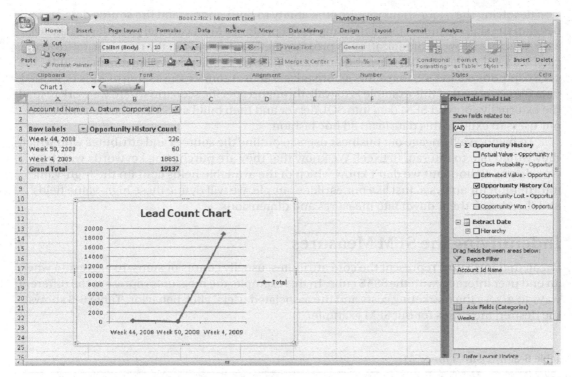

Figure 6-14. *An Excel pivot chart powered by our SSAS cube*

Tracking Search Engine Marketing

Marketing organizations frequently have large volumes of data stored across many disparate business systems. One key challenge is to be able to pull in this data from external hosted sources and analyze it in the tools that the organization is comfortable using. Specifically, the organization frequently is asking these questions:

- How can I analyze the search engine marketing (SEM) data that currently resides within Yahoo or Google?

- How can I see the trends of this same data over time?

Resolving these questions requires the ability to both understand the source data and develop the skills to pull in that data using the BI platform. Most external providers make available APIs that allow an organization to programmatically download the raw data, or the data can be downloaded as a flat file and then manipulated. The Microsoft BI platform includes the core components in SSIS that allow an organization to automate the calling of APIs or to load data files. The goal of this example is to walk through a specific scenario where we work to load the externally sourced SEM data into SQL Server and then build an SSAS cube that will allow our users to explore this data in an ad hoc fashion.

To begin, we'll engage our business users to outline the sources and attributes with which they would like to interact in Excel. We know that they are purchasing keywords with both Google and Yahoo, but we don't know which of the available fields contain the high-value information for analysis. Just like our earlier example, we will define these high-value fields and then break them down into measures and dimensions.

Indentifying the SEM Measures

Recall that measures represent the core attributes, usually counts or sums, to aggregate when an end user interacts with the SSAS cube. In this example, the measures represent the different ways to assess the marketing costs and the associated users' click behavior. Table 6-3 shows the desired measures for our SEM example.

Table 6-3. *Measures for SEM*

Measure	Comments	Priority
Clicks	The number of clicks on a given keyword in a given day	1
Impressions	The number of impressions displayed for a given keyword in a given day	1
Cost	The cost associated with a given keyword in a given day	1
Cost per click	The average cost per click for a given keyword in a given day	2

Identifying the SEM Dimensions

Dimensions represent a set of attributes related to our core measures identified in Table 6-3. They provide the capability to filter and group our key measures. You can think of the dimensions as the rows and columns of an Excel pivot table, though a critical distinction is that our dimensions can have hierarchies that we will need to define as we develop the cube. Hierarchies allow users to look at results for a top-level category (like a calendar month) and expand the category to see details (like individual dates). Table 6-4 shows the desired dimensions and hierarchies for our SEM example.

Table 6-4. *SEM Dimensions*

Dimension	Comments	Priority
Date	The date on which results are analyzed for a given keyword	1
Keyword	The keyword term on which a user searched	1
Campaign	The campaign with which a given keyword was associated	1
Provider	The search engine (Google or Yahoo) on which a given keyword result was generated	1

Our design here is straightforward when compared with the sales trends example. In the case of SEM, the events around our data happen on a specific day, and there should be no changes to a given data element over time. With this in mind, we will follow a basic design approach that we used in Chapter 4 for our initial CRM cube. Exercise 6-2 leads you through our example.

Exercise 6-2. Using SSIS and SSAS for SEM Analysis

In the case of our search engine data, the company is already downloading the data into an Excel file, and we will use that as our baseline data source. With SSIS, files can be uploaded to SQL Server programmatically, and then we can begin to leverage SSAS to manage data calculations and deliver the data to users in a manageable format via Excel. Following are the steps in our exercise. The end result will be an SEM cube that you can view from the SSAS cube browser or Excel.

1. Navigate to Start ➤ Programs ➤ Microsoft SQL Server 2008 ➤ SQL Management Studio. Click Connect on the log-on dialog, as shown in Figure 6-15.

Figure 6-15. *Launch SQL Server 2008*

2. In Object Explorer, right-click Databases, and click New Database, as shown in Figure 6-16.

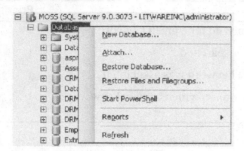

Figure 6-16. *Create a new database.*

3. As shown in Figure 6-17, name the database **GoogleAnalytics**. Keep the defaults for everything else, and click OK to create the database.

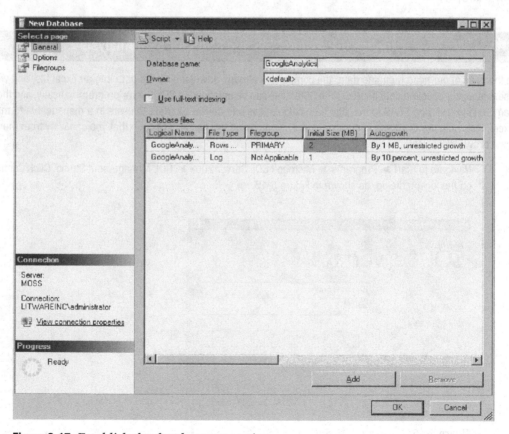

Figure 6-17. *Establish the database properties.*

4. Right-click the database GoogleAnalytics, and click Tasks ➤ Import Data. The SQL Server Import and Export Wizard will ask for a data source. Set the "Data source" field to Microsoft Excel. For the "Excel file path" field, point to the `GoogleAdsExtract.xlsx` file in this book's materials, which are available for download from this book's page on the Apress web site. The "Excel version" should be Microsoft Excel 2007. Make sure to check the "First row has column names" box. When these tasks are completed, the data source dialog will look like Figure 6-18. Click Next.

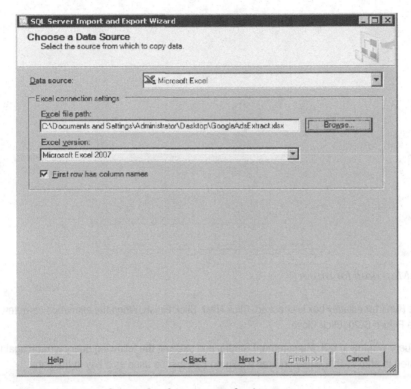

Figure 6-18. *Configure the data source for import.*

5. Accept the defaults on the data source page, and click Next.

6. On the "Specify Table Copy or Query" page, select "Copy data from one or more tables or views." Click Next.

7. The next page allows the user to map the source to the destination. In this section, it is possible to map the Excel file to a preexisting table or create a new table. Click the destination, and begin typing to change the name of the table you want to create. In Figure 6-19, the name of the table is Analytics. Click Next.

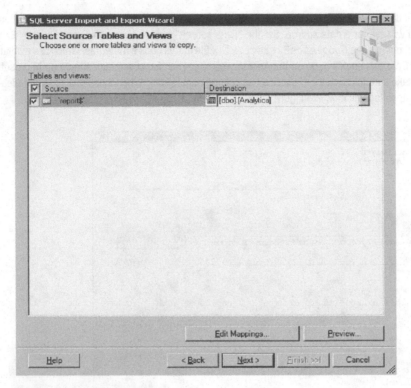

Figure 6-19. *Map data for import*

8. Make sure the Run Immediately box is checked. Click Next. Click Finish. When the execution completes, it will look like Figure 6-20. Click Close.

9. Open a new query window in SQL Management Studio, and execute the following query written against the table created in step 7. This query creates a column that can be used as a key in the cube.

```
ALTER TABLE [GoogleAnalytics].[dbo].[Analytics]
 ADD [Key]  [int] IDENTITY (1, 1) NOT NULL ;
```

10. Now, we have a repository for our SEM data, and we can continually add additional data to this location. At this point, our focus will shift to creating the cube that our users will interact with. Navigate to Start ➤ Programs ➤ Microsoft Visual Studio 2008 ➤ Microsoft Visual Studio 2008. Navigate to File ➤ New ➤ Project. Select Business Intelligence Projects and then Analysis Services Project. Name the project **Google Analytics**, as shown in Figure 6-21. Click OK.

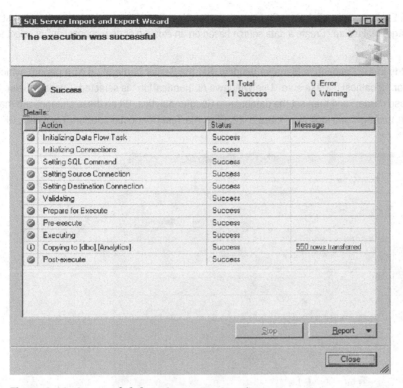

Figure 6-20. *Successful data import execution*

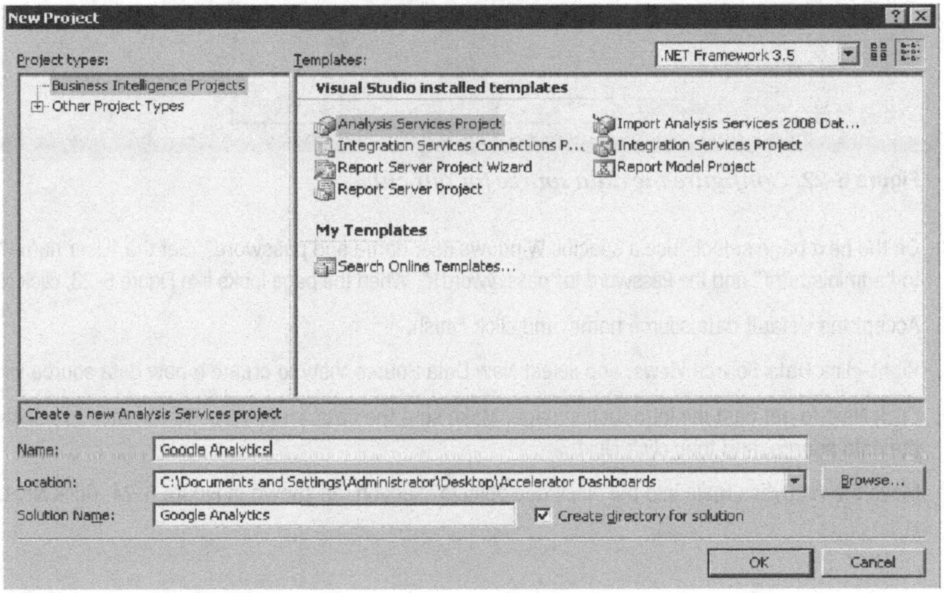

Figure 6-21. *Create the SSAS project.*

11. In the Solution Explorer, right-click Data Sources, and click New Data Source. Click Next to get past the introductory page. Make sure "Create a data source based on an existing or new connection" is selected. Click New.

12. Fill out the fields in the Connection Manager window. Set the Server name to . (i.e., a period), which is shorthand for "localhost." Make sure "Use Windows Authentication" is selected. Choose "Select or enter a database name," and then set the database to GoogleAnalytics. When these changes are made, the connection manager will look like Figure 6-22. Click the Test Connection button. Then click OK.

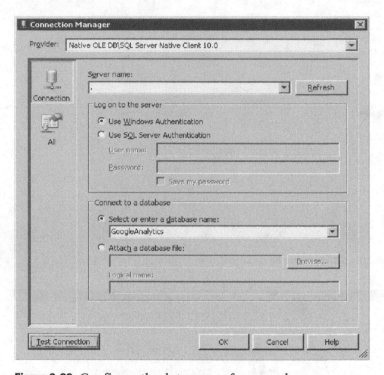

Figure 6-22. *Configure the data source for our cube.*

13. On the next page select "Use a specific Windows user name and password". Set the "User name" field to "administrator" and the Password to "pass@word1". When the page looks like Figure 6-23, click Next.

14. Accept the default data source name, and click Finish.

15. Right-click Data Source Views, and select New Data Source View to create a new data source view.

16. Click Next to get past the introduction page. Make sure the data source recently created is selected as the data source, and then click Next.

17. Move the Analytics table into the "Included objects" section, as shown in Figure 6-24. Click Next.

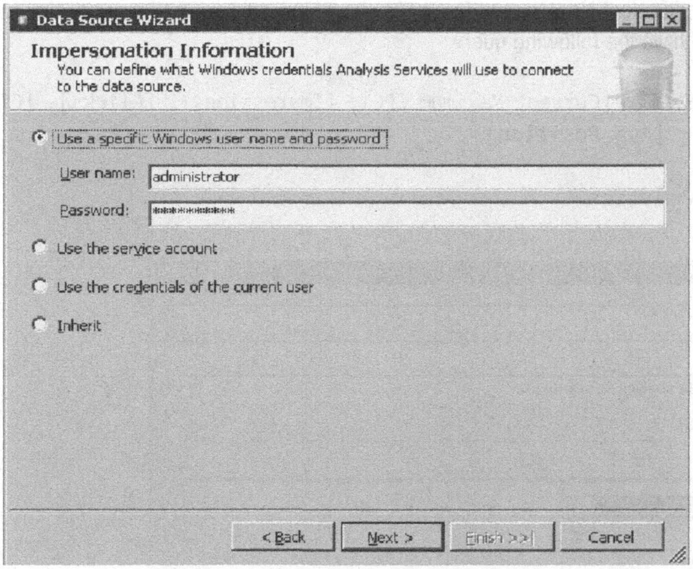

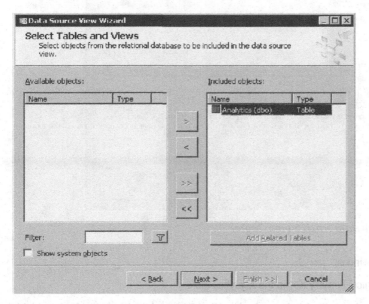

Figure 6-23. *Establish data access information.*

Figure 6-24. *Configure tables for the data source view.*

18. Accept the default name for the data source view, and click Finish.

19. Right-click the canvas, and select New Named Query. As shown in Figure 6-25, the query should be called AnalyticsFact and have the following query:

```
SELECT    [Key], [Date], [Current Maximum CPC], [Impressions], [Clicks], [CTR],
[Avg CPC], [Cost],  [Avg Position]

FROM          dbo.Analytics
```

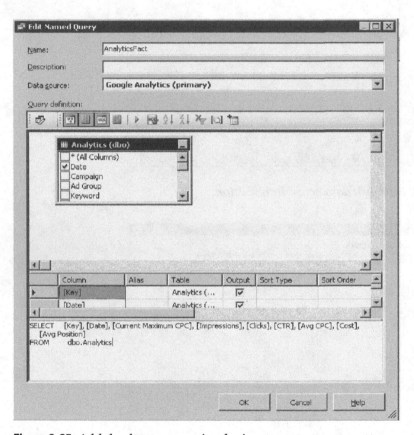

Figure 6-25. *Add the data source view logic.*

20. Click OK to close the window.

21. Set the Key as the Logical Primary Key in the Analytics table.

22. Create a relationship between the key in the AnalyticsFact table and the key in the Analytics table. The source table should be the AnalyticsFact table and the destination should be the Analytics table.

23. Right-click Cubes, and click New Cube. Click Next to get past the introductory page. Select the option to use existing tables. Click Next.

24. For the Measure Group Tables page, the data source view should be set to Google Analytics. The AnalyticsFact table should be the only Measure group table selected. Click Next to continue.

25. On the Select Measures page, make sure every Analytics Fact measure is selected, as shown in Figure 6-26.

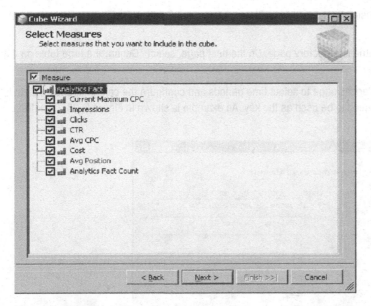

Figure 6-26. *Select the cube measures.*

26. Click Next. Click Next to accept the default dimension. Click Finish to complete the wizard. When the wizard is complete, it will create a cube that looks like the one shown in Figure 6-27.

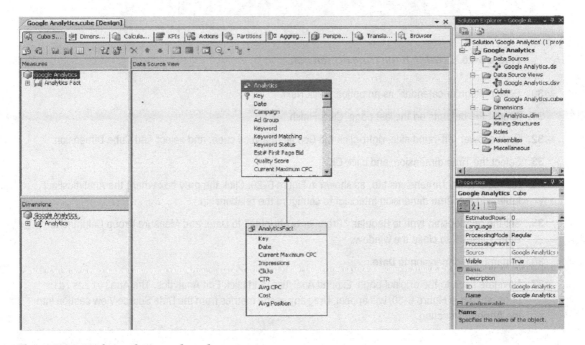

Figure 6-27. *Web analytics cube schema*

27. Add a new time dimension by right-clicking Dimensions on the Solution Explorer and selecting New Dimension.

28. Click Next to get past the introductory page. On the next page, select "Generate a time table on the server". Click Next.

29. Use the Define Time Periods page to select time periods and configure the calendar. Ensure Date is selected, since it will need to be used as the key. An example is shown in Figure 6-28. Click Next.

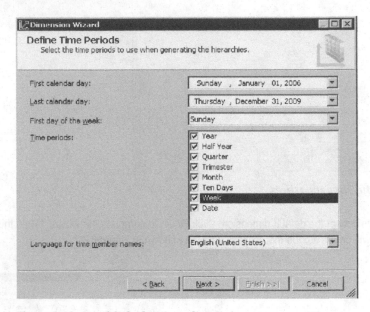

Figure 6-28. *Establish the time dimension.*

30. Select "Regular calendar" as an option. Click Next.

31. Accept the defaults on the last page. Click Finish.

32. On the lower left-hand side, right-click the Google Analytics cube, and select Add Cube Dimension.

33. Select the Time dimension, and click OK.

34. Navigate to the Dimensions tab, as shown in Figure 6-29. Click the grey box where the AnalyticsFact table and the Time dimension intersect to configure the relationship.

35. Set the relationship type to Regular, "Granularity attribute" to Date, and Measure Group Columns to Date. Click OK to close the window.

36. Rename the dimension to **Date**.

37. Navigate back to the original page. Expand Analytics, and click Edit Analytics. The `Analytics.dim` page, shown in Figure 6-30, will appear. Drag any useful metrics from the Data Source View section into the Attributes section.

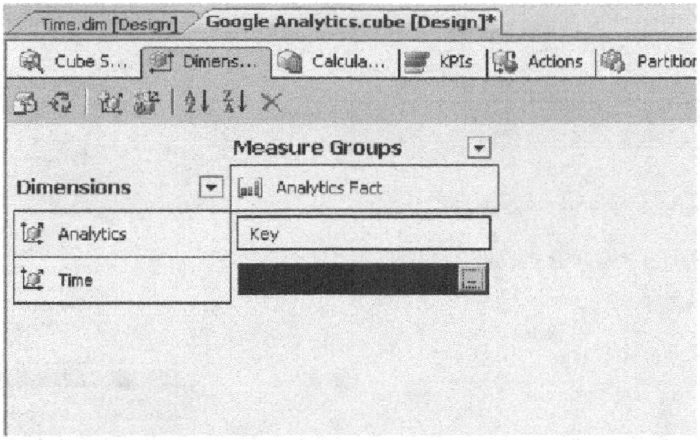

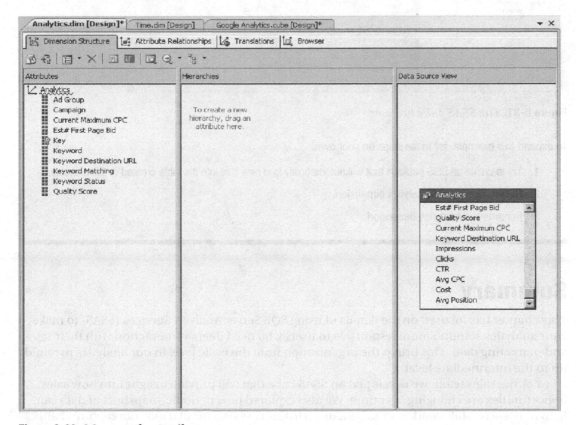

Figure 6-29. *Map relationships*

Figure 6-30. *Manage the attributes.*

38. Save the cube. Build, deploy, and process the cube.

39. Navigate to the browser to view the cube. Figure 6-31 provides an example of this. Just like in Exercise 4-2, as depicted in Figure 4-46, this cube can be viewed from within Excel.

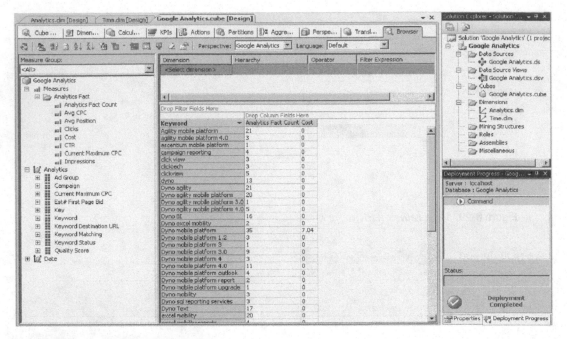

Figure 6-31. *The SSAS cube browser*

To expand this example, try these steps on your own:

1. Try to create an SSIS package that will automatically load new files into the table created in this exercise.

2. Hide the key in the Analytics dimension.

3. Rename the Analytics dimension.

Summary

This chapter has focused on the details of using SQL Server Analysis Services (SSAS) to make your analytics solution more responsive to users who need deeper interaction with their sales and marketing data. This brings the organization from the basic level in our analytics pyramid up to the intermediate level.

For the sales team, we developed an SSAS cube that will provide insight into how sales opportunities are changing over time. We also explored how periodic snapshots of data can help us to successfully work around limitations in business systems that may not capture changes in the data state that are critical to our users.

For the marketing team, we looked at how SSIS combined with an SSAS cube can be used to load data from external providers to allow us to draw better conclusions about the effectiveness both of providers and marketing tactics.

■ ■ ■

CHAPTER 7

Performance Management

This chapter sets out a working definition for "performance management" and then begins to detail how we can build on the tools that have been developed in earlier chapters to deliver an end-to-end system for business performance management. Much like our discussion of KPIs, this chapter is not intended to be an exhaustive discussion of performance management. Rather, it is intended to provide you with an introduction to the topic and to provide practical examples that can serve as a template for how you can effectively manage business performance by leveraging the Microsoft platform.

Defining "Performance Management"

Performance management can be difficult to precisely define. Our definition is that performance management is the consistent application of business process and tools to continuously assess progress toward specific objectives. If you choose to use this definition, it implies that performance management in the context of analytics isn't about the use of any one piece of software, but rather more about how you leverage all of the tools you have at your disposal to ensure that each key user community within the organization has good visibility into how it is performing against its KPIs.

The key here is that the presentation of this information is intuitive and occurs within the context of day-to-day work. For us, this definition is consistent with our framework that analytics initiatives can be structured as a pyramid of increasing sophistication that builds on prior levels (see Figure 7-1). With performance management, we've arrived at the top of the pyramid, and we are focused on making all the pieces work together seamlessly.

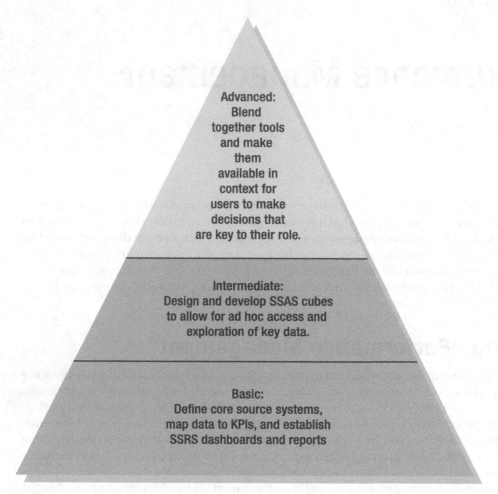

Figure 7-1. *The analytics pyramid*

Up to this point, we've primarily focused on SQL Server Database Services, Analysis Services, Reporting Services, and Excel as the core tools to deliver your analytics platform. Microsoft provides SharePoint and Excel services as an overall framework for collaboration and broadly sharing information. During this chapter, we'll look at how we leverage these collaboration tools in conjunction with the tools that we've built to deliver analytical information to broad audiences. The goals are to provide for a thorough exploration of how companies can make analytics seamlessly fit into the business and to allow you to understand some of the benefits of advancing beyond the core SQL Server platform into the usage of SharePoint.

One Microsoft tool that frequently comes up in conversations with customers looking at performance management on the Microsoft platform is PerformancePoint. PerformancePoint was a stand-alone product, but it is no longer sold. Instead, the dashboard components are now in the process of becoming a part of the upcoming version of SharePoint. Since we don't know precisely how the resulting product will work, we do not provide any PerformancePoint examples in this chapter, but we do anticipate that PerformancePoint will be another valuable service built into SharePoint for organizations exploring the Microsoft BI platform.

Managing Sales Performance

Let's begin our exploration of Performance Management by taking a closer look at how a sales organization would typically strive to integrate its analytics tools into its daily workflow. We'll do this by returning to our fictional company, Dyno Technologies.

The sales team members spend time in two primary applications: Microsoft Outlook and CRM. The key challenges for these folks are having information at their fingertips inside their typical workflow in these applications and providing the appropriate context and depth of information that they need to manage to the KPIs established for them. Let's look at how the BI platform is designed to handle challenges like these by stepping through a couple of examples with specific relevance for our sales team:

- *Dashboard display*: The sales management team wants to be able to see the overall dashboard inside of Outlook, and the chief financial officer wants to see this same information inside of the executive SharePoint site. The BI platform allows us to embed the same report in both locations while still maintaining only one physical copy of the report.

- *Drill into KPIs*: The sales manager has defined the dashboard to provide an overview of the key metrics that drive sales performance. That said, this team needs the ability to drill into and look at specific KPI attributes to be able to really understand why the team is either exceeding or failing to meet its overall objectives.

Creating the Dashboard Display

In Exercises 7-1 and 7-2, we will show how you can take the KPI dashboard we built in Exercise 4-1 and make it available for multiple audiences within the context of the applications where they spend most of their time working. The goal is to demonstrate that one of the key benefits of having built our analytics system on top of the Microsoft BI platform is that we can then seamlessly integrate and deliver a common experience across Microsoft business applications while maintaining only one set of reports. This both saves on maintenance of reports and ensures that, even though different stakeholders may be reviewing the core data in from separate interfaces, they are all looking at the same metrics calculated the same way.

Exercise 7-1. Rendering a Dashboard in the CRM System

This exercise demonstrates the deployment of the KPI dashboard built in Exercise 4-1 in a business web application. For the sake of this example, we are using Microsoft Dynamics CRM as our web application. For those of you using Dynamics CRM, you can follow these steps exactly. If you are using another CRM system, you will need to refer to its documentation in order to complete Steps 3 to 11. The result of this exercise is that CRM users will have direct access to the dashboard available from the main navigation frame in the application. Here are the steps to follow:

1. Embedding the dashboard into the Microsoft CRM application will provide our sales manager with visibility into key business metrics where they work. Open Internet Explorer. Navigate to http://localhost/reports2008. After the page loads, click the Upload File button, which is shown in Figure 7-2.

Figure 7-2. *The Upload File button*

2. Navigate to the `dashboard.rdl` file that was created in Exercise 4-2. Click OK to load and view the report in the report manager. Double-click the report to render it. If there are any errors, return to Visual Studio, and edit the report. Figure 7-3 shows the report with no errors. Copy the URL from this report.

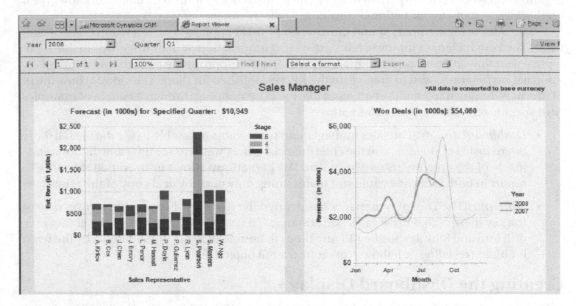

Figure 7-3. *The KPI Report rendered in the report manager*

3. Open a new window in Internet Explorer. Navigate to Microsoft Dynamics 4.0.

4. Navigate to Settings ➤ Customizations ➤ Export Customizations. Select Site Map. Click Export Customizations. Click OK when the warning is displayed. As shown in Figure 7-4, a File Download window will pop up. Chose to save the document to an easily accessible location.

5. Right-click the file, and select Extract All. Open the unzipped folder. Open the `customizations.xml` file in Visual Studio.

6. Add a `SubArea` within a `Group`. In Figure 7-5, the `SubArea` is within the `Workplace` group. Give the `SubArea` an `Id` and a title. The title will be what is displayed to users, so ensure it is something they will understand. The `SubArea` should also have a URL. Paste the URL that was copied in step 2 here.

7. If desired, add an icon. The following code sample contains a pointer to a reporting icon that ships with Microsoft CRM 4.0. Add the icon information to the `SubArea`. Review the `SubArea` code to ensure it looks similar to the following code:

```
<SubArea Id="Dashboard" Title="Dashboard"
Url="http://localhost/ReportServer2008?%2fCRM+Accelerator+
Dashboards%2fAFSalesManager&amp;rs:Command=Render&amp;rc:
Parameters=False" Icon="/_imgs/bar_bottom_ico_reports.gif" />
```

8. Save and close `customizations.xml`.

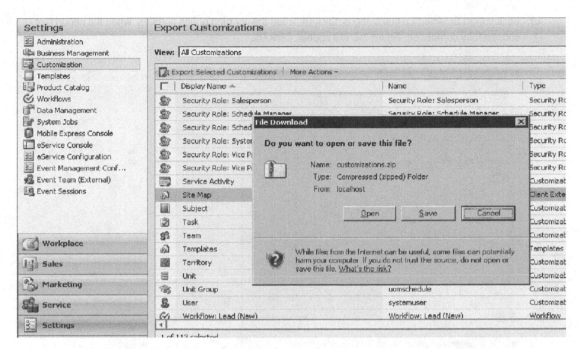

Figure 7-4. *Exporting customizations in CRM*

```
customizations.xml
<ImportExportXml version="4.0.0.0" languagecode="1033" generatedBy="OnPremise">
  <Entities>
  </Entities>
  <Roles>
  </Roles>
  <Workflows>
  </Workflows>
  <SiteMap>
    <SiteMap>
      <Area Id="Workplace" ResourceId="Area_Workplace" ShowGroups="true" Icon="/_imgs/workplace_24x24.gif" DescriptionR
        <Group Id="MyWork" ResourceId="Group_MyWork" DescriptionResourceId="My_Work_Description">
          <SubArea Id="nav_activities" Entity="activitypointer" DescriptionResourceId="Activities_SubArea_Description"
          <SubArea Id="nav_calendar" Icon="/_imgs/area/18_calendar.gif" ResourceId="Homepage_Calendar" Url="/workplace/
            <Privilege Entity="activitypointer" Privilege="Read" />
          </SubArea>
          <SubArea Id="nav_import" Icon="/_imgs/area/18_import.gif" ResourceId="Homepage_Import" Url="/workplace/home_i
            <Privilege Entity="import" Privilege="Read" />
          </SubArea>
          <SubArea Id="nav_duplicatedetectionjobs" Icon="/_imgs/data_management.gif" ResourceId="Homepage_DuplicateDete
            <Privilege Entity="asyncoperation" Privilege="Read" />
          </SubArea>
          <SubArea Id="nav_queues" Entity="queue" Url="/workplace/home_workplace.aspx" DescriptionResourceId="Queues_Su
            <Privilege Entity="activitypointer" Privilege="Read" />
          </SubArea>
          <SubArea Id="nav_answers" Entity="kbarticle" Url="/workplace/home_answers.aspx" DescriptionResourceId="Articl
            <Privilege Entity="subject" Privilege="Read" />
          </SubArea>
          <SubArea Id="Dashboard" Title="Dashboard" Url="http://localhost/ReportServer2008252fCRM+Accelerator+Dashboard
          <SubArea Id="nav_reports" Entity="report" Url="/CRMReports/home_reports.aspx" DescriptionResourceId="Reports_
            <Privilege Entity="report" Privilege="Read" />
          </SubArea>
          <SubArea Id="nav_news" Entity="businessunitnewsarticle" Url="/home/homepage/home_news.aspx" DescriptionResour
        </Group>
```

Figure 7-5. *Modifying the site map in CRM*

9. Navigate back to CRM ➤ Settings ➤ Customizations. Select Import Customizations. Browse to the
customizations.xml file. Click the Upload button.

10. Click Import Selected Customizations. Click OK when the warning notice appears. When the import has successfully completed, Figure 7-6 will appear. Click OK.

Figure 7-6. *Customization upload confirmation*

11. Click the refresh button on the web browser. Navigate to the newly created report. An example of a report shown within CRM is displayed in Figure 7-7.

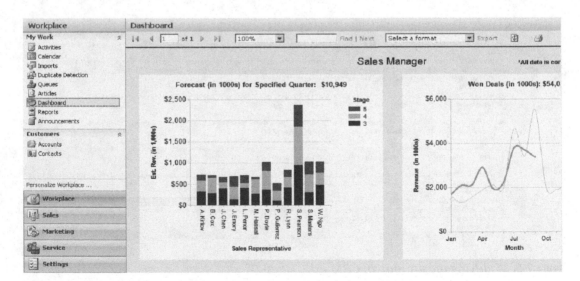

Figure 7-7. *KPI report rendering in CRM*

Exercise 7-2. Rendering a Dashboard in Microsoft SharePoint

We find that many of our clients are looking to combine the power of SQL Server with the web portal product Share-Point. This exercise is provided as supplemental material for those who are looking to go beyond the sample database and leverage existing SharePoint assets. The exercise demonstrates the deployment of the dashboard from Exercise 7-1 into SharePoint. The result of this exercise is that SharePoint users will have direct access to the dashboard where they typically work. The key for the technical team is that the report may be displayed in multiple places, but there is still only one place where the code has to be managed. Here are the steps to follow:

1. Again, navigate to the `dashboard.rdl` file. Click OK to load and view the report in the report manager. Copy the URL from this report.

2. Open a new window in Internet Explorer. Navigate to SharePoint 2007. As displayed in Figure 7-8, the link can be found at the top of Internet Explorer.

Figure 7-8. *SharePoint link on the favorites bar of Internet Explorer*

3. Click Site Actions. Select Edit Page, which is the second option in Figure 7-9.

Figure 7-9. *Select Edit Page.*

4. Select Add a Web Part, and then select the Report Viewer Web Part listed under Miscellaneous Web Parts. Click the Edit button on the report viewer. Select Modify Shared Web Part, which is the third option from the bottom in Figure 7-10.

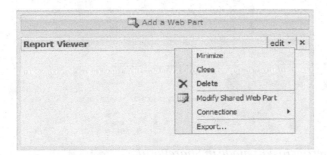

Figure 7-10. *Modify the report viewer web part.*

5. Type the URL for the report manager, for example **http://localhost/reports2008**, into the Report Manager URL. Type the path to the specific report to be uploaded, for example, **/ExecutiveKPI**. This path includes the folder and name of the report. The web part configuration will resemble Figure 7-11.

Figure 7-11. *Passing report parameters into the report viewer web part*

6. Click OK. Once the web part has been modified, the SharePoint page will resemble Figure 7-12.

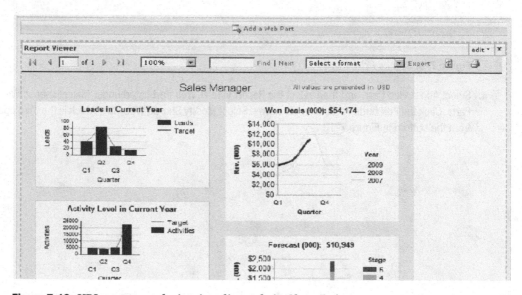

Figure 7-12. *KPI report rendering in edit mode in SharePoint*

7. To get out of edit mode, click the Exit Edit Mode link on the right-hand side. The final version of the report on SharePoint will look like Figure 7-13.

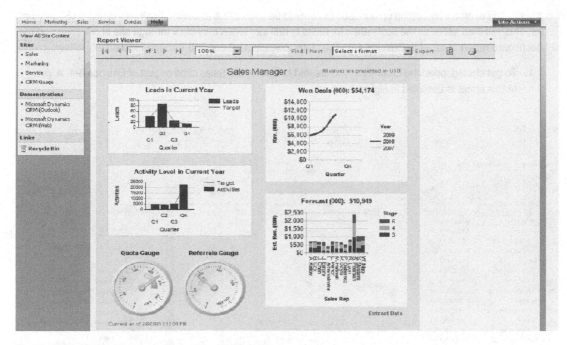

Figure 7-13. *KPI web part rendering in SharePoint*

Drilling into the KPI Details

Now, it's time to look at drilling down into the details. The example in Exercise 7-3 shows how we can take the KPI dashboard we built in Chapter 4 and increase the power of that dashboard by providing deeper drill-through paths into reports that allow for enhanced filtering. We can also provide the capacity to drill directly into raw data in Excel sheets and into our SSAS cube.

Our goal in Exercise 7-3 is to demonstrate that one key component of performance management is to make it intuitive for business users to get to the deeper meaning in the data that underlies our KPIs. One way to achieve this with the core SQL BI platform is to leverage the context-sensitive drill-through capability of SSRS and combine that capability with the power of filtering in deeper reports and powerful end user tools like Excel. This approach means that everyone can start at the high-level metrics that are relevant to executives but can then quickly drill into detailed underlying data to better understand why a given, higher-level metric is performing at the level captured in our dashboard.

Exercise 7-3. Drilling Down into Different Targets from SSRS

We'll begin this exercise by setting up our cube browser to be available and automatically refreshed on SharePoint Server. This will then serve as the destination for users to drill into when they click through one of our charts on the KPI dashboard report created in Exercise 4-1. The steps to implement our drill-through functionality follow:

1. To get started, open the Excel sheet you created to browse the Sales cube as part of Exercise 6-1. A view of this sheet is depicted in Figure 7-14.

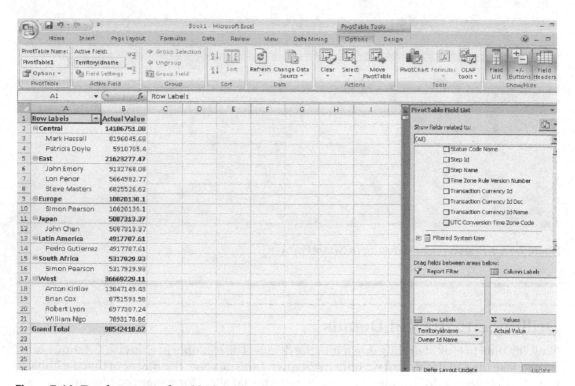

Figure 7-14. *Excel connected to SSAS*

2. Establish the view that you would like users to see on drill through. Now, we will publish this sheet to SharePoint via Excel services so that users may not only view the layout we've created, but also interact with the data. The first step is to select the publish option from Excel by clicking the Windows icon, selecting Publish, and selecting Excel Services, as highlighted in Figure 7-15.

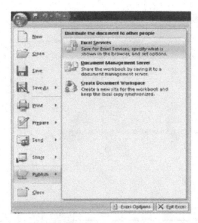

Figure 7-15. *Initiating publish of the cube browser*

3. Select the correct URL for the document library to which you would like to publish the browser, and check the Open in Excel Services box. Figure 7-16 displays a view of this selection.

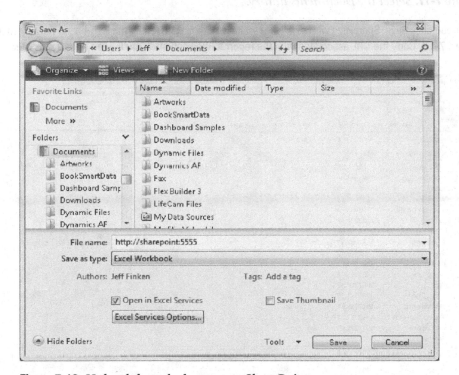

Figure 7-16. *Upload the cube browser to SharePoint.*

4. Click Save, and the browser will display a new window with available libraries on the SharePoint site. Select Documents, and click Open, as depicted in Figure 7-17. Upon clicking Open, the dialog box will give you the option to save the `.xls` file.

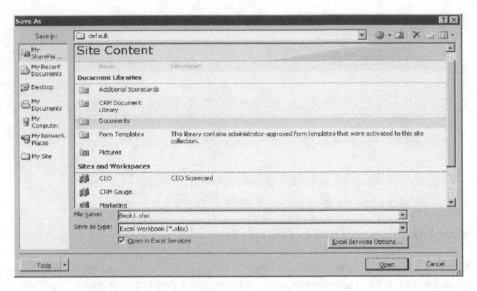

Figure 7-17. *Select the Documents library.*

5. After you click Save, SharePoint will upload the resulting `.xls` file and render the web-based view shown in Figure 7-18. Copy the URL associated with the report to the clipboard. You'll need it for a later step.

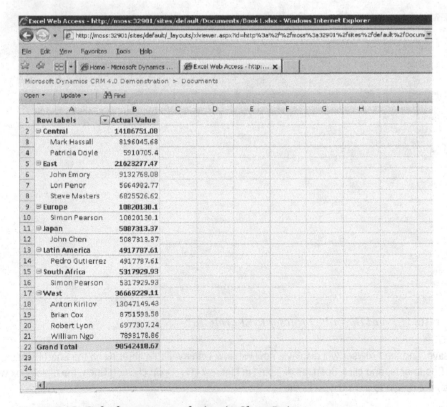

Figure 7-18. *Cube browser rendering in SharePoint*

6. Note that the available spreadsheet can now be updated in the web browser to pick up any changes in the cube, or it can be opened in Excel by the end users to add and filter fields as they choose. Figure 7-19 displays the outcome when a user selects to open the spreadsheet in Excel and adds the Address1Country dimension as a row.

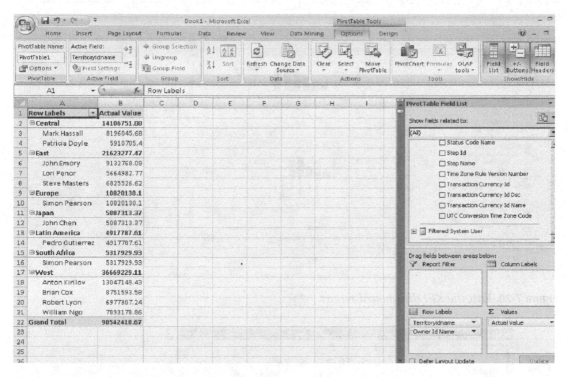

Figure 7-19. *Edit the Excel services sheet.*

7. Now, we'll move on to make this sheet that has been posted to SharePoint available as a drill-through report from SSRS. Open Business Intelligence Development Studio (BIDS), and navigate to the KPI dashboard created in Exercise 4-1. Right-click the Won Deals chart, as depicted in Figure 7-20, and select Chart Area Properties.

8. Select the Action option, and paste the URL for the web view of the cube browser that was copied in step 6 into the Select URL field of the resulting dialog, as depicted in Figure 7-21. Click OK.

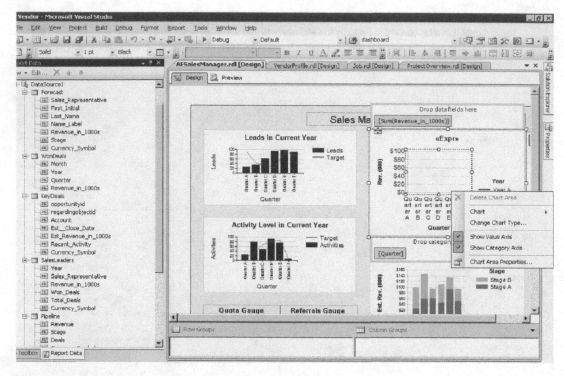

Figure 7-20. *Edit the KPI dashboard report.*

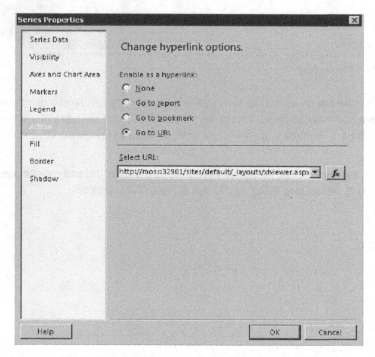

Figure 7-21. *Set up the URL in the Series Properties dialog.*

9. Publish the report to the report manager, and hover over the Won Deals chart. Click through the Won Deals hyperlink, and the cube browser will open in a new window, as shown in Figure 7-22.

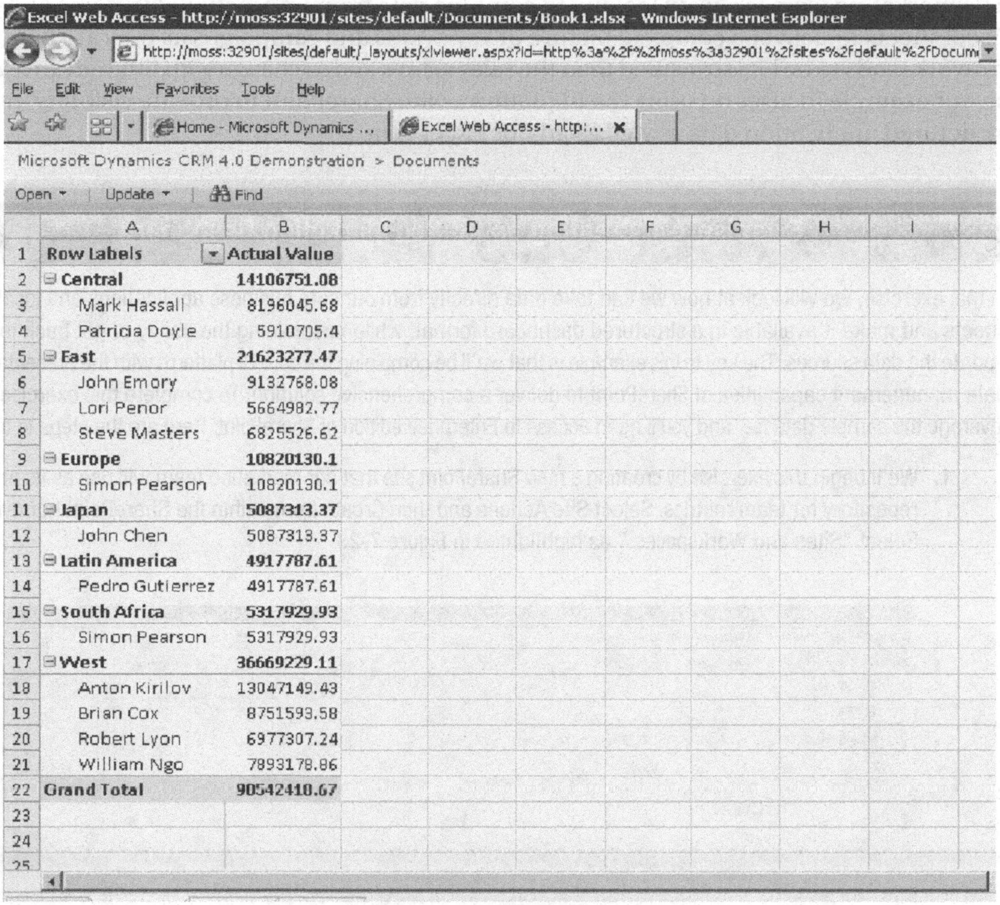

Figure 7-22. *Drill through from the KPI dashboard to the cube browser.*

You now have established a drill-through report from SSRS that sends a user to a web-based view of an OLAP cube. This approach of providing drill-down capability provides a way for analysts to publish key cube views but still gives the end users the option to open the viewer in Excel and conduct their own analysis.

Managing Marketing Performance

Let's look at how a marketing organization would typically strive to integrate analytical tools into its workflow. A marketing team is typically working across a much broader set of tools than just a CRM application and Outlook and tends to be looking at the data much more deeply for insights into how leads and campaigns are performing. With the goal of providing a flexible framework that allows for combining structured and unstructured data, we'll look at what the

Microsoft BI platform provides by stepping through an example with specific relevance for our marketing team.

The example we'll be stepping through in Exercise 7-4 is one of creating ad hoc dashboards. The marketing team is always looking to combine data from transactional systems and ad hoc Excel sheets to deliver a complete picture of key events and campaigns as they are happening. Its work tends to be less structured than the sales team's and to change with little advance notice so our example focuses on using the BI platform with SharePoint to provide visibility into both structured application data as well as ad hoc Excel data.

Exercise 7-4. Creating an Ad Hoc Marketing Dashboard

In this exercise, we will look at how we can take data directly from our core business applications and local spreadsheets and make it available in a structured dashboard format, while maintaining the ability to get back to and update the data sources. The key to this example is that we'll be combining the core BI platform with the presentation and data management capabilities of SharePoint to deliver a comprehensive solution. To complete this exercise you will leverage the sample data file, and you'll need access to Enterprise edition of SharePoint. Here are the steps to follow:

1. We'll begin this exercise by creating a new SharePoint site that our marketing team will use as its primary repository for team metrics. Select Site Actions and then Create from within the SharePoint home page. Select "Sites and Workspaces," as highlighted in Figure 7-23.

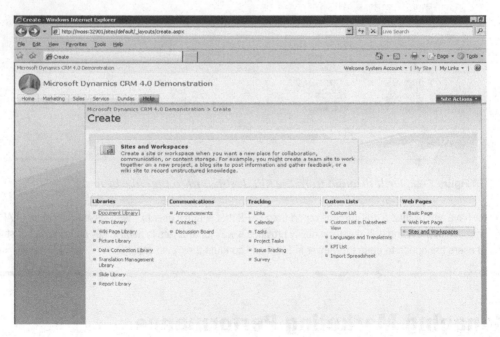

Figure 7-23. *Initiate site creation.*

2. Input a title and URL name for the site based on your preferences. Select the Enterprise tab on the templates menu, and highlight Report Center, as depicted in Figure 7-24. Click Create. This will establish your core dashboard site for posting and rendering the ad hoc analysis that the marketing team may engage in.

3. After you click Create, the site will be set up automatically on the SharePoint server, and the Report Center template will generate a site similar to Figure 7-25.

Figure 7-24. *Establish the site type and name.*

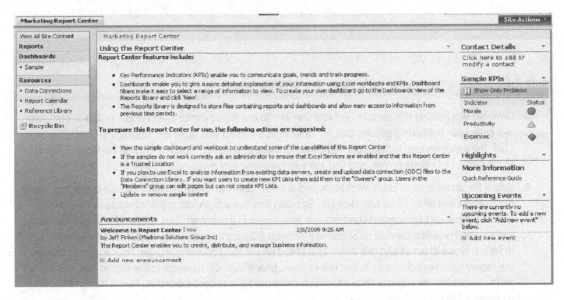

Figure 7-25. *Default site generated by the report center template*

4. With the site created, let's get some content ready and post a few examples of the material that may end up here. Open the Excel sheet created in Exercise 6-2 that connects to our cube of Google keyword ad data. Select Impressions as the measure, and Campaigns and Ad Group as the dimensions. Highlight the campaigns and impressions, and add a simple pivot chart by selecting Insert and then Pie. The result will look similar to Figure 7-26.

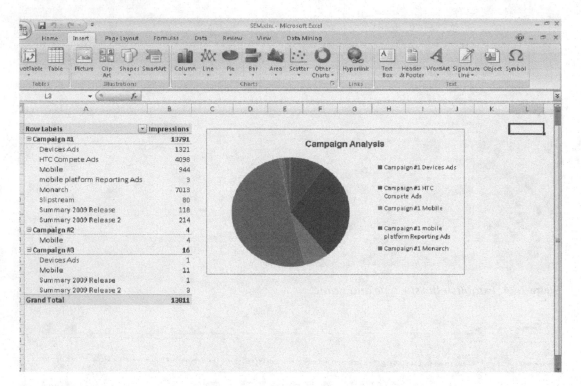

Figure 7-26. *Excel connected to SSAS with marketing campaign data*

5. Now, we will publish this sample via Excel services to our report center site created in step 3. First, we will select our publishing options that will drive how the chart and table are rendered in SharePoint. Click the windows icon in the upper-left corner of Excel and select Publish and Excel Services. Click the Excel Services Options button, and you will see the dialog box depicted in Figure 7-27.

6. Select the arrow next to Entire Workbook, and choose "Items in the Workbook". Place a check box next to the chart and pivot table, and click OK. By doing this, we are providing the information SharePoint needs to allow us to render the chart or table specifically in a web part. This will provide an elegant user experience in viewing the data on SharePoint where publishing the entire workbook would make it difficult to view a single chart as part of a larger dashboard on the main SharePoint page. Now, input the URL for the report site created in step 3, and select Save. SharePoint will navigate to the Report site and allow you to select the appropriate library to which you would like to post the report. Select Reports Library, as depicted in Figure 7-28.

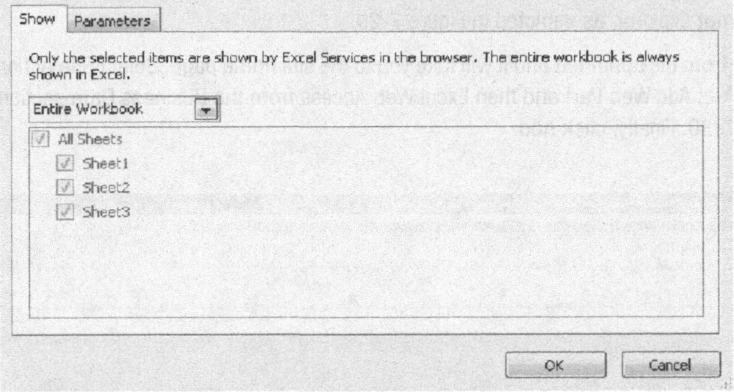

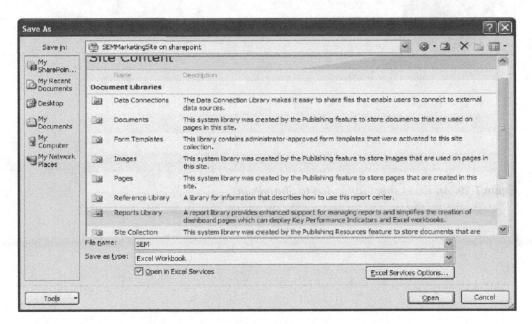

Figure 7-27. *Excel dialog box for defining which attributes are published to SharePoint*

Figure 7-28. *Excel dialog pointed to the Reports Library option*

7. Click Open, and input the name of the file. Click Save, and the file will upload and open the resulting server copy in Internet Explorer, as depicted in Figure 7-29.

8. Click the site name from the upper left and it will take you to the site home page. Select Site Actions and Edit Page. Next, select Add Web Part and then Excel Web Access from the Business Data section, as depicted in Figure 7-30. Finally, click Add.

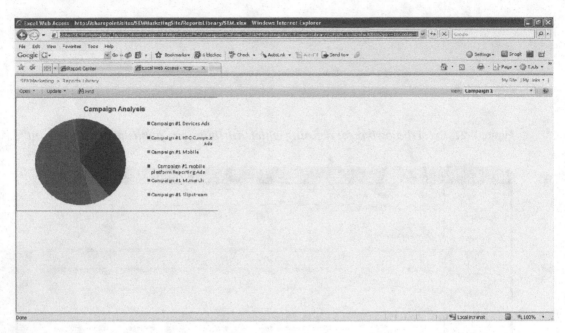

Figure 7-29. *An Excel sheet uploaded to SharePoint*

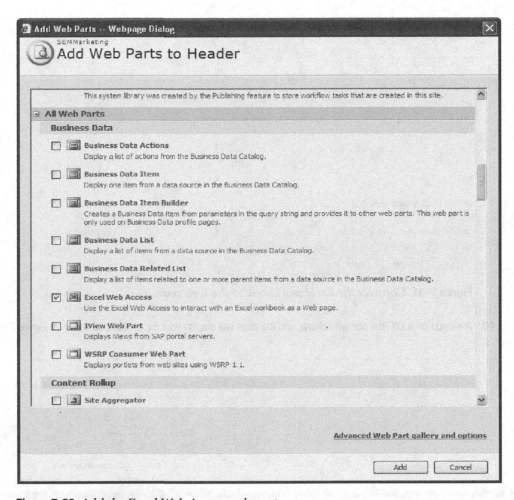

Figure 7-30. *Add the Excel Web Access web part.*

9. On the Excel Web Access web part, click Edit and Modify Shared Web Part. Click the ellipsis next to workbook, and navigate to the workbook that was uploaded. In the Named Item field, type the name of the chart, as depicted in Figure 7-31.

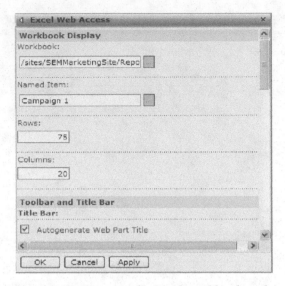

Figure 7-31. *Connect the Excel workbook to the web part.*

10. After you click OK, the site will refresh, and the page will display your Excel chart, as shown in Figure 7-32.

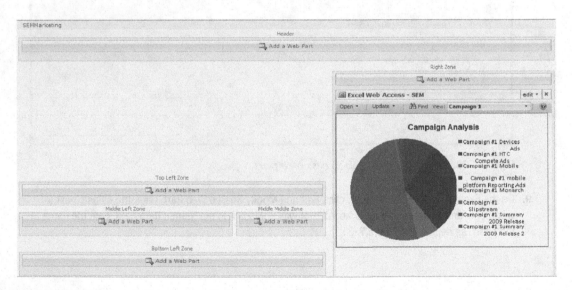

Figure 7-32. *The Excel chart being display on the SharePoint dashboard*

Now, you have the core framework available to add charts or tables from Excel sheets to build an elegant dashboard that accepts ad hoc user data and publishes to users in a way that allows them to view the material or open the contents in the source Excel file for greater interactivity. A fully built dashboard may look something like Figure 7-33.

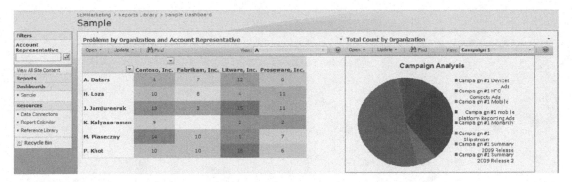

Figure 7-33. *The complete SharePoint sample dashboard*

Summary

The goal of this chapter has been to provide some specific examples of how the concept of performance management comes to life with the Microsoft BI platform. To accomplish this, we set out a working definition that performance management is the consistent application of business process and tools to continuously assess progress toward specific objectives. Next, we looked at our key constituencies of sales and marketing and delivered examples that brought the tools we have built in earlier chapters into the day-to-day workflows of these groups.

For our sales team members, we embedded analytical tools directly into the business applications where they spend their time, as well as ensuring that the team has the ability to drill down from top-level KPIs into specific metrics to understand the details around key factors that drive the overall KPIs.

For our marketing team, we provide the ability to build elegant ad hoc dashboards that incorporate both data from our core systems as well as unstructured Excel data. These ad hoc dashboards, in turn, provide the ability to look at both summarized charts as well as to drill into the source data in Excel.

■ ■ ■

CHAPTER 8

Implementation and Maintenance of the Integrated System

In previous chapters, we explored both the functional and technical items necessary and available to successfully implement an analytics solution. Additionally, having completed and reviewed the key technologies available using the Microsoft BI platform, this chapter will provide information on implementing these technologies successfully and maintaining applications following deployment.

Understanding the Project Management Phases

Let's begin by outlining a basic set of considerations and requirements that fit into the phases outlined in Figure 8-1. The methodology we follow is loosely based on the Microsoft Solution Framework.

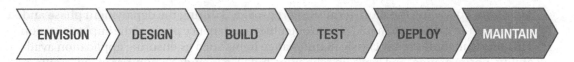

ENVISION 〉 DESIGN 〉 BUILD 〉 TEST 〉 DEPLOY 〉 MAINTAIN

Figure 8-1. *The project management process*

At a high level, these phases can be defined as follows:

Envision: The envisioning phase is the time when the project team and the customer (internal or external) agree on the overall direction for the project, including what the final product will and will not include. Envisioning addresses one of the most fundamental needs for project success—unifying the project team. The team must have a clear vision of what it wants to accomplish for the customer (either internal or external) and be able to state that goal in terms that will motivate the entire team and the customer. Detailed discussions during this phase force the clients to be crisp about what they are hoping to achieve with the project and what outcomes must be achieved in order for the project to be a success. Finally, during the envisioning phase, KPIs are developed. For more information on the development of KPIs, refer to Chapter 3.

Design: During this phase, business requirements will be gathered and any data and user interface design will be executed to prepare for the build phase. This key stage will determine the success of the project, as the needs of the client are matched up with the capabilities of the chosen software components. Additionally, the key scenarios for individuals using the system will be detailed, and any custom components associated with the reports or dashboards will be designed and signed off on by the overall project team. As part of the prioritization exercise, the teams will evaluate these items using the data map, road map, and mock-up process outlined in Chapter 4. Those items that fit within the project budget will be included.

Build: The project team will develop data schemas, SQL Server Integration Services (SSIS) packages, SQL Server Analysis Server (SSAS) cubes, and SQL Server Reporting Services (SSRS) reports through a series of development iterations. These will be tightly controlled through the weekly status meeting and status reports process and will likely be based on the basic, intermediate, and advanced pyramid outlined in Chapter 4. During this phase of the engagement, the team will also perform detailed unit testing to ensure that the functionality built performs as designed.

Test: During the testing phase, complete testing of the functionality will be completed including full, end-to-end system testing, user acceptance testing, and a design and test of both mock and real data to ensure anticipated performance and functionality within the reporting platform.

Deploy: Once all components have passed through the testing phase and been approved, resources begin training the end users and application administrators on the various Microsoft products. Often, various types of training will be provided (end user training, web-based on-demand training, etc.). The project team will perform the implementation of all components (hardware and software) into the production server environment, and complete any data seeding necessary. Additional short-term, postproduction support (after the go-live date) should be provided to ensure the stability of the system.

Maintain: Following the short-term support provided during the deployment phase and after the go-live date, you should plan to enter the maintenance phase of the implementation. This phase includes many classic maintenance items such as ensuring application availability, performance, and back-up reliability, but also includes a number of envisioning-like items that will enable you to move seamlessly into the next phase of the analytics implementation.

One component underlies all six of these phases—project management. Project management skills and resources will be needed during all phases of the implementation. Information on all of these concepts will be reviewed in more detail throughout this chapter.

Beginning with the Envisioning Phase

All analytics projects, initial iterations, or later implementations should begin with an envisioning phase. Whether or not this phase can be abbreviated depends completely on your organization's experience with technology implementations and your ability to drive quickly through the items included in this phase.

Identifying the Project Scope

Probably the most critical component of the envisioning phase of the project is the identification of and agreement on the scope. This is the place where all of the project stakeholders including end users, department managers, and executives must be on the same page relative to what is being delivered. As we discussed in Chapter 2, during the first phase, this scope often includes structured, ad hoc reports and expands into more complex offerings and performance management during later phases. Whether this project is an internal project, or an external consulting engagement, documenting and agreeing on the scope is imperative for long-term project success. How the scope is documented is up to you: our team utilizes a project charter document to get sign off from all stakeholders (Figure 8-4 will provide a sample of this document's table of contents for your review).

Calculating the ROI

Once you have identified the scope items for the first phase of the engagement, it will be imperative for you to evaluate the impact that the reports and dashboards will have on the business. This effort may include actual return on investment (ROI) calculations or simply the team's gut feelings on the impact that having fast, easy access to the data will or will not have on their day-to-day activities.

Regardless of the chosen approach, a simple table should be sufficient to assist you in highlighting the items that are obviously causing the team to be less efficient than otherwise possible.

Figure 8-2 provides a simple table to track and to review the various scope items with the team. This format can be used to estimate the value, costs (both internal and external), and ultimately to prioritize the items for a specific project phase.

ROI Evaluation

ID	Scope Item	Long Description	Value (Low, Medium, High)	Internal Cost ($)	External Cost ($)	Prioritized Phase
1						
2						
3						
4						
5						
6						
7						
8						
9						
...						

Figure 8-2. *A sample ROI table*

Once you have completed this exercise, the information should be presented to the project steering committee for review. The committee can then make a more informed decision relative to what scope will be included in this phase of the analytics deployment.

Selecting the Project Scope

After receiving the ROI information, it will be necessary to specifically identify which requested scope items will and will not be included in the initial phase of the engagement. Once you've identified those items, you then prioritize them.

Identifying Scope Items

The "Key 3: Delivering Structured, Ad Hoc Reports" section in Chapter 2 will provide you with a number of detailed questions associated with selecting the appropriate scope items. In general, you'll focus on the following:

- Which scope items will have the greatest impact on my business?

- What software will I need to buy to complete the phase?

- Will I be able to leverage my existing technology investments to complete the desired reports?

- Will the information presented be trusted?

- Is the information able to be presented in a timely fashion?

- Will my users have the ability to effectively access the reports or dashboards and manipulate the data to present user-appropriate information?

Frequently, as Chapter 2 discusses, the decision on which scope items are included in various phases of the implementation depends on the technologies currently owned by your organization. As you would guess, completing a project phase with minimal additional technology investments frequently improves a scope item's ROI.

In general, if you have your team complete the ROI review in the preceding section and answer some questions about the value of each report and its respective impact on the users, you will ensure a successful start to the implementation.

Prioritizing Scope Items

While prioritizing scope items may seem like a repeated task given the previous assessment, once the scope has been identified, you need to review the scope items to prioritize them within a specific phase. This will enable you to make decisions later should scope, budget, or timeline challenges arise with a minimal amount of emotion involved. More important than being able to address issues is the ability for the project steering committee to continue to get more and more deeply involved in the project. The more difficult decisions they're required to make as a team, the more they will be invested in the project's ultimate success.

Planning the Project

After the details of the scope have been identified, it is time to take the first look at the project schedule and associated resources. This process will involve setting an initial direction for the project specific to timelines and deliverables, while the ultimate deliverable, a project plan, will be the tool that a number of different groups use to track progress, plan resources, and identify potential issues before they arise. The project plan will also help to provide clarity about the following project items:

Project schedule and duration: At a high level, a completed project plan will provide you with information on the overall project schedule and duration of specific phases. A well-done project plan will take into account key stakeholder vacations, holidays, and other existing resourcing commitments. There will also inevitably be impacts to your user's day-to-day activities when the phase is completed and the reports and dashboards are deployed, so a completed project plan will provide visibility into when changes might occur.

Expected task start and end dates: In addition to the overall project schedule, the completed project plan will provide individual users or stakeholders with an idea of when their time will be needed throughout the process to assist with designing or testing the application. Providing up-front information on resource requirements will either (a) reduce the likelihood of resource conflicts later or (b) allow any issues to be addressed should they arise.

IT resource requirements: Throughout the course of the implementation, IT assistance is likely to be needed. The creation of a project plan will provide them with up-front information on these needs. Oftentimes, IT resources are required to provide hardware for training, testing, or deployment requiring more lead time than simply securing a resource for a specific task.

Meeting schedules: While many meetings will occur during the implementation, the project plan is one tool utilized to provide insight into upcoming discussions. Many "standard" tasks that occur consistently will be outlined during the project, such as project status meetings and steering committee reviews. Additionally, standard design discussions and testing or training involving a large amount of users will typically be identified in the project plan well in advance of the actual meeting.

Overall project status: Finally, once the project plan has been completed and reviewed by the project steering committee, it can be baselined as a tool to track project progress against initial dates and provide visibility into any slips in schedule that may necessitate resource changes and updated meeting schedules.

Figure 8-3 provides an example project plan with many of the items typically scheduled during a project phase. The schedule has been abbreviated to enable a more complete view of the project tasks. As you work through the project plan definition, you will need to set up the tasks that make sense for your business and implementation.

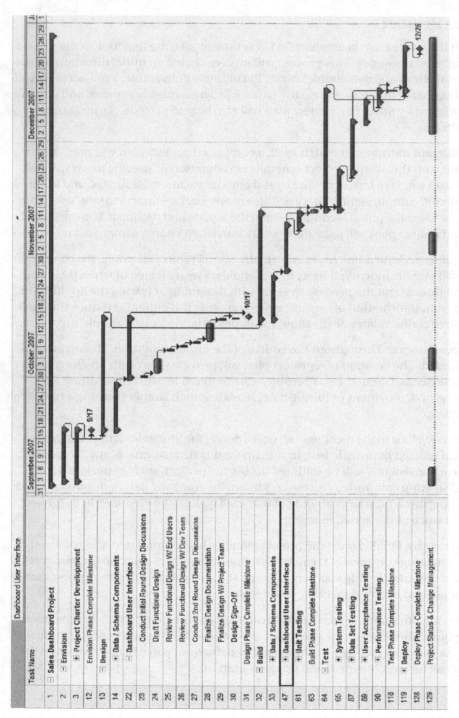

Figure 8-3. *A sample project plan*

Identifying Critical Team Skills

As you continue to work through the process, the critical skills needed on the team will begin to become evident. As you select scope items and appropriate technologies, you will identify the necessary internal stakeholders who are required to design functionality or review its eventual completeness relative to this design.

In addition to the functional skill sets required, technical assistance will be needed to complete both development and deployment work. Depending on the technologies selected, resources or consultants can be used to build the reports and dashboards. Key 3 in Chapter 2 provides additional information on merging the necessary skills with the scope items.

An additional item to consider when developing the team is spreading the appropriate skills across a number of individuals. While this provides some redundancy should other demands be placed on a specific resource, it also creates a small checks and balances process often resulting in better design and deliverables because of the "team effort". Depending on the size of your project, you will have to evaluate which of the following roles are needed:

Project manager: The project manager is responsible for the management of all day-to-day activities associated with the project, which include the following:

- Managing the project schedule and budget

- Managing project resources

- Reporting the project status to project stakeholders

- Tracking and triaging project issues

Project analyst: The project analyst will be responsible for performing many of the activities that affect the usability, performance, and stability of the application. This role can at times be both functional and technical and, depending on the skill set of the analysts, one or multiple people can fill it. Some of the project analyst's responsibilities follow:

- Mocking up user interfaces based on good information design principles

- Designing logical data structures that identify all key tables and fields of source systems

- Defining data transformations that must occur to convert raw data into KPIs

- Developing quick reference and training guides

- Developing and executing all application testing (system, user acceptance testing, regression) and training (end user and administrator)

- Executing a defined roll-out plan and subsequent go-live support

Developer: The developer will build the project components designed by the project analyst and the project team. Developers' tasks include the following:

- Developing SQL code

- Administering databases

- Using SSAS to design and develop data cubes for ad hoc access to key data

- Using SSIS to develop data transformations to clean and consolidate data for cubes and reports

- Using SSRS to develop dashboards and transactional reports

Project sponsor: The project sponsor is ultimately responsible for the overall success of the implementation. Some responsibilities of this individual include

- Serving as an escalation point for any project issues

- Providing project guidance and oversight on scope management and design reviews

Project champion: The project champion will provide overall guidance to the delivery team for a specific feature or component of the application. This individual is often a higher level executive than any of those outlined thus far. Some responsibilities of this individual follow:

- Providing functional guidance on the design of features or functions

- Ensuring that team members and other project stakeholders are available and providing design feedback as necessary

Project stakeholder: The project stakeholders are individuals with a vested interest in the success of the project above and beyond that of a typical user. Project stakeholders should be prepared to provide requirement guidance as needed and serve as an evangelist of the application.

Setting Expectations

After the scope is finalized and the individuals involved in the project are identified, it is time for you to begin to set expectations. Again, though setting expectations is a relatively straight-forward concept, this step is important for a number of reasons:

Project success: Expectation setting is critical anytime varying views of success are applied by different employees to the end result. Beginning to work with stakeholders and end users early in the project regarding the things they may or may not get as part of this project will go a long way in affecting that project's ultimate perception.

Ongoing change management: One item we will focus on more later in this chapter is ongoing change management. As part of this process, beginning to set expectations for users about the impact on their day-to-day roles is vital to driving a building excitement about the deliverables of the project.

Sponsoring the Project

When all the items identified thus far as part of the envisioning phase are completed, it is appropriate for you to work with the project sponsor to discuss your needs with him or her during the project. While the sponsor's involvement is perhaps to simply ensure any resources you need are available, oftentimes issues will arise that the sponsor needs to be involved in resolving. Having complete support from the project sponsor will ensure that these issues do not derail the project and are resolved successfully.

Figure 8-4 provides you with a high-level example of a project charter document. This document can be used to clarify all of the items reviewed during the envisioning phase. It can be viewed as a working project document should questions come up during the project relative to high-level scope, scheduling, or resource involvement.

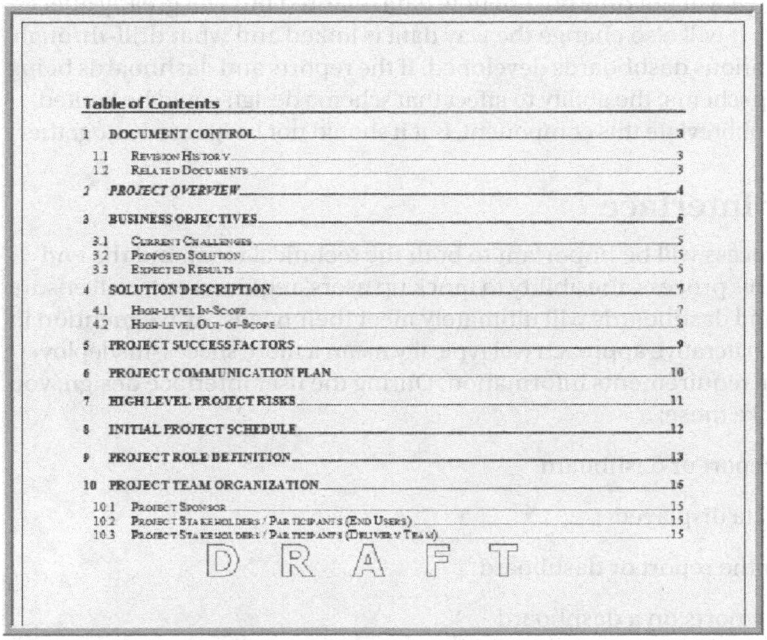

Table of Contents

DRAFT

Figure 8-4. *A project charter table of contents*

While the envisioning phase contains quite a few components, it is ultimately the one phase that will take you the smallest amount of time during the project. That said, executing these items well can ultimately affect project success more than any of the other phases. Successfully completing the envisioning phase will not only position the first overall phase of the project for success but will provide additional background and planning for future phases.

Initiating the Design Phase

Following the completion of the envisioning phase of the implementation, you will likely move directly into the design phase. This phase will involve designing the data structure and schema, the look and feel of the reports and the ability to interact with the various reports and dashboards. It will also focus on the often overlooked task of developing of the test plans that will govern the testing that will occur prior to the release of the reports going live during the deployment phase.

Designing the Schema

Designing the schema for reports and dashboards goes hand-in-hand with the design of the user interface. As you would imagine, what needs to be displayed greatly effects what needs to be stored (and likely how it should be stored). This process will definitely impact the technical users or developers much more than the end users of the reports and dashboards.

During the schema design process, the complexity of the needed reports will affect how detailed the schema is, how many tables and columns are needed, and whether or not more complex schema requirements exist for things like an OLAP cube.

Ultimately, schema design will not only govern how data is stored but will greatly affect how quickly data is returned. It will also change the way data is linked and what drill-through capabilities will exist in the various dashboards developed. If the reports and dashboards being developed point to an existing schema, the ability to affect that schema design could be limited. Therefore, you can choose to abbreviate this component, but it should not be ignored altogether.

Designing the User Interface

The user interface design process will be important to both the technical team and the end users. As you work through this process, the ability to mock up users' requirements will ensure that the developed reports and dashboards will ultimately meet their needs. As we mention in Chapter 2, working through an iterative approach will typically mean a more successful deployment than a single capture of requirements information. During the user interface design, you will want to focus on items like these:

- Attractiveness of the report or dashboard

- Look and feel of the data displayed

- Opportunities to filter the report or dashboard

- Placement of various reports on a dashboard

- Position of the refresh and data source information

While many of these items seem straightforward, having information in the right place and making the report user friendly will not only impact its use but will also subconsciously impact the user's trust in the information presented and underlying data.

BENEFITS OF AN ITERATIVE APPROACH

The benefits of working through an iterative design approach merit being called out again in this chapter. Many failed IT initiatives, reporting and otherwise, are the result of someone capturing a set of requirements based on one or two brief conversations and building a solution to reflect those. Oftentimes, users don't know what they don't know, so until they are forced to think about answers to questions multiple times, they may not come up with the correct answer. Additionally, from a user interface perspective, until they see how a requirement looks on the screen or how a requirement affects other components of a report or dashboard, they may not have the background information to make an informed decision. To reiterate a point previously made, engaging the end users in multiple discussions that allow them to see continual growth and progress with their requirements will also help in driving excitement and adoption down the road.

Developing Use Cases

Finally, we will address a surprising component of the design phase for some people—designing the use cases for the reports and dashboards. This process will assist with two things going forward:

Process alignment: One piece missing from the design process identified throughout this chapter is the analysis and review of the business process. While more process discussions are involved in designing a line of business applications (like a CRM system), understand any processes associated with the reports interactions will ensure the end result continues to meet the needs of the end users.

Complete testing: Developing use cases during the design phase will guarantee that complete testing is done during the testing phase of the deployment. Far too often, end-to-end system tests are completed based on what was built, not what was designed (and intended to be built). Designing use cases will provide a baseline set of information for the testing plans developed during a later phase of the engagement.

Use cases often include a flow of information as well as mock-ups of the reports and dashboards. Figure 8-5 provides one example of a use case structure.

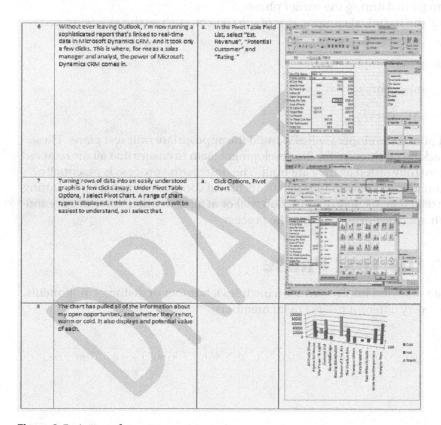

Figure 8-5. *A sample use case structure*

As we discussed in Chapter 4, the overall design process also includes mapping data from the source system to identify data weaknesses and gaps in the data quality. A roadmap of the reports should also be defined to ensure that the dashboards and reports are appropriately prioritized to address the KPIs defined during the envisioning phase (see Chapter 3). Completing these steps in addition to the iterative mock-ups discussed earlier in this chapter will ensure the best reports and dashboards are delivered throughout the engagement.

Working Through the Build Phase

Following the design phase, you will move into the build phase of the implementation. From a project management perspective, this is probably the most straightforward part of the project. Typically, during the build phase, very little interaction is required from end users and even the project steering committee. Now that the input has been received from the users, the technical team is involved in developing the reports and dashboards.

In order to continue the change management processes associated with the overall engagement, the build and project management teams may want to consider having periodic build reviews as appropriate user interface content is developed. This will prevent the users from losing any momentum gained during the earlier phases.

During this phase, the technical components of the project, such as the following, are built:

- Database and schema components

- User interface components

- Any necessary OLAP cubes

During the build phase, developers will also build the appropriate unit test plans. These plans will provide a tracking mechanism for the development team to ensure that all the required components are successfully tested as they are built. The unit testing process is essentially completed in a vacuum associated with the specific technical component being built. During the build phase, unit-tested items may not function well or at all with other components and instead complete their specific purpose within the process.

Moving into the Test Phase

The testing phase of an analytics implementation includes a number of distinct components, each of which involves very different project team members:

Sample dataset testing: For any projects that include a custom data structure or schema, creating sample data early in the testing process will enable you to test both the data structure and the early version of the reports. This testing is typically performed by the project developers.

System testing: System testing includes an end-to-end review of the schema and user interface components. This allows the project developers and analysts to, for the first time, review how the reports will look with data and how primary reports and subreports may interact with one another.

Real dataset testing: After the system test has been completed, the development team can work to implement real data into the solution. While a sample dataset will provide valuable testing, no data-testing process is complete without access to the real information. The population and testing of real data often includes both the developers and the analysts most familiar with the information.

User acceptance testing: Following the system and any necessary regression testing, users will get their first glimpse of the final product. User acceptance testing (UAT) typically includes visibility into both the data and UI components of the solution as well as a review of the process users might walk through when interacting with the solution.

Performance testing: After users have provided their feedback on the developed solution and any necessary updates have been made, performance testing should be completed. This testing should include an evaluation of the solution relative to metrics like execution time, refresh rate, and subreport load time and should be evaluated with varying datasets and at different times of day.

Regression testing: Subsequent to each of the identified testing phases, regression testing should be completed. Assuming some level of feedback is received at each stage, modifications will need to be made to the solution, and these modifications should be as thoroughly tested as the initial work.

Figure 8-6 shows a sample testing plan. The same template should be used for different testing stages by re-executing the plan and/or providing additional information (in the case of UAT) to enable users to successfully navigate the solution.

There are a number of natural points throughout the project where the project steering committee should be engaged to sign off on progress. Other than the design phase, probably the most important place to engage the team and receive confirmation or acceptance of the solution deliverables is at the end of the test phase. Whether or not approval is received will determine whether you move onto the deployment phase and release the solution.

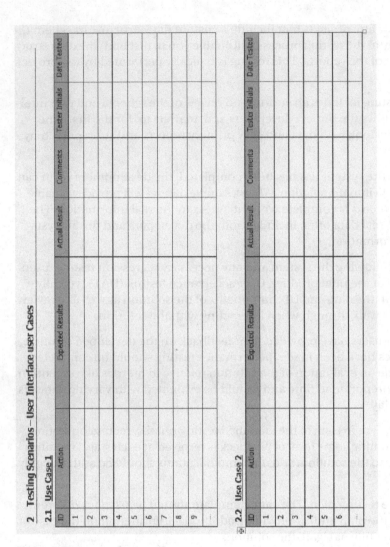

Figure 8-6. *A sample test plan*

Releasing the Solution During the Deployment Phase

Several different things occur during the deployment phase, prior to releasing the solution. The appropriate level of training needs to occur at various levels of the organization. After the training is completed, the deployment process can begin.

Training Various Resources

Training should occur for various roles across the organization:

End users and analysts: Training for end users and analysts would include information for the individuals or teams that are going to regularly use the solution. This training should include basic information on accessing the reports and dashboards and, probably more importantly for this group, instructions on manipulating the results by filtering or tweaking the result sets to allow them to produce different reports depending on the management business needs or questions.

Managers and executives: This training will likely be at a higher level than end user or analyst training and should include an overview of the reports and dashboards available and how to interact with them. Executive training typically also includes a functionality overview of the capabilities of the solution, so managers are better prepared to ask the users and analysts for the appropriate information when the situation arises.

Administrators: Administrator training frequently includes information about how the solution was developed and what components exist requiring regular support and maintenance. Frequently, administrator resources are the first line of defense for usability questions or concerns, so a detailed understanding of what is available is important.

Each of these training sessions should provide an appropriate-level overview of the solution and how it directly relates to the specific roles. Just as important is providing a mechanism for ongoing training and review of the solution. These training items can include the following:

Quick reference guides: These guides are often delivered as simple, two-paged PowerPoint presentations that can be printed, laminated, and posted on a user's wall. Quick reference guides will provide basic information on the solution used regularly, such as running the report, filtering on a primary attribute, and so on.

Detailed training guides: Comprehensive training information is typically presented as part of detailed training manuals. These documents are often longer and contain much more complete information than quick reference guides. Detailed training materials may also contain references to other resources whether internal or external that may help in utilizing the solution.

On-demand or web-based training: This type of training is becoming more and more prevalent for Internet-based or technology-savvy businesses. These trainings are often recorded trainings of a user taking specific actions that can be posted on internal (or external) web sites for download and review by users.

Releasing the Solution

Once training has been completed, it is time for you to deploy the solution. This process begins by development of a deployment plan with the information necessary to ensure a smooth, issue-free deployment process. This often includes the process associated with

- Backups
- Code releases

- Postdeployment refresher training

- Disaster recovery

As backup plans, release procedures, and disaster recovery are all extremely environment specific and depend on the solution and your existing infrastructure, we won't provide specific steps. Completion of a deployment plan is another step that is often unfortunately overlooked, but it definitely represents a document of extreme importance should any problems arise.

Many of our clients utilize an Intranet site, or an application like SharePoint to display information for internal users. Exercise 8-1 is provided as supplemental material for those who are looking to go beyond the sample database and leverage existing SharePoint assets, and provides an example of how to deploy a new dashboard in SharePoint. By doing this, the dashboard may reach a broader set of internal users. This approach may also make the report or dashboard available to those not normally using this line of business application.

Exercise 8-1. Using SharePoint for Rendering SSRS Reports

This exercise provides an example of how to deploy a report as part of the solution release process. This deployment could include any report or dashboard, and this exercise focuses on utilizing SharePoint as the hosting application.

1. Open Internet Explorer. Navigate to your reporting server (often `http://localhost/reports`). After the page loads, click the Upload File button, which is shown in Figure 8-7.

Figure 8-7. *The Upload File button*

2. Navigate to an `.rdl` file that was previously created. Click OK to load the report into the report manager. Double-click the report to render it. If there are any errors, return to Visual Studio, and edit the report. The report shown in Figure 8-8 does not have any errors. Copy the URL from this report.

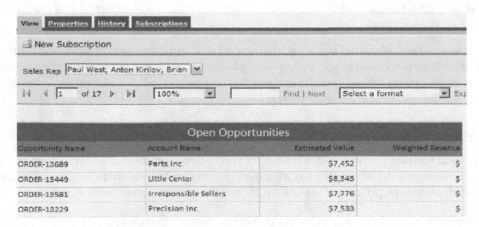

Figure 8-8. *An error-free report example*

3. Open a new window in Internet Explorer. Navigate to SharePoint 2007. As displayed in Figure 8-9, the link can be found at the top of Internet Explorer.

Figure 8-9. *The SharePoint 2007 button*

4. Click Site Actions. Select Edit Page, which is the second option shown in Figure 8-10.

Figure 8-10. *The Site Actions menu*

5. Select Add a Web Part, and select the Report Viewer Web Part. Click the "edit" button in the Report Viewer pane, and select Modify Shared Web Part, which is the third option from the bottom in Figure 8-11.

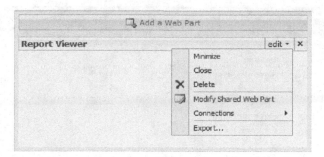

Figure 8-11. *The Report Viewer's "edit" menu*

6. Paste the URL of the report, which was copied in step 2, into the Report Manager URL. SharePoint uses the Report Path to determine which report in the Report Manager should be displayed. The report path is a small portion of the report's URL. Paste the URL into the Report Path field, and delete everything before "/Report" in the Report Path. Alter the other Web Part properties as necessary. None of the report properties must be modified for the report to be displayed in SharePoint. However, modifying some properties, like height and width, will make the report presentation better. Click OK. Once the web part has been modified, the SharePoint page will resemble Figure 8-12.

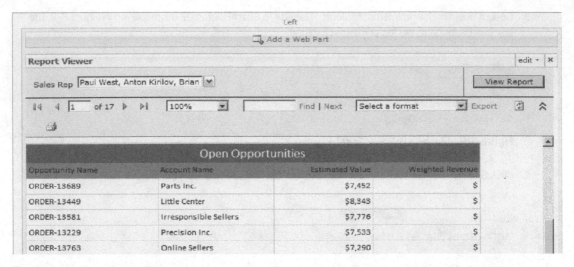

Figure 8-12. *A report web part*

7. To get out of edit mode, click the Exit Edit Mode link on the right-hand side. The final version of the report in SharePoint will look like Figure 8-13.

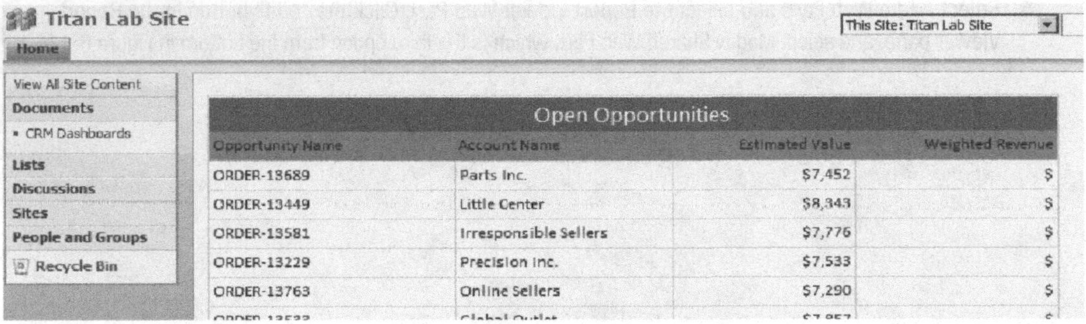

Figure 8-13. *A final report*

With most projects, after a reporting or dashboard solution is deployed, some users will find tremendous value in the deliverable, and others will wish it displayed slightly or drastically different information. At this point, the project team is responsible for coordinating feedback requests, managing user opinions, and above all else, continuing to drive some level of excitement with the solution.

Maintaining the System

Once the solution is deployed and has been supported for a brief period of time following release, you are ready to move into the maintenance phase of the implementation. This phase includes core solution maintenance items as well as some things that allow you to continue to grow and enhance the existing solution.

Performing Core Maintenance

Several basic items should be maintained following deployment. To begin with, backing up the data associated with any custom schemas is important. This should be easily accomplished by incorporating the new data structure into the standard backup strategy of your organization. Without prescribing a specific strategy (as they are typically specific to the solution), ensuring that backups occur regularly and are maintained both onsite and offsite are two important things to consider.

Of equal importance is keeping any training documentation up to date. As either the tools or processes change, training documentation should change with them. If your company is regularly hiring new people, this training documentation will be the tool utilized to bring them up to speed on the solution.

Finally, ensuring that the data is in good condition is also something for you to consider. You should make sure that the data itself contains no irregularities and ensure that users are keeping information on which the solutions depend up to date. For the second item, you can use a simple report to track application and data usage and staleness. Figure 8-17 provides one example of how this could look.

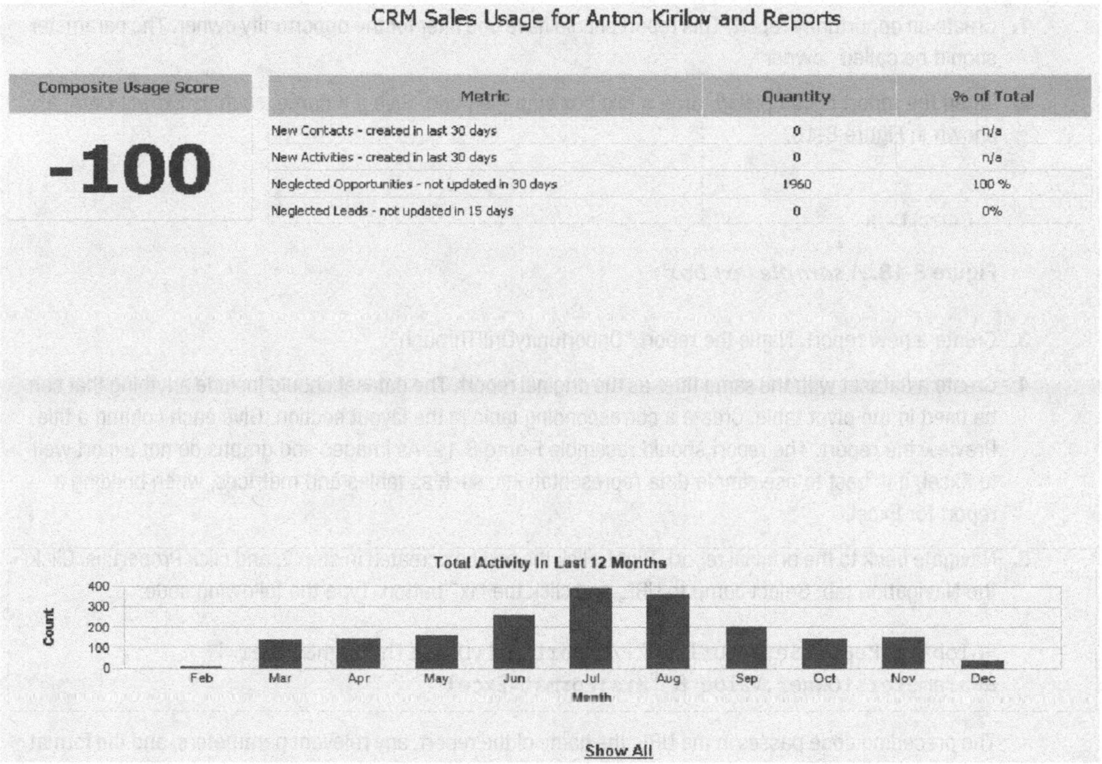
CRM Sales Usage for Anton Kirilov and Reports
Composite Usage Score
-100
Metric
Quantity
% of Total
New Contacts - created in last 30 days
0
n/a
New Activities - created in last 30 days
0
n/a
Neglected Opportunities - not updated in 30 days
1960
100 %
Neglected Leads - not updated in 15 days
0
0%
Total Activity In Last 12 Months
Count
400
300
200
100
0
Feb
Mar
Apr
May
Jun
Jul
Aug
Sep
Oct
Nov
Dec
Month
Show All

Figure 8-17. *A sample usage report*

Moving Past the Initial Implementation

The other maintenance components associated with most analytics projects is the ongoing capture, triage, and, if appropriate, implementation of new features and requests. To make sure this process goes smoothly, many of the concepts outlined earlier in this chapter can be reimplemented and utilized on a smaller scale as these new features are added.

Exercise 8-2 gives one example of how this process can work. For this exercise, let's assume we deployed a sales dashboard during our initial project phase. As users continue to use the information presented, there are many requests for more detailed or granular information about one of the displayed charts. This exercise will show how to take our existing dashboard and augment it to include a drill-through link with additional detail.

Exercise 8-2. Moving Seamlessly from Dashboards to Transactional Reports

This exercise showcases an opportunity sales report. The report filters by owner and has an Extract Data link that will automatically export the detailed data to Excel. SSRS contains functionality to do this, so there is no need for custom code. Here are the steps to follow:

1. Create an opportunity report. This report should have one filter for the opportunity owner. The parameter should be called "owner".

2. When the report is completed, drag a text box onto the page. Give it a name, such as Extract Data, as shown in Figure 8-18.

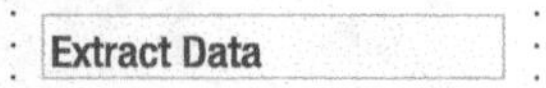

> Extract Data

Figure 8-18. *A sample text box*

3. Create a new report. Name the report "OpportunityDrillThrough".

4. Create a dataset with the same filter as the original report. The dataset should include anything that can be used in the pivot table. Create a corresponding table in the layout section. Give each column a title. Preview the report. The report should resemble Figure 8-19. As images and graphs do not export well to Excel, it is best to use simple data representations, such as tables and matrices, when building a report for Excel.

5. Navigate back to the original report. Right-click the text box created in step 2, and click Properties. Click the Navigation tab. Select Jump to URL, and click the "fx" button. Type the following code:

```
=Globals!ReportServerUrl & "?/OpportunityDrillThrough&Owner="
&Parameters!Owner.Value & "&rs:Format=Excel"
```

The preceding code passes in the URL, the name of the report, any relevant parameters, and the format in which the report should be rendered. In this case, the parameter is the owner parameter, and the report will render in Excel. When this is done, save the changes, and close the window.

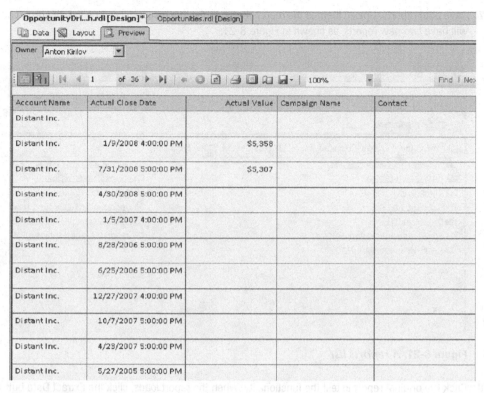

Figure 8-19. *A sample table*

6. The modified Navigation tab will look like Figure 8-20. Click OK to close the Textbox Properties dialog.

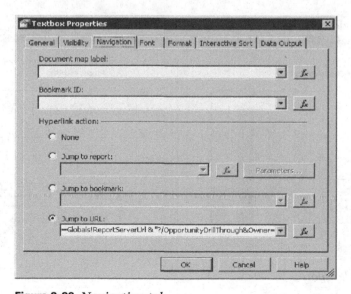

Figure 8-20. *Navigation tab*

7. Save both reports. Upload them to the report server. When this process is completed, the report server will have two new reports, as shown in Figure 8-21.

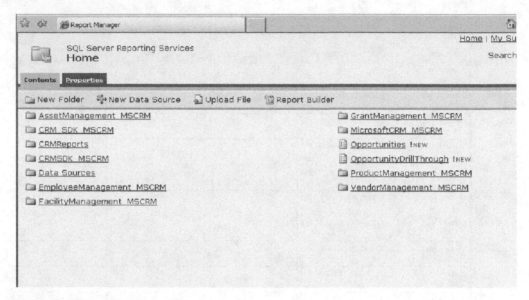

Figure 8-21. *A reports list*

8. Click the original report to test the functionality. When the report loads, click the Extract Data button, which is on the report itself. A sample report is shown in Figure 8-22.

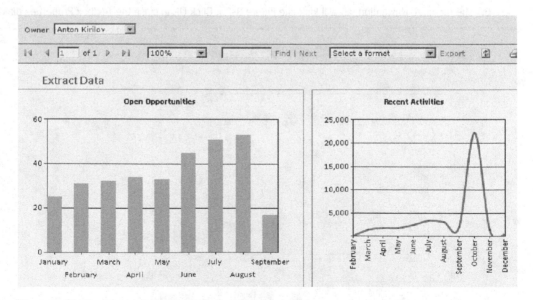

Figure 8-22. *Our sample report*

9. A window will appear, asking if the new Excel file should be opened or saved. Select Open. You should see results like those in Figure 8-23.

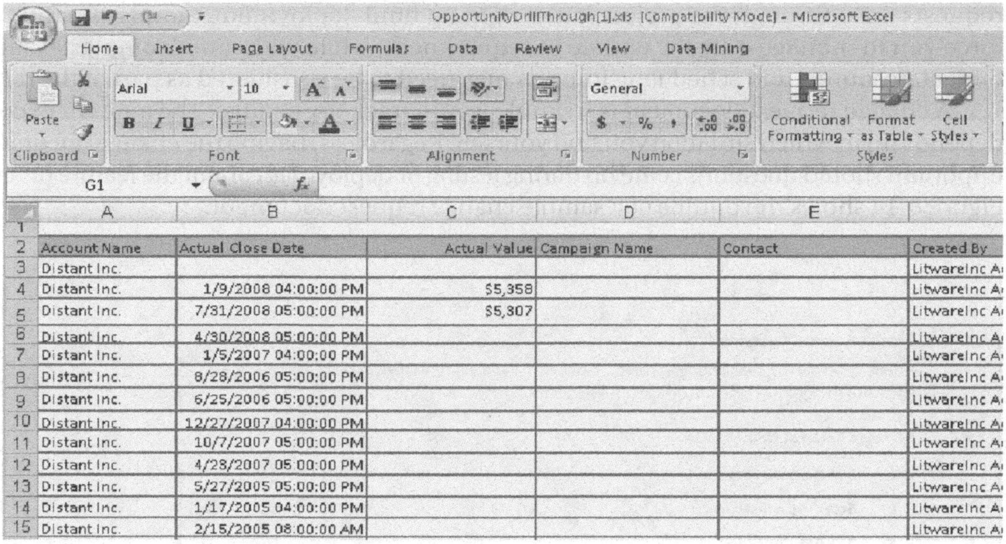

Figure 8-23. *Extracted data*

At this point, the data can be manipulated and analyzed in any manner. For example, it can be converted to a table, and the Data Mining Add-In can be used to categorize and sort opportunities.

Performing Overall Project Management Tasks

Numerous project management concepts have been explained throughout this chapter. While many of these components fall specifically into one of the previous phases, overall project management and the associated concepts span each of the phases of the implementation and should be considered regularly during the engagement.

Categorizing Project Management Tasks

Typically project management tasks for an analytics initiative can be lumped into the following categories:

- Scope management
- Budget management
- Schedule management
- Resource management
- Status reporting

Managing the Scope

After the scope is finalized in the envisioning phase of the implementation, project managers can shift into scope management mode. For virtually all implementations, additional scope requests arise through the project, often right up until deployment. Simple situations may force you to manage only the update in requirement, while with more complex examples, budget, resource, and scheduling impacts may need to be considered as part of the request.

A change request document is a simple way to track the change. The amount of content depends on in which situation you find yourself. Regardless, having the change documented is important should questions come up during testing or deployment about the feature or function. Figure 8-14 shows the outline of a sample change request document.

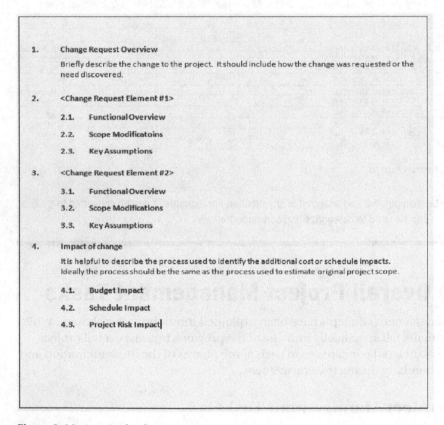

Figure 8-14. *A sample change request*

Managing Budgets

For most implementations, internal or external, a budget is always associated with the solution. Whether that budget is internal resources and their associated efforts, or the investment to hire a consulting organization to complete the work, being able to regularly provide a budget status to the project sponsor and steering committee is important.

Various technologies can be used for tracking this information, depending on the situation and complexity of the project. For internal implementations, a simple accounting for how much time a resource has spent should be sufficient. For implementations involving consulting or external resources, you can use simple tools like Microsoft Excel to track weekly hours and spending against an initial budget. These tools can also be used to track any change requests that arise and to enable reporting on their overall impact to the budget and implementation.

Managing the Schedule

Within an identified scope, tasks should always be specified that enable you, as the project manager, to track short-term progress toward the end solution. These tasks can range from menial to complex and can be extremely short in duration or longer running, sometimes for the whole project. Overall, these tasks can be combined to identify and report on the overall project schedule or the schedule associated with a specific phase.

Frequently, detailed tasks are used by the project team on a period-to-period (often week-to-week) basis to gauge project progress. Because many analytics implementations are weeks or months in duration, judging the progress based on detailed tasks is difficult. So, it becomes important to provide a historical accounting of the tasks completed as well as a prediction of tasks to come. While tasks sometimes take more or less time than anticipated, if predicted tasks are continually not completed, this is likely a red flag on the project status.

Managing Resources

Resource management is a project management task that is typically split between the project manager and the project sponsor. For most implementations, the project manager is responsible for ensuring resources are appropriately allocated to project tasks and are making the necessary progress toward the end deliverable. Should any resource allocation issues arise, it is the project manager's responsibility to work to ensure the proper alignment.

Unfortunately, in most situations, project managers lack the authority to reassign resources if required. This is where the project sponsor can be engaged to assist with making sure those involved in the project are working on the appropriate tasks. Alternatively, if resources are required elsewhere, the project sponsor (combined with the steering committee) is responsible for approving the change in project schedule.

Reporting on the Project's Status

Once you are tracking all of these items related to project status, it is important to make them available to the project team in a concise, easy-to-read way that doesn't take too much time to review. Figure 8-15 provides an example status report that covers all of these project items.

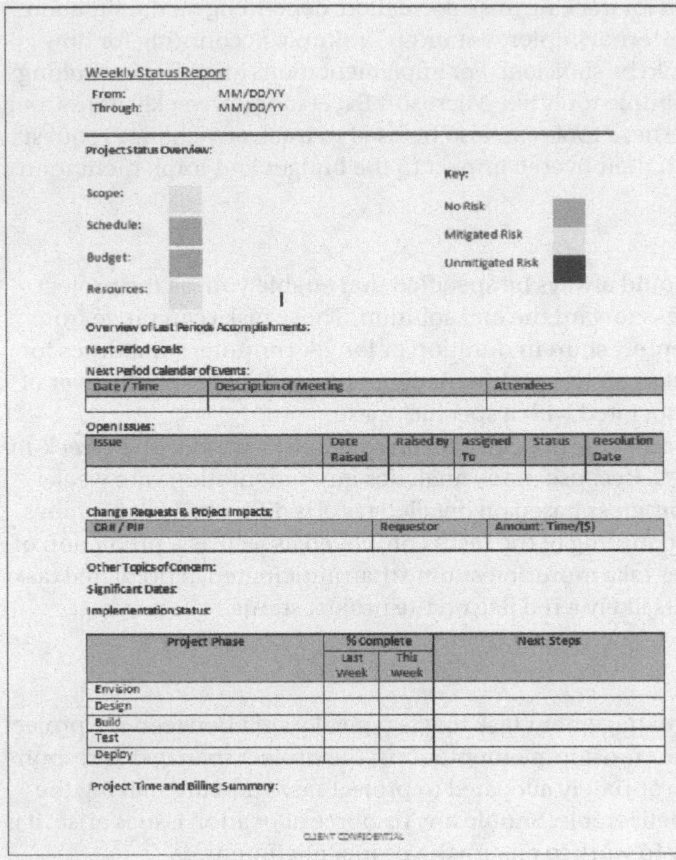

Weekly Status Report

From: MM/DD/YY
Through: MM/DD/YY

Project Status Overview:

Scope:
Schedule:
Budget:
Resources:

Key:
No Risk
Mitigated Risk
Unmitigated Risk

Overview of Last Periods Accomplishments:

Next Period Goals:

Next Period Calendar of Events:

Date / Time	Description of Meeting	Attendees

Open Issues:

Issue	Date Raised	Raised By	Assigned To	Status	Resolution Date

Change Requests & Project Impacts:

CR# / PI#	Requestor	Amount: Time/($)

Other Topics of Concern:

Significant Dates:

Implementation Status:

Project Phase	% Complete Last Week	% Complete This Week	Next Steps
Envision			
Design			
Build			
Test			
Deploy			

Project Time and Billing Summary:

CLIENT CONFIDENTIAL

Figure 8-15. *A sample status report*

Using SharePoint As a Project Management Tool

Whether using it as a mechanism to capture the project status reports or as a more comprehensive solution to track all project documents, manage code, and so on, SharePoint can be a productive project management tool.

At a basic level, the document check-in and check-out capabilities allow you to manage documents and code so that multiple versions aren't created. Varying levels of security allow you to manage permissions to different sets of material and prevent resources from having access to information that isn't appropriate. In addition, SharePoint web parts can be used to directly display information, such as status reports, on the home page of the project site. This enables you to point users to a central place and avoids having to contribute to what often amounts to too many daily e-mails.

Figure 8-16 shows an example of what a project site might look like. It presents a number of document libraries, any new project news, upcoming events, issues, and a number of other items.

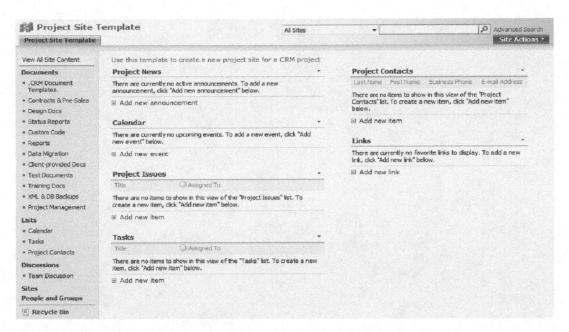

Figure 8-16. *A sample SharePoint project site*

Overall project management is one of the most time-consuming tasks that exist as part of an analytics project. Using some of the tools identified in this chapter will enable you to manage and track the appropriate information.

Summary

The various project management processes and tools outlined through this chapter should enable you to be more successful during analytics implementations. While many implementations may not require use of all the tools, this chapter should provide an overview of some of the tools available.

Tools like SharePoint, Excel, and Word, the technologies necessary to develop many of these documents and sites, are likely available currently within your environment. Overall, carefully selecting the important components of the different project management phases will allow you to have a tighter control of the project and will mean more success during implementation and after, while maintaining the solution.

CHAPTER 9

■ ■ ■

Case Studies

Throughout previous chapters of this book, we have discussed the appropriate steps to go through as you plan and execute your BI initiative, as well as the technologies available via the Microsoft platform. In this chapter, we will provide three examples of how the Microsoft BI platform has been leveraged within different organizations. The examples explore reporting in an online or a cloud environment; complex, multirole sales and marketing reporting; and detailed web analytics. Specifically, we will outline the challenges each organization was experiencing, the solution that was implemented, and the results that the clients achieved. These solutions were implemented by our consulting firm, Madrona Solutions Group, for our clients, and examples of the deliverables and code will be provided, where possible while still maintaining confidentiality of the organization involved.

Case Study 1: Reporting in a Hosted Business Application Environment

Our consulting team was engaged by a large, global organization providing testing and measurement equipment and services for the healthcare industry. The employees of this company strive to be the best at delivering innovative solutions to improve the quality of global health. They serve biomedical engineers, radiation physicists, and oncologists, and they are continually expanding their range of solutions to a broader group of health and safety professionals. The client organization was a subsidiary of a much larger Fortune 500 organization based in the Pacific Northwest.

While this project was specific to the subsidiary business, many of the standard challenges are associated with working IT organizations of larger companies. In this case, server maintenance, software costs, and access to other enterprise systems were factors in selecting the eventual solution.

Prior to undertaking this project, organizational staff members lacked important information about their customers and found that routine tasks like preparing sales reports were cumbersome and inaccurate. They decided to address these issues with a more comprehensive analytics solution associated with their CRM application.

Identifying the Customer's Challenges

Because of the highly interactive and high-touch nature of the business, being able to track and report on the volume of activity (e-mails, meetings, and phone calls) with customers is extremely important. Not having access to this information reduced the company's effectiveness with regard to staffing sales positions and knowing which customers were ultimately the most profitable per interaction. Additionally, sales managers struggled to coach the sales team, since identifying where sales team members were getting hung up during the sales cycle was difficult when their levels of interaction (or lack thereof) were difficult to determine.

In addition to these challenges associated with the sales team, the company's previous analytics applications required a significant amount of manual intervention to generate valuable reports. Frequently, information needed to be solicited and gathered from each sales person, consolidated on a per-sales-manager basis, and then consolidated further for sales and overall company executives.

Additional challenges for the organization included the following:

- Even after eventually gathering all the appropriate sales data, the users, managers, and executives did not have the ability to slice and dice the data to meet their needs. A small number of reports were available that provided relatively flat views of information.

- While sales management coached individual representatives on the appropriate process for selling their products, the sales process itself was not reflected in the existing pipeline reports, making it difficult to accurately forecast product sales and subsequent manufacturing needs.

- Existing sales and analytics tools did not provide the ability to deeply analyze sales information. Sales managers desired the capability to analyze the velocity with which each opportunity moved through the various sales stages in order to assist sellers with managing the process.

- The creation of sales forecasts for the subsidiary executives and parent company management was an extremely time-consuming, manual process that left several opportunities for human errors.

In summary, the objectives of the engagement were to provide a platform that enabled consolidated reporting on the team's interactions with customers. The project team was also tasked with providing improved sales forecasting and pipeline management tools. Finally, whatever tools were deployed needed to be able to grow with the business.

Exploring the Solution

The client organization deployed Microsoft Dynamics CRM Online for simplified data collection and leveraged SSRS for reporting. This has resulted in excellent user adoption and better business analytics. Management now has more sales information available for making decisions and is able to compile that information more rapidly.

Microsoft Dynamics CRM Online is a platform for managing customer relationships and tracking key sales, support, and marketing activities. But, like many of our clients, this organization needed to go beyond the out-of-the-box reporting capabilities offered by Dynamics CRM. Because of that, many users leverage the ad hoc reporting capabilities available using Microsoft Excel or the Dynamics CRM Reporting Wizard to generate quick, simple SSRS reports.

For the more complex reporting needs, Madrona Solutions data replication and reporting for Microsoft Dynamics CRM Online delivered a complete solution with custom dashboards. The solution leverages Dynamics CRM Online as the data provider and replicates this data to a local SQL Server instance. The replicated data is then used to deliver custom dashboards and reports that are rendered from within Dynamics CRM Online. As a result of this company's internal challenges associated with infrastructure management, Dynamics CRM Online allows for a subscription-based license model that provides a robust support structure, low up-front license costs, and the ability to effectively manage the entire CRM instance. The data replication and reporting solution inherently has a relatively small amount of maintenance and upkeep but still allows the organization to completely own their reporting solution.

While there are multiple approaches that can be used to build this data reporting and online reporting solution, we will share one simple approach that only requires an organization to use an existing SQL Server Standard license (and server) to both host the data retrieval components (SSIS packages) and to maintain the replicated data. Figure 9-1 provides a high-level overview of how the process works.

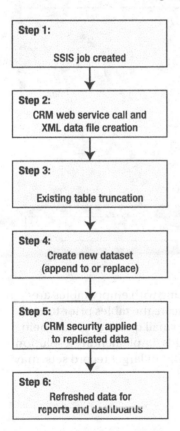

Figure 9-1. *The case study 1 solution overview*

Following is a detailed description of the steps shown in Figure 9-1:

1. As Figure 9-2 shows, an SSIS job is created using SQL Server Management Studio (SSMS). During the first step, you create an Execute Process Task to call Dynamics CRM web services and download the Web Service Description Language (WSDL) files. Our consulting team wrote C# code to authenticate against Dynamics CRM Online using a set of administrator credentials and the organization's name. This C# code then calls the Dynamics CRM Online instance and retrieves the requested information as XML.

2. The SSIS task, or job, contains a step in which a custom assembly will be called that will connect to the Dynamics CRM Online web services, and the resulting, returned data will be an XML file for the relevant CRM entity.

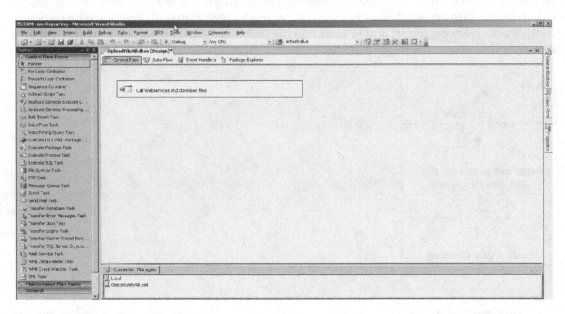

Figure 9-2. *SSIS task creation*

3. While appending the data to the existing dataset and starting with empty tables are both options, as Figure 9-3 shows, we have chosen to truncate the tables prior to each data load. We made this decision because of the relatively small quantity of data being replicated and to eliminate the potential for duplicate records. Implementing a solution to append the data would require additional effort and, without larger record sets, may not be necessary.

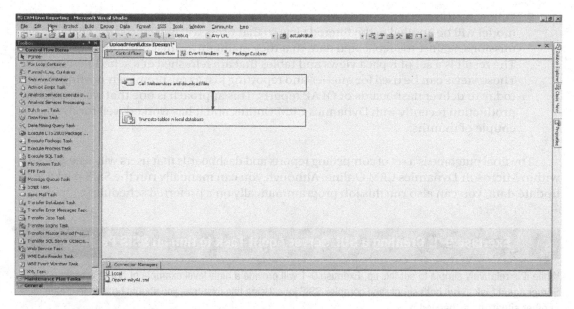

Figure 9-3. *Table truncation*

4. After you have deleted all of the data in your tables, create Data Flow Tasks to load all of the data in those tables. The number of data flow tasks will depend on the number of different types of data being loaded. As Figure 9-4 shows, the SSIS job will contain a setup that will format this data and load the extract into a replica of the Dynamics CRM– filtered view for the relevant entity. This step also grabs the XML files, created earlier, and generates the XML schema, defining the elements and attributes.

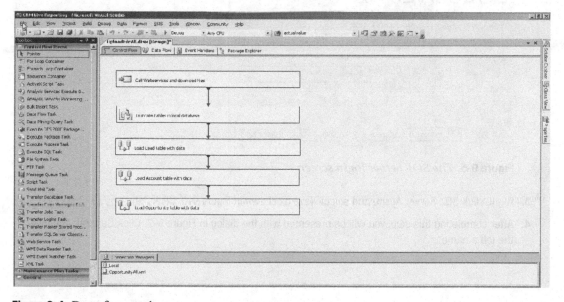

Figure 9-4. *Data formatting*

5. Following the extraction and formatting of the data, the core Dynamics CRM security model will be applied to the filtered view so that users will have the same visibility permissions against the replicated data that they maintain against the online application. The result is a set of replica views and tables that are refreshed at a scheduled interval. These views can be used for queries and reporting just as on-premise reporting is done today to deliver dashboards or OLAP reports. This approach is one that we've used in production recently with Dynamics CRM Online, and it has worked well for the past couple of months.

The final outcome is a set of compelling reports and dashboards that users will access from within Microsoft Dynamics CRM Online. Although you can manually run the SSIS package to update data, you can also run this job programmatically on a preferred schedule.

Exercise 9-1. Creating a SQL Server Agent Task to Run an SSIS Package

While it is relatively simple to set this up, Exercise 9-1 will provide a high-level example of how to create a SQL Server agent task to run both simple and complex SSIS jobs. Using this example, you should be able to create these in other situations as needed.

1. SSMS ships with most versions of Microsoft SQL Server. Navigate to Start ➤ All Programs ➤ SQL Server ➤ SQL Server Management Studio.

2. Connect to your Database Engine, as shown in Figure 9-5.

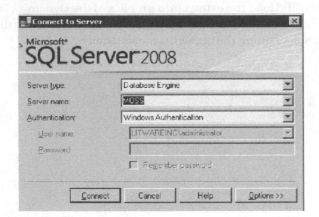

Figure 9-5. *The SQL Server login screen*

3. Right-click SQL Server Agent, and select New, as shown in Figure 9-6. Click Job.

4. After completing this step, you will be presented with the dialog in Figure 9-7. Click General, and give the job a name.

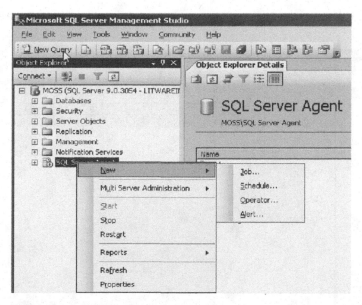

Figure 9-6. *New job creation*

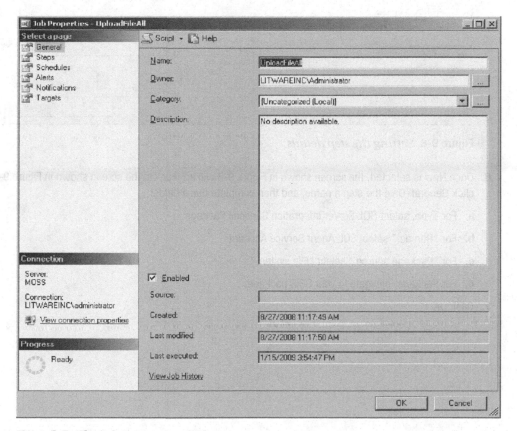

Figure 9-7. *The Job Properties dialog*

5. Click Steps and then New. When you click Steps, you'll be presented with the window shown in Figure 9-8.

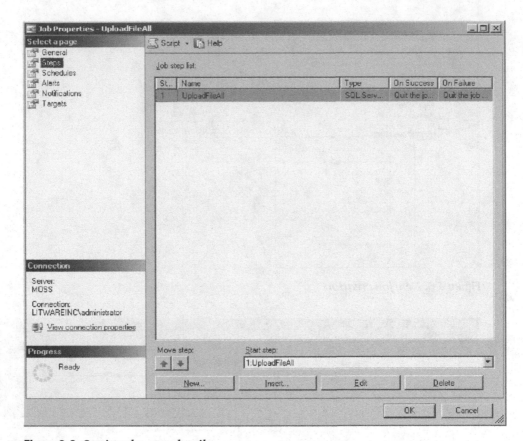

Figure 9-8. *Setting the step details*

6. Once New is selected, the screen shown in Figure 9-8 will appear. On the screen shown in Figure 9-9, click General. Give the step a name, and then complete these fields:

   a. For Type, select SQL Server Integration Services Package.

   b. For "Run as," select SQL Agent Service Account.

   c. For "Package source," select "File system".

   d. For Package, navigate to your SSIS package.

7. Click OK.

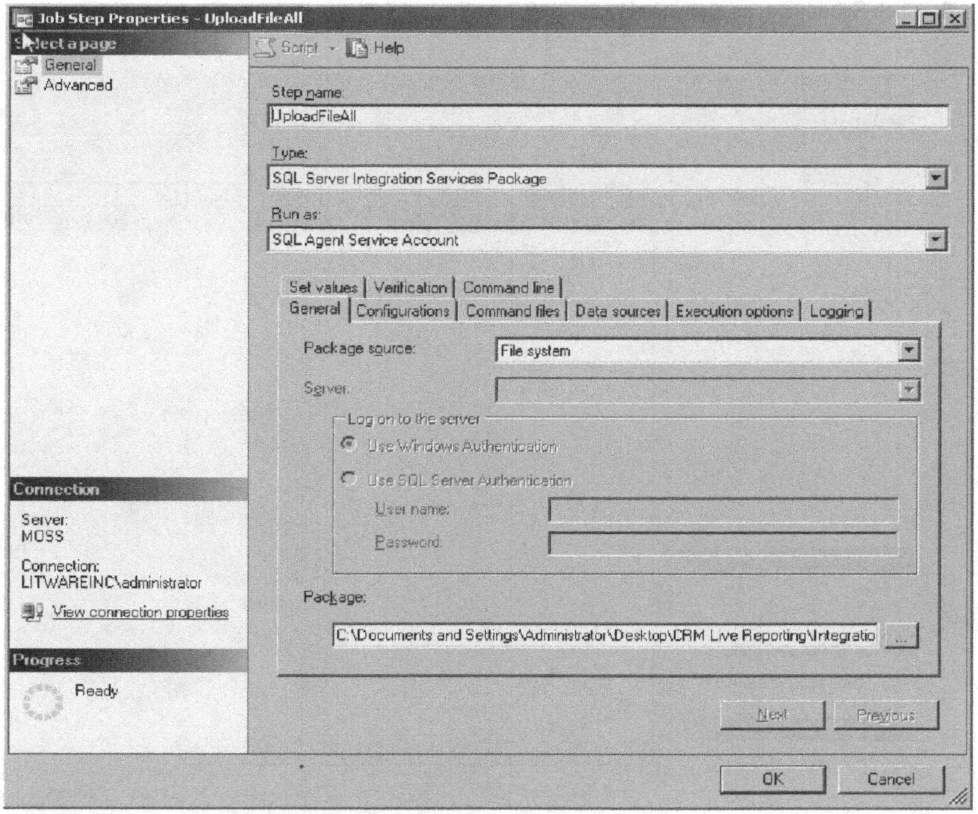

Figure 9-9. *Setting the job details*

8. Click Schedules, as shown in Figure 9-10, and then click New.

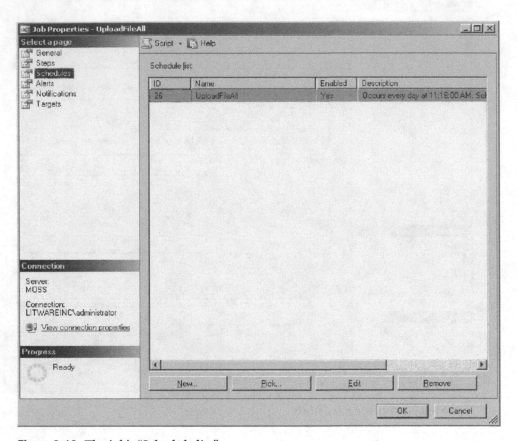

Figure 9-10. *The job's "Schedule list"*

9. Fill in desired values for the SSIS package to run on a schedule, as shown in Figure 9-11, and click OK.

10. The SQL Server agent job will be created successfully, and you will be presented with the window shown in Figure 9-12.

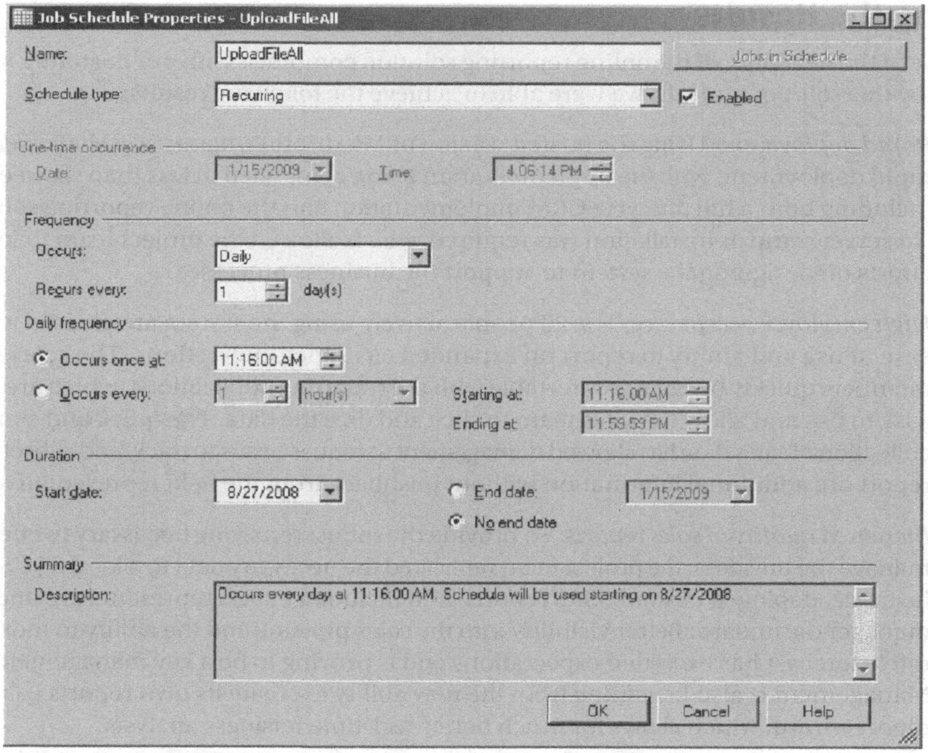

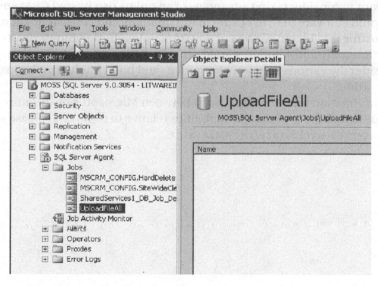

Figure 9-11. *SSIS schedule options*

Figure 9-12. *SQL Server agent job*

Seeing the Results

Because of the flexibility of the online reporting solution combined with our customer's desire to deploy this solution quickly, we were able to achieve the following results:

- *Rapid deployment*: Using the hosted version of Microsoft Dynamics CRM allowed for rapid deployment, with the implementation being completed in less than six weeks and including both a full life cycle CRM implementation and the online reporting solutions. No server setup or installation was required, which allowed the project team to focus its efforts on designing the system to support the business processes.

- *High employee acceptance*: The 20 people actively using the system are pleased with the ease of use and ability to report on expanded customer interactions. The sales staff members quickly became comfortable with the reporting applications, which are, again, easy to use and allow the sales team to slice and dice the data. The quick and simple collection of sales data has allowed management to request users to track, and subsequently report on, additional information without pushback from the field representatives.

- *Increased quality of sales reports*: To provide the robust reporting necessary to effectively manage the business, the project team replicated the necessary data to a local SQL Server instance, deployed custom SSRS reports, and included a sales representative and sales manager dashboard. Better visibility into the sales pipeline and the ability to more accurately forecast has exceeded expectations and is proving to be a key management tool. Management is also benefiting from the new ability to create its own reports using the report wizard, which allows for much better real-time business analysis.

An example of the solution deployed for the sales managers is shown in Figure 9-13.

While you and your organization may have reasons to implement an on-premise CRM application, you may want to consider taking advantage of an online or a hosted CRM environment. However, you should be aware that, to ensure maintainability and consistency across all hosted services, your hosting provider may prevent you from uploading customer reports into the environment. This case study and solution should provide you with the information necessary to completely consider the various solution alternatives and build a solution that works well within your organization.

For more general information on the comparisons between Microsoft's on-premise and hosted CRM environments, and the associated capabilities relative to reporting, please see http://msdn.microsoft.com/en-us/library/cc299424.aspx.

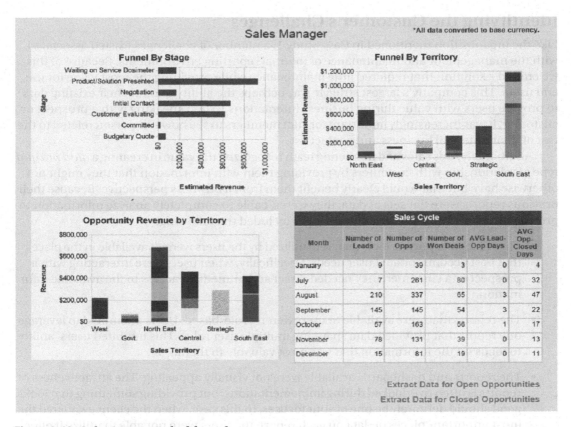

Figure 9-13. *Sales Manager dashboard*

Case Study 2: Implementing Embedded Analytics

Another of our customers was a large Fortune 50 organization that required the ability to present complex, custom reports to sales and marketing users across all levels of the organization.

Prior to this project, our customer's demanding users had to navigate to various, unintuitive parts of their primary business application to find relevant information about the folks with whom they interact as part of their day-to-day roles within the organization. Many of the necessary reports existed outside of the standard business application and were hosted in applications like SharePoint or on random file shares.

Finally, while the organization possessed the ability to generate complete, single-entity reports, it required reports and dashboards that could effectively analyze the data available within the CRM application. It also needed to provide contextual reporting quickly to assist in making business decisions.

Identifying the Customer's Challenges

Like the organization mentioned in Case Study 1, a number of challenges existed associated with the management and maintenance of internal reporting environments. Because of this, we crafted a solution that required little maintenance while providing the most value for the end users. This company's largest struggle was perhaps the ability to mine their existing data to provide users with value during business interactions. When speaking with a prospect or customer, it was increasingly important for staff members to see how this person related to the rest of their potential business and contact list.

Additionally, this sales and marketing team recognized the value in creating a *quid pro quo* type of relationship with customers by providing them with information that they might not otherwise have but that would clearly benefit them from a business perspective. Because their previous reports were flat sets of data, they weren't able to completely analyze information to provide the necessary value. Other challenges included the following:

- The valuable reporting tools that were utilized by the users weren't available in the places that best accommodated user needs. Specifically, when users were interacting with a prospect or a customer, they needed direct and immediate access to the available information.

- The reports that were available to users weren't role-based. Users attempted to leverage one report that provided data spanning multiple user roles. This inhibited users' ability to focus on the information that was most valuable to them.

- The reports and dashboards available were not visually appealing. The attractiveness of reports is often overlooked during implementations, but providing something that looks good should definitely be one of your focuses. In this case, when the client evaluated the most important pieces of data on each report, the users were not able to utilize it effectively because it was buried or difficult to find.

Exploring the Solution

The team implemented a phased, role-based solution that presented information to all users, from top to bottom, within the organization. A number of stand-alone reports and dashboards were made available at both entity-specific (account, contact, opportunity, etc.) and summary (sales pipeline, activity summary, etc.) levels.

Specifically, the team provided analytical information embedded within various entity forms throughout the CRM application. This information allowed users to open a specific account or contact record and find valuable information for themselves and the prospect or customer. For example, on the contact-at-a-glance dashboard, shown in Figure 9-14, the sales user was able to provide the customer with a set of contacts that have similar roles in the same geographic area so that customer could network with them as appropriate.

Note In Figure 9-14, the Activity Goals gauge changes color based on an activity goal set for each contact record. For contacts that have the defined number of CRM activities associated, the gauge is green. For those that are close to the goal, the gauge is yellow, and for those contacts well short of the defined activity goal, the gauge is red.

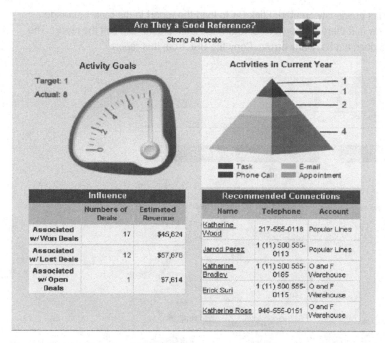

Figure 9-14. *An embedded analytics example*

For those of you utilizing Dynamics CRM, Example 9-2 shows how to take a report or dashboard similar to the one in Figure 9-14 and embed the analytics within a CRM entity, making it available on a specific record when that record is opened. The concept presented in this exercise, displaying information within a line of business application, is important to consider regardless of the business application you use.

Exercise 9-2. Implementing Embedded Analytics

In this exercise, you will load an opportunity-specific report into a tab on the opportunity form. You'll need to be familiar with SSRS, including creating queries and manipulating report parameters.

Here are the steps to follow:

1. In SSRS, create a report with the following parameters: `id`, `type`, `typename`, `orgname`, `userlcid`, and `orglcid`. All parameters are type text and can be null or blank. Hide every parameter except `id`. Use the `id` parameter as a filter to bring back only information pertaining to a specific opportunity. For example, a query that brought back the estimated value and estimated close date for an opportunity would look like this:

```
SELECT EstimatedValue
  ,EstimatedCloseDate
FROM FilteredOpportunity
WHERE Opportunityid = @id
```

2. Open Internet Explorer. Navigate to `http://localhost/reports`. After the page loads, click the Upload Report button.

3. Navigate to the `.rdl` that was previously created. Click OK to load the report in the report manager. Double-click the report to view it. If there are any errors, return to Visual Studio, and edit the report. The report shown in Figure 9-15 does not have any errors. Copy the URL from this report.

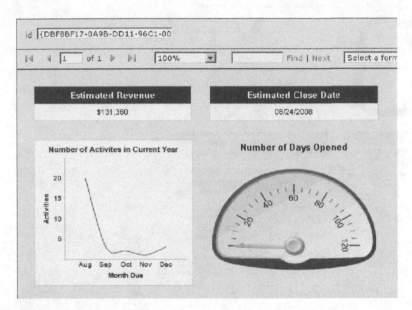

Figure 9-15. *An error-free report*

4. Open a new window in Internet Explorer. Navigate to Microsoft Dynamics CRM.

5. Navigate to Settings ➤ Customizations ➤ Customize Entities ➤ Opportunity ➤ "Forms and Views" ➤ Form. Click "Add a Tab". The window displayed in Figure 9-16 will be shown. Type the name of the tab, and click OK.

6. Click "Add a Section." Type the name of the section, and keep the defaults, as shown in Figure 9-17. Click OK.

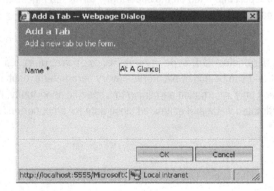

Figure 9-16. *Dynamics CRM Online tab creation*

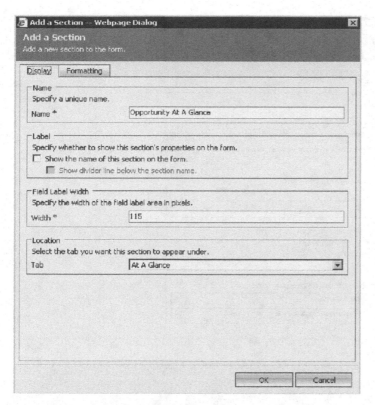

Figure 9-17. *Dynamics CRM Online section creation*

7. Click "Add an IFrame". Give the IFrame a name. Paste the URL copied in step 3 into the URL field. At the end of the URL, type this: **&rs:Command=Render&rc:Toolbar=False**. This text will force the report to automatically render without the toolbar. Check the "Pass record object-type code and unique identifier as parameters" box. When this is done, the General tab will look like Figure 9-18.

8. Navigate to the Formatting tab. Check the "Automatically expand to use available space" box. Make sure Scrolling is set to As Necessary and the "Display border" box is checked. Click OK to exit the IFRAME Properties dialog.

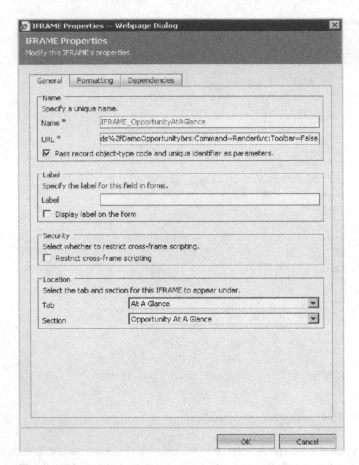

Figure 9-18. *Setting IFrame properties*

9. Click the Save and Close button for the opportunity form. Save the opportunity entity. Click Actions, and then click Publish. Click Save and Close to exit the opportunity entity window. Navigate to Sales ➤ Opportunities ➤ Open Opportunities.

10. Click an opportunity to view the new report. An example is shown in Figure 9-19.

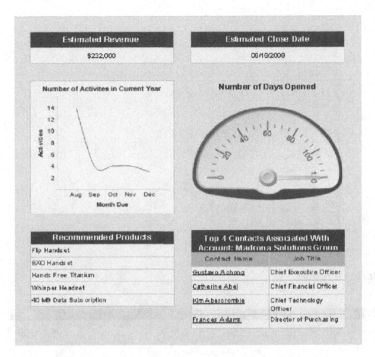

Figure 9-19. *Example embedded opportunity information*

This project also featured some complex, data-rich dashboards that summarized information for sales managers and executives. These reports provide only summary-level information to really focus the user on the results. Additionally, because many sales representatives and sales managers wanted to see individual or team-level summary results, we presented these dashboards throughout the application. Because the reports and dashboards for this client were based on the Dynamics CRM application, Exercise 9-3 shows those of you using this application how to upload such dashboards into Dynamics CRM Online and present them to users.

Exercise 9-3. Connecting Dashboards into the UI for Dynamics CRM Online

Follow these steps to upload and connect a new dashboard into the user interface for Dynamics CRM Online:

1. Use the link on the navigation bar of Internet Explorer to connect to Dynamics CRM Online.

2. Navigate to Workplace ➤ Reports, as shown in Figure 9-20. Click the New button to upload a report into Dynamics CRM.

3. Set the Report Type to Existing File. This will cause the Location field to display. Indicate the file location and name. If the report should show up in any categories or related record types, define these in the Categorization section, displayed in Figure 9-21.

Figure 9-20. *Uploading a report*

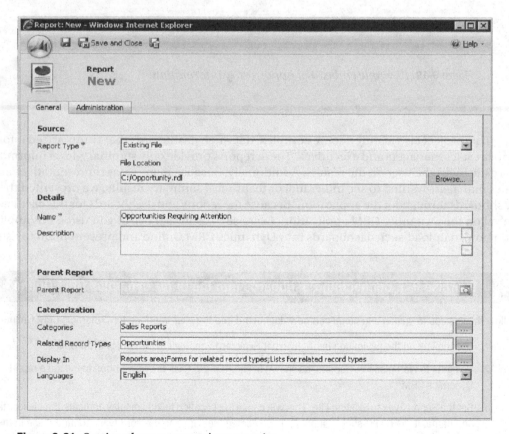

Figure 9-21. *Setting the new report's properties*

4. If the report is configured to appear in the Reports area, it will show up in the list of reports. Double-click the report to run it. If the report is uploaded correctly, it will display data directly from Dynamics CRM. An example of a correctly uploaded report is shown in Figure 9-22.

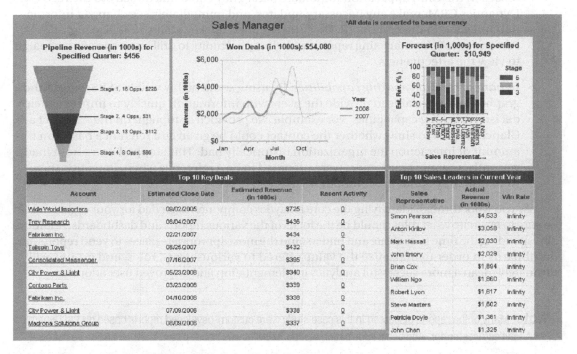

Figure 9-22. *A correctly uploaded report*

Seeing the Results

The resulting application enabled sales users and management team members to view applicable information quickly and easily through their CRM application. Other reports and dashboards that we created using Microsoft Excel or PerformancePoint Server were uploaded into the application and are available in a centralized location. Additionally, the organization was able to see and take advantage of these:

- *Improved data access*: Users across the organization were able to access relevant information throughout the course of their day-to-day activities. Account and contact information was available on those Dynamics CRM entities within the application. Additionally, manual consolidation of data at the sales manager and executive levels was no longer required, making the team more efficient and eliminating the potential for errors associated with manual consolidation.

- *High-quality client and prospect networking*: Because Dynamics CRM users could provide recommended contacts from their networks to prospects and customers to leverage during networking activities, these companies and individuals were much more willing to partner during the sales cycle, resulting in a mutually positive situation.

- *Detailed drill-through capabilities*: Within the Dynamics CRM and PerformancePoint dashboards, we provided the ability to drill through to the underlying data and more detailed reports. For example, sales managers no longer had to navigate to a specific record in the CRM application to validate data. They could link directly to the record in Dynamics CRM, make any necessary updates, and immediately see changed information reflected in the dashboard. Executives gained the key ability to utilize high-level PerformancePoint marketing reports, with the opportunity to drill into a specific campaign to view the effectiveness.

- *Enhanced decision-making capabilities*: By using some highly visible SSRS gauges and graphics, we were able to provide the users with information quickly to improve their decision-making capabilities. For example, we provided a stoplight on the "Contact at a Glance" report to show whether the contact could be given as a reference based on the amount of interaction the organization historically had. This stopped users from inadvertently assuming customers were prepared to be a reference when, in reality, they were unhappy about the company's service.

As you work through identifying the core analytics components needed for your organization, be sure to evaluate what roles should be the focus of the various reports and dashboards. Additionally, spending the time to evaluate and understand the most appropriate places to vend reports and dashboards in order to maximize the value offered to various users, roles, and groups will ultimately mean a more successful analytics implementation and improved user adoption.

■**Note** Many of the reports discussed in this case study were custom-developed reports based on the Dynamics CRM Analytics Accelerator. Additional information can be found at www.codeplex.com/crmaccelerators.

Case Study 3: Adding Web Analytics

We had the opportunity to work with a large software vendor based in the Pacific Northwest to improve and enhance its existing marketing information and web analytics platform. This project included an evaluation of both the user interface components and existing data infrastructure associated with the current solution.

To set the stage for this case study, it is important to present you with an overview of the web marketing and web analytics space. In this case, our customer worked on hundreds of marketing campaigns throughout a specific fiscal year. From a web marketing perspective, each individual campaign included some elements of the following components:

- *Display advertisements*: These are interactive online picture or video advertisements on various web sites that aid in brand building and in gaining the attention of customers considering a purchase.

- *Search engine marketing (SEM)*: This refers to keyword purchases on major search engines used as a reference for finding other information. Keywords are often purchased from search engines in the hopes that they will drive prospective customers actively engaged in making a buying decision.

- *Print or large-format display advertisements*: These large display advertisements are placed at high-profile events, like football games, or appear in print in various periodicals.

Various metrics are commonly associated with each of these marketing components. Depending on which components an organization was purchasing, it might be interested in any or all of the following:

- *Impressions*: Impressions provide a metric on the number of times a specific display advertisement has been viewed.

- *Clicks*: For keyword purchases on primary search engines, click metrics provide the purchaser with an idea of the number of times a specific keyword result was clicked.

- *Cost*: For both impression and click metrics, being able to identify the general costs as well as the costs per click or view is extremely important in developing analysis to gauge the effectiveness of a specific campaign.

Our client had made keyword purchases on the Yahoo, Google, and Microsoft Live search engines. The company also chose to vend display advertisements on a number of major web sites. When evaluating the success or failure of marketing campaigns, the click, impression, and cost data were often challenging to get. While most of the major search vendors have APIs to enable information access, someone with a development skill set is needed to extract and manage the information.

Then too, a number of web analytics applications, such as WebTrends and Omniture, provide click-stream information (the behavior a user exhibits when clicking from a search result to a web site through completing an online product purchase). These tools often provide information on web site downloads and specific page visits, making the search result metrics and data even more important in tying the overall effectiveness together.

Identifying the Customer's Challenges

As you would imagine, with the technical and data management complexity associated with managing marketing campaign effectiveness, our customer struggled to identify which keyword, display advertisement, or overall campaigns have the best ROI. This evaluation process typically mixes external data and internal data, web sites, and databases, so there is often a significant volume of data and not a lot of insight.

Complicating matters is the human intervention associated with browsing the Web. Unfortunately for companies with large web presences, users don't always click where a company wants them to. A user may click a web search result resulting in a tracking token being put on the navigator's machine. From there, the user will navigate to a web site and browse a number of pages looking for information. So far, our search result metrics and web analytics tools can effectively track that click stream. At this point, our user may log off the web site for a couple of days, only to return in a week and make the product purchase. While we have the data showing an end-to-end click process (search result to purchase), we have two reporting challenges:

- We cannot always assume that the original search result was the reason a customer made a purchase. Something in the intervening week may have pushed the customer to make a purchase, and we likely wouldn't know.

- Data from the various search vendors and web analytics tools is often provided on specific days. While it is possible to tie data provided on a number of different days together, it very clearly complicates the situation.

Some other challenges that exist follow:

- For more technically complex organizations, campaign effectiveness reporting also includes data from various line-of-business applications for CRM and ERP.

- Other situations arise when a user navigates through a web site, perhaps making a purchase that is not the result of a search. While tracking this information is important (and available from the web analytics tools), identifying the marketing campaign or campaign component responsible for influencing the purchase is nearly impossible.

Exploring the Solution

The solution developed for this customer involves a noteworthy amount of data consolidation and transformation. In addition to receiving the data from various sources, normalizing and transforming the data that arrives in multiple formats requires a significant amount of time.

The project team leverages the APIs available from Google, Yahoo, and Microsoft to retrieve the information from the various search providers. These extracted data files are consolidated and will serve as the foundation for our analysis of which search engine marketers and keywords are the most effective.

After consolidating the information from the search vendors, the solution deployed for this client consolidated web statistics data from the web analytics vendors. This data arrives in flat or comma-delimited files that require programmatic import in addition to the normalization and transformation mentioned previously.

After all the data has been gathered, an SSIS package that completes the following steps:

1. The package begins by grabbing all the appropriate data.

2. It groups the consolidated data by date and keyword and then merges all the records together.

3. Finally, the SSIS package takes the data and formats it for use in a cube.

Once the SSIS package has run, an SSAS cube is provided to users. Any number of user interfaces can be used to access the data and allow users to pivot on it. In this case, our customer utilized a complex Excel interface to present the information.

Figure 9-23 shows how the data is combined from the various sources and displayed by search provider on a weekly basis.

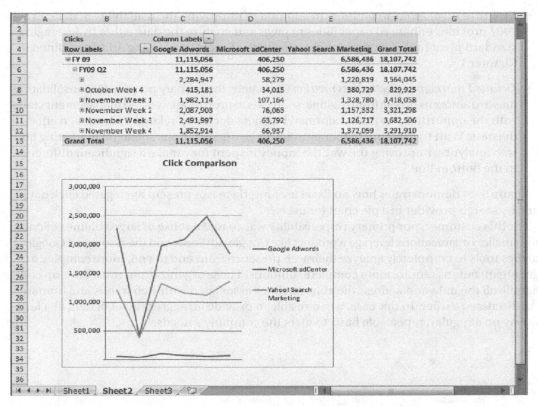

Figure 9-23. *Excel-based pivot table*

Seeing the Results

This project provided our customer with the ability to manage and report on very bewildering data from a number of disparate data sources. As part of the transformation and consolidation process, a complex evaluation was completed by the project team early in the implementation, the solution was able to address a number of the challenges previously identified, including multiday click streams and some of the random human component that is inherent with web usage and traffic.

Our customer was also able to identify the following results:

- *Reduced number of human interactions*: Based on the data evaluation performed at the time of consolidation, many of the inherent abnormalities and challenges associated with extremely high-volume web trend and analytic data were addressed. While a perfect solution to many of these issues is almost impossible, addressing as many of the issues as possible significantly improves the accuracy of the metrics and allows users to better trust the available data (see Chapter 2).

- *Improved data coherence*: For average marketing analysts and managers, information downloaded via API from a search vendor or presented via flat file would prevent them from ever evaluating the success of a campaign. Normalizing that data and making it available via a familiar Excel interface makes it much easier to understand.

- *Extensive pivot table capabilities*: In addition to improving the readability of data, Excel 2007 provides enhanced capabilities to pivot and analyze the data either by leveraging standard pivot table functions or by utilizing the Excel Data Mining Add-In outlined in Chapter 1.

- *Detailed marketing effectiveness metrics*: Ultimately, the primary purpose for consolidating massive amounts of data from multiple sources is to provide analyst and management staffs with the opportunity to make informed business decisions related to campaign effectiveness. With the amount of money many large organizations spend on marketing and web analytics, improving the way the money is spent may make a significant difference to the bottom line.

Figure 9-24 demonstrates how an Excel user interface can present aggregated click data sorted by search provider in a pie chart for users.

For this customer, our primary responsibility was to make sense of large volumes of data. While smaller organizations leverage a product like Google AdWords and the associated Google Analytics tools to completely analyze their web presence from end to end, more complex or larger organizations require more complete solutions. Those organizations must develop code to handle all the data and address the abnormalities associated with web trends and human clicks discussed earlier. In this case, we were able to provide an aggregate set of data in a fast, easy way on a regular, repeatable basis to meet the company's needs.

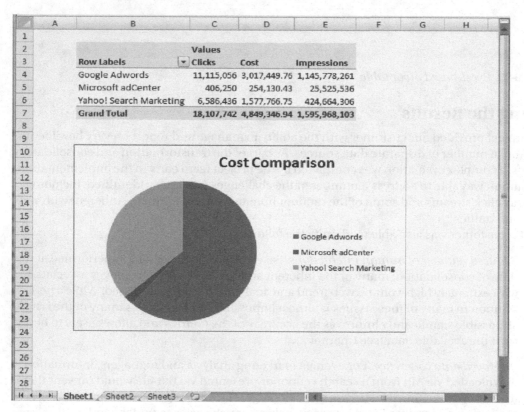

Figure 9-24. *An aggregated click data example*

Summary

Each of the case studies outlined in this chapter provides a different example of how reports and dashboards can be used to improve business effectiveness and make decisions that greatly benefit the end users utilizing the information. While two of them leverage a CRM application, the data and information displayed can be displayed in any number of places and will still add the same value. More importantly, each of these case studies should show you how flexible the Microsoft platform can be. You can use creative solutions to solve virtually any reporting problem within your organization.

Each of the case studies also provides you with a set of information that addresses a problem of organizations large and small, and when viewed independently of the example client, provides insight into some options available when reporting challenges arise. Specifically, we addressed situations like reporting with an online cloud-based application, complex, multirole sales and marketing reporting, and providing detailed web analytics.

It is our hope that the combined functional and technical nature of this book will provide you with the tools necessary to implement a successful analytics solution for your organization. The case studies provided present some out-of-the-box solutions to common reporting problems. We hope you've enjoyed this book, and best of luck with your upcoming analytics initiative!

Index

You Need the Companion eBook

Your purchase of this book entitles you to buy the companion PDF-version eBook for only $10. Take the weightless companion with you anywhere.

We believe this Apress title will prove so indispensable that you'll want to carry it with you everywhere, which is why we are offering the companion eBook (in PDF format) for $10 to customers who purchase this book now. Convenient and fully searchable, the PDF version of any content-rich, page-heavy Apress book makes a valuable addition to your programming library. You can easily find and copy code—or perform examples by quickly toggling between instructions and the application. Even simultaneously tackling a donut, diet soda, and complex code becomes simplified with hands-free eBooks!

Once you purchase your book, getting the $10 companion eBook is simple:

❶ Visit **www.apress.com/promo/tendollars/**.

❷ Complete a basic registration form to receive a randomly generated question about this title.

❸ Answer the question correctly in 60 seconds, and you will receive a promotional code to redeem for the $10.00 eBook.

THE EXPERT'S VOICE™

2855 TELEGRAPH AVENUE | SUITE 600 | BERKELEY, CA 94705